Building a Performance

Building a Performance

An Actor's Guide to Rehearsal

John Basil and Dennis Schebetta

ROWMAN & LITTLEFIELD
Lanham • Boulder • New York • London

Published by Rowman & Littlefield
An imprint of The Rowman & Littlefield Publishing Group, Inc.
4501 Forbes Boulevard, Suite 200, Lanham, Maryland 20706
www.rowman.com

86-90 Paul Street, London EC2A 4NE, United Kingdom

British Library Cataloguing in Publication Information Available

Library of Congress Cataloging-in-Publication Data

Names: Basil, John, author. | Schebetta, Dennis, 1972– author.
Title: Building a performance : an actor's guide to rehearsal / John Basil, Dennis Schebetta.
Description: Lanham : Rowman & Littlefield, [2022] | Includes bibliographical references and index. | Summary: "Performance provides a clear step-by-step system for actors through all stages of the rehearsal process. It enables actors to make more dynamic choices, craft complex characters with rich behavior, and find engaging and powerful levels of performance"—Provided by publisher.
Identifiers: LCCN 2021038843 (print) | LCCN 2021038844 (ebook) | ISBN 9781538161302 (cloth) | ISBN 9781538161319 (paperback) | ISBN 9781538161326 (epub)
Subjects: LCSH: Theater rehearsals. | Acting.
Classification: LCC PN2071.R45 B37 2022 (print) | LCC PN2071.R45 (ebook) | DDC 792.02/33—dc23
LC record available at https://lccn.loc.gov/2021038843
LC ebook record available at https://lccn.loc.gov/2021038844

∞™ The paper used in this publication meets the minimum requirements of American National Standard for Information Sciences—Permanence of Paper for Printed Library Materials, ANSI/NISO Z39.48-1992.

Contents

Acknowledgments   vii

Introduction   ix

Part I: Laying the Foundation: Steps before First Rehearsal

1   Reading the Blueprint   3

2   Building the Scaffolding   15

3   Constructing a Shell   27

4   Brick by Brick: Three Types of Language   39

Part II: Building the Role: Steps for Early Rehearsal

5   Building with Others   53

6   Building Habits   65

7   Building Your Character   77

Part III: Making It Your Own: Steps for Final Rehearsal

8   Building Dynamics with Textual Clues   89

9   Interior Fittings: Building Emotional and Verbal Dynamics   103

10   Building with Care and Consent: Fights, Extreme Physicality, and Intimacy   119

11   Exterior Fittings and Final Touches: The Technical Rehearsal   131

Part IV: Other Models of Construction

12   When There's No Blueprint: Devising, Physical Theater, and
         Ensemble Plays   141

13   New Construction: Rehearsing the New Play   151

14   The Fast Build: Rehearsing Film, TV, and Other Media   165

15   Moving In: Common Notes from Directors   175

Conclusion   183

Notes   185

Appendix A: Recommended Play Reading List   191

Appendix B: Recommended Reading & Resources   193

Bibliography   197

Index   199

About the Authors   211

Acknowledgments

Our appreciation for the many people involved in getting this book completed and out to the public are many. First, we'd like to thank the various teachers who have taught us, the directors we have worked with, and all the actors and students we have watched and learned from over the years. John would especially like to thank the "three sisters" who provided so much foundation to his work: Stella Adler, Uta Hagen, and Mira Rostova. Dennis learned so much from teachers like Davey Marlin-Jones, William Esper, Joel Rooks, Dr. Tawna Pettiford-Wates, Dr. Aaron Anderson, Dr. Noreen Barnes, David Leong, and Sergei Ostrenko.

A huge thanks to our agent, June Clark, for tirelessly hanging in there with this manuscript over the years and through a global pandemic.

Thank you to the editing and publishing team at Rowman & Littlefield, especially our editor, Christen Karniski.

To the institutions that have supported us, we thank you: Marymount Manhattan and Skidmore College.

Thanks to Tonia Sina, Chelsea Pace, Laura Rikard, Claire Warden, and Kim Shively for education, guidance, and help with intimacy and consent-based practices.

Thanks also to early readers who provided support, fact-checking, information, and thoughtful notes: Dennis Turney, Dr. Diego Villada, John Michael Diresta, Jared Klein, Ariana Starkman, Teisha Duncan, Brittany Pivovar, and Steve "Stevo" Parys for the chapter on film and TV.

Special thanks to our colleagues for support, including Rob Roznowski, Dr. Valerie Clayman-Pye, Dr. Krysta Dennis, and Erin Cherry.

And finally, to our family: Lisa and Penelope and Liz. You inspire us and support us, and we are forever grateful.

Introduction

> If you want to reach every person in the audience, it's not about being bigger, it's about going deeper.
>
> —Sanford Meisner[1]

Congratulations! You got the part! Now what?

Maybe you picked up this book because you finally got cast in a substantial role. Maybe you've acted in one scene for class, but you're wondering how to craft a whole performance over multiple scenes. Or perhaps you never thought about your rehearsal process and are looking for ideas. There are a lot of books about acting. This is a book about how to *rehearse* as an actor—it is the difference between training as a runner and actually running a marathon. *Building a Performance* gives you tools to apply techniques and ideas from acting class to the rehearsal room.

Ideally, if you picked up this book, you have an understanding of the fundamentals of acting a scene and how to listen and respond truthfully in the moment. You know some Stanislavski-based techniques, such as those taught by Uta Hagen and Stella Adler, or have done a year of Meisner training. You might have done Viewpoints or movement and vocal classes.

Acting classes are important. It's the place to take time and enjoy the journey of exploring your identity and imagination and building skills of playing with the ideas of character and intention. There is time to grow, and a good teacher will give you positive notes and coach you. Acting class is for training. A rehearsal room is for working.

In this book, we use the metaphor of building a house. In acting class, you learn about how to use your tools, like a drill and hammer, and types of material, like types of joints and wiring and plumbing. In rehearsal, you apply those skills to make a three-dimensional structure that people will experience and live in.

What we've discovered over our collective decades of directing and teaching acting is that actors learn basic skills in a classroom but find challenges in applying those skills to the professional rehearsal process.[2] Many actors, even professionals, seem to have a loose process or no process at all when it comes to rehearsal techniques. Some actors are so developed in their craft they don't even think about their process, and granted, it changes from role to role, as it should. Even when actors do have a process, they use the same tools over and over again. That works fine as long as they're in familiar artistic territory and playing similar roles, but when that actor takes on a challenging role, they fumble.

Yes, you can and will learn by experience. Most actors learned how to rehearse by being in the studio and learning from others. And we can attest, learning this way is solid. But it's also difficult and time consuming. Wouldn't it be great if someone took you aside in rehearsal to guide you at each stage of the process? Wouldn't it be nice if you knew how to prepare and work even before the first day of rehearsal?

Building a Performance aims to be that guide, giving you tools to help you build your rehearsal process. This book is a bridge from the fundamentals explored in acting class to practical work, showing you with specific examples how to apply the techniques. With these tools, you can avoid using the same old tricks that lead to stale performances. You can maximize your time, digging deeper into your character and getting more out of your rehearsal.

In this book, we hope to answer such questions as

- How do I get the most of those first readings of the script?
- How can I dig for clues about my character before rehearsal begins?
- How do I make dynamic choices about my actions and relationships?
- How do I find the music of the text and explore vocal qualities in my text?
- How can I physicalize my character choices on my own?
- How do I integrate my choices with the director or fellow actors?
- How do I "raise the stakes" when the director gives that note?
- How do I safely access my emotional life in a scene?

HOW TO USE THIS BOOK

This book is designed so that you can start crafting your character's actions and behaviors at each stage of your process: from first readings of the script to later rehearsal. Although we present these tools in this linear sequence, many of them relate to each other. We recommend you read this book sequentially, but we have designed this book to help you with specific moments in your journey of rehearsal or your process of working on a role. If you find that you need specific help for a problem area, feel free to jump to that chapter or section. The creative process is more akin to working on parallel stories, where you constantly reflect on earlier work, or to concurrent tasks rather than a rigid, step-by-step story line.

For instance, if you have been involved in several productions and don't feel you need all the information in chapter 5 on the first rehearsal, skip to chapters 6 and 7, and dive into refining your acting choices and examining status.

However, we do encourage you to fully examine what each chapter offers. It may seem that some of the material is rudimentary, and we make no apologies about reviewing the fundamentals. Fundamentals are vital and should be reviewed. Often when actors struggle, it's because they're not doing the most fundamental thing or asking the basic questions.

You may think you know how to do the work, but sometimes, let's face it, you *just don't do it.* In the same way, you know you should eat your veggies, but pizza is much more enticing. Or you skip the abs session of your workout. Why? Because its hard and you're human. Same thing with actors and some of the basics. So we have to be the ones tell you. Don't look for a shortcut. Don't say you'll read the play, but really you just skim through it and read only your scenes. (Hey, we're actors, too. We know you do it.) We get it: You're busy. But to go deeper, you must work harder. This book is for those actors who want to go deeper. You can't go deep with superficial preparation.

For example, consider the first chapter on how to read a play. Most actors think, "I know how to read a play," but you need to read it like an actor—not a passive reader, a director, or a designer. When we ask actors a question about a scene, such as "What is the event that happened right before this scene?" or "How long has it been since you saw this person in the previous scene?" they don't know or give a general answer. They don't understand how that knowledge can help shape their choices. Another example is the read-through on the first day of rehearsal. Most actors are confident they know what to do. But we see actors make the same mistake over and over again (see chapter 5). If we consider this idea that building your performance is like building a house, you can see how each step of the process is connected to the next. The first step is to lay down a foundation, then build the scaffolding, then add the final layers and unique details.

You cannot have a firm structure without a solid foundation. Our first three chapters are all about using the blueprint (the text) to lay down the foundation that will serve you throughout the process. We give you tools that you can use to prepare on your own before rehearsals begin. These tools help you to uncover hidden and not-so-hidden clues by analyzing and categorizing scenes and awakening your imagination and instinctual process. These ideas also engage in the physical and vocal qualities of your character.

The next section (chapters 5–7) give specific tools to engage you in rehearsals and to encourage you to interact with the director and actors, including refining your choices, such as your basic needs and actions, and exploring physicality. This is where we build a scaffolding for you to run and play in, testing the joints and solidity of your structure.

In the third section, we focus on your character choices and how to play with status, secrets, lies, and the physical life of your character. We also tackle some of the specific challenges and opportunities you might face with demanding roles, whether that be a long speech; complex language; an emotional scene; or physical challenges related to intoxication, intimacy, and stage combat. Finally, we cover the technical rehearsals, where you put up the walls and final details of your house and live in it!

Our last section of this book highlights other models of rehearsal, giving you a glimpse into the differences between rehearsing a devising or ensemble-based performance; rehearsing a new play with the playwright in the room; or rehearsing for film, TV, and other media. This section concludes with a chapter on some of our most common notes that we give to actors in the final steps of rehearsal.

EXERCISES

At particular moments, either midway through or at the ends of chapters, we have practical exercises to help you incorporate and directly apply the concepts. You may find it useful to do the exercises in sequence, but you may also find it helpful to use a particular exercise to get unstuck in the middle of a rehearsal process.

It is important to remember that acting is doing. When you see the exercises, we encourage you to take time to explore and *do them*. Discover what you can about the concept as more than just a theory; the more you grasp the concept in practice, the better. You also may find that doing an exercise more than once is beneficial.

The exercises are merely one way to explore the text, the character, or scene in a new way. Think of them as if you are a musician practicing scales, a ballet dancer working at the barre, or an artist sketching out different ideas on paper. You don't have to perform your role with this choice from the exercise, and nothing we say in this book should contradict conversations you have with your director. The tools allow you to keep digging deeper so you can examine the text and the role. Ultimately, the final choices for performance are yours alone.

RECOMMENDED SCRIPTS

As you work through the book, we use specific examples from contemporary scripts. There are a few plays we refer to on a regular basis, and we recommend you grab yourself a copy of them to read and refer to as needed. These are *Hedda Gabler* by Henrik Ibsen, *The Government Inspector* adapted by Jeffrey Hatcher from the original by Nicolai Gogol, *Intimate Apparel* by Lynn Nottage, and *Lobby Hero* by Kenneth Lonergan. We also refer to Tracy Letts's *August: Osage County*, as well as works by Theresa Rebeck, Sarah Ruhl, August Wilson, and Nilo Cruz. Occasionally, we use original text or text from some of Dennis's published and produced plays.

Although we may use a text as an example of a particular tool, please know that this does not mean that the tool couldn't be applied to other scripts, especially the one you're working on.

A CHANGING ENVIRONMENT: EQUITY IN THE INDUSTRY

As we were finishing up this book, the entertainment industry in the United States engaged in complex conversations on racial and gender inequities. We See You White American Theatre (WSYWAT; https://www.weseeyou wat.com/) calls out not just Broadway but also regional theaters, as well as academic institutions. In addition, these conversations have begun in Hollywood. Many regional theater companies have made efforts and are working with WSYWAT in their antiracist strategies and examining how the structure of theatrical practices is oppressive for BIPOC members of their community. The changes that are occurring and still need to occur are changes that go beyond mere programming of BIPOC plays. It also means examining structural and institutional culture and practices. The rehearsal process is part of that practice.

As two White cis-males, we want to acknowledge that the techniques and exercises that we outline as part of this rehearsal system is White-centric and derived from Eurocentric ideas about the acting process (based in the Stanislavski system and its derivatives). We refer to our own experiences as examples, in primarily White spaces. While we may feel these are safe spaces for us as White men, that may not be the experience of BIPOC actors. While we have taken great care to be inclusive and thoughtful, we know that we will not be able to recognize and speak to others' experiences.

We want to emphasize that there is no universal method of actor training and that we're sharing our own experiences and practices we've learned or integrated professionally. Recently there have been rich conversation and much-needed changes in the ways we teach acting in our colleges, conservatories, and studios, and we hope that conversation will continue to grow. It is more important for you to find a rehearsal process that will work for you and your way of knowing. For those of you wanting to learn more about different approaches, please check out *Black Acting Methods* by Dr. Sharell Luckett, as well as her website (https://www.sdluckett.com/) and workshops. An actor should also look at the recently published *Breaking It Down: Auditions Techniques for Actors of the Global Majority* by Nicole Persley and Monica Ndounou, as well as the work of Dr. Tawnya Pettiford-Wates's Poetic Ritual Drama with her company, the Conciliation Project.

You cannot speak about the rehearsal room without acknowledging and examining the power dynamics. Many producers and directors are working toward an antiracist practice, but change can be slow, unsatisfying, and messy. You may find yourself in situations dealing with that change. You may also find yourself in difficult scenarios beyond the scope of this book. It is our belief that an actor should feel empowered to advocate for their own rights or the rights of others.

HEALTH, SAFETY, AND CONSENT-BASED PRACTICES

In addition to equity, our emergence from a global pandemic has brought more attention to the health and safety of our workplace, whether that be on-set or on-stage. While the attention to physical health is important, there are also conversations about mental health, stress, and anxiety. Often, physical and mental health are connected. For instance, there are conversations by many theater companies about the issues and inequities with 10-out-of-12 rehearsals. A 10-out-of-12 rehearsal is a technical rehearsal that gets its name from the Equity mandate that actors can only work ten of those hours. It is by its nature the longest rehearsal possible, so it makes sense that it is reserved for technical rehearsals, which are often time consuming. The stage crew and designers usually work even longer hours those days than actors.[3] Playwright Anne Washburn wrote a play called *10 out of 12*, which debuted at Soho Rep in 2016. It is a comic but dark look at this type of rehearsal, as an audience watches (and listens via headset) to the actors and crew. It's not just a funny glimpse of the process, but it also examines the power dynamics and how hard actors and crew work and what they sacrifice mentally, emotionally, and physically for the sake of getting the show up.

This idea that artists should expect to put the show above and beyond their own health and safety is obsolete. The 10-out-of-12 rehearsal model has shown to be not only a biased or racist practice but also unsafe, ableist, and anticaregiver. Many actors have tried to balance any kind of life and self-care with the demands of rehearsal schedules that are all-consuming. Several theaters, such as Alley Theater, Public Theater in New York City, Oregon Shakespeare Festival, City Theater in Pittsburgh, and the Baltimore Center

Stage have eliminated their 10-out-of-12 rehearsals.[4] By the time this book goes to print, many more will likely have followed this trend.

Recently, acting teachers are incorporating "consent-based" practices into their teaching, and many directors are learning about the power dynamics of the casting and rehearsal rooms. This is an ongoing and important process made evident not just by the #MeToo and Black Lives Matter movements but also because of mental and emotional health.

Recent research shows that actors engage in a stressful occupation. Yes, it seems like fun and games (it's called a play, after all), but the stress of the performance as well as the stress of all that comes with the job can cause psychological harm. Actors can suffer from issues with interpersonal relationships, depression, generalized anxiety, alcoholism, and even trauma.[5] Taking these stresses to heart, Dr. Mark Seton has termed what he calls "postdramatic syndrome."[6] This is not an actual diagnosis but a way to reference actors unable to decompress or step away from roles they play (in essence, taking your work home with you). He believes that actors should develop habits that can be sustainable and can change the culture so that they can develop what he calls "resilient vulnerability."

In the same way that you might wear a hard hat at a construction site, you have to manage self-care as an actor. If you are going to step into an intense role or a scene that is emotionally charged, you have to prepare yourself—your mind and body will have difficulty differentiating between real and imaginary, and that can take its toll. One of those ways is to examine and know your boundaries, either personal, psychological, or physical. (We talk more about safety and boundaries in chapter 10 when we discuss stage combat and sexual intimacy.) Boundaries are an important concept. We borrow some of the language used in intimacy direction and education. In *Staging Sex*, Chelsea Pace breaks down the three big ideas that drive intimacy direction. The first big idea is to "create a culture of consent." In order to initialize an actor's consent, it needs to be clear what that actor's boundaries are, either physically or emotionally. Actors, however, are trained to say, "Yes, and . . ." They don't want to be labeled "difficult to work with."[7]

As Pace states,

> No ethical director wants to take advantage of the actor-director power dynamic. Consent requires an enthusiastic, uncoerced "yes" from all parties involved, so an "I guess so, sure" out of obligation hardly qualifies. . . . To actually get consent in the rehearsal room, there has to be space, real space, for the actor to say "no."[8]

Actors fear that saying no to a suggestion will bring the rehearsal room to a standstill. If a director suggests you do something out of your boundaries, then you have the right to preserve your own health. And there are ways to say "no" without it being final. An actor can offer suggestions or options that are within their boundaries. In short, the rehearsal room should be as safe as any other workplace. You cannot fully engage in a vulnerable and creative state as an actor if you are working in an unsafe environment.

Let's be clear, though, that *safe* doesn't mean *comfortable*. There is nothing comfortable about playing Ophelia and having Hamlet tear out your heart emotionally as he challenges you to "get thee to a nunnery." Your job as an actor is to live in uncomfortable places because those are the moments your characters are experiencing. Drama is built on conflict, and conflict is uncomfortable. As Keith Johnstone states, if you think of something "you wouldn't want to happen to you, or to someone you love, then you'll have thought of something worth staging or filming."[9] But if the actor playing Hamlet makes you feel unsafe because he has erratic behavior or performs an unrehearsed and unplanned slap in your face, we have crossed the line from discomfort to unsafe.

Just like with muscles that can grow with repeatable stress and discomfort, we can also experience pain and trauma by lifting too much. We don't want pain and trauma. Contrary to belief, you *do not* have to suffer for your art. This means you have to manage self-care. Part of that will be knowing and honoring your boundaries. You may want to incorporate some kind of ritual for entering and exiting the space, a check-in with your partner or other way of acknowledging the separation between real and imaginary. Other basics of self-care are also important, such as a proper vocal and physical warm-up before rehearsal, getting enough sleep, exercise, proper nutrition, and some form of stress release.

Of course, working in a safe place also means if you find yourself in a situation that doesn't feel safe, you should be empowered to do something about it. We encourage you to know and understand the rules and guidelines of Actors Equity Association or the Screen Actors Guild.

CONCLUSION

Each role will have its own unique challenges. The tools in this book are not meant to be didactic. Acting is not like following technical instructions as if you're putting together a bookshelf from IKEA. As stated before, we recommend you look at this process sequentially as presented here so you understand the differences in the stages of rehearsal. However, every actor is different. You may find it more helpful to get up on your feet immediately and explore the character through your verbal and physical energy (in chapter 4) before you have analyzed the play or looked at the text for character clues (as in chapter 1). Feel free to adapt these tools to make it fit *your* process.

Ultimately, it's not about what process you have but that you have *your own unique process* that will enable you to solve challenges when you get stuck. What works today for this production may not work for the next. Each show may illuminate some strength or weakness of your acting skills. As stated earlier, there is no substitute for experience. You try and fail and experiment and learn as you go. Any system or technique that isn't able to adapt to the role is not going to be helpful for the length of your acting career. As Stanislavski once said, "It is essential for every actor on his way up, for his status, his career, his popularity, to create his own system."[10]

RECOMMENDED READING

Basil, John. *Will Power: How to Act Shakespeare in 21 Days.* New York: Applause Theatre & Cinema Books, 2006.

Luckett, Sharrell, with Tia M. Shaffer, eds. *Black Acting Methods: Critical Approaches.* London: Routledge, 2016.

Persley, Nicole Hodges, and Monica Ndounou. *Breaking It Down: Audition Techniques for Actors of the Global Majority.* Lanham, MD: Rowman & Littlefield, 2021.

Stanislavski, Konstantin. *An Actor's Work.* Translated by Jean Benedetti. New York: Routledge, 2008.

Part I

LAYING THE FOUNDATION: STEPS BEFORE FIRST REHEARSAL

Chapter One

Reading the Blueprint

We must be architects of the inner life.

—Jacques Lecoq[1]

In this first chapter, look at a script as if it's your blueprint for the final construction. Looking at a script (whether for stage, film, or TV) is similar to looking at blueprints. They both involve taking a two-dimensional page of information and then imagining it in a three-dimensional world. Most everyone knows what a blueprint looks like but aren't skilled enough to glean information from it about construction. That is what we are teaching you here: how to look at your script and glean as much information as you can to help you build your role.

If you have never done any script analysis, this chapter may seem like a lot of homework to do before your first day of rehearsal or shooting. But this is part of the rehearsal process—your own personal process. Actors call it "working on the script." It's work that is imperative before you start working with a director or other actors. Don't skip these first steps. Know your script as well as you can. Your director will notice if you don't.

Also, you may think you know how to read a script, but you'll find some useful techniques to get even more information from your script than you previously have. This chapter is about how an *actor*—not just any general theater practitioner—begins to work on a role.

STEP 1: READ THE SCRIPT AS AN AUDIENCE

There is probably nothing more important than the first reading of the script you are about to work on, mainly because these first impressions will shape your initial choices. At this point, you may have only a vague notion about those choices or even what the director, designers, or other actors might do. Sure, you may know the director from auditions, and you may have seen the cast list. Yes, you've seen the character descriptions and read sides for the audition. Maybe somebody told you about the lavish period costumes or that it would be a site-specific performance in an old, abandoned warehouse, but you still have only a few clues about the story and essence of your character. This feeling of excitement (or nervous anticipation) is like standing on a dock about to board a ship headed for a great adventure. Your bags are packed, but you have no idea where the winds will take you and how you will arrive at your destination.

The first and most obvious thing an actor needs to do, of course, is read the script. Now, you may be thinking, "I know how to read a play," and that may be true. You may have taken a script-analysis class in high school or college, or you may have read many plays in your English-lit classes. But you may not be aware of effective strategies for how an actor reads to connect the text to the role they will build. Directors, dramaturgs, and designers all analyze a script differently so that they can engage in their specific work. That's what this chapter is all about. We know you want to skip this and get to the "fun stuff" of character creation, but please know how important all this work is for laying your foundation.

What does it mean to *really* read the script? It means to read the entire script from beginning to end, with full attention and focus—not skimming it to see when your character enters, not reading it while glancing at your smartphone to check your social media sites or while *Stranger Things* is playing. It means not reading only your lines and counting them up (you know you've done it). You might be chuckling at how obvious this guidance is, but you'd be surprised how many actors, even professionals, skim through a play or only read their scenes.

In most acting classes, especially Meisner-based classes, there is a lot of talk about taking the attention off yourself and putting it on your partner— to really listen and focus. Think of this script as your first acting partner. Really listen. Treat this reading like a first date with someone you're trying to get to know: Pour some coffee or tea, find a comfortable chair, and sit down with the script for the length of the time it takes you to read it, like an audience member watching it unfold for the first time. Enjoy this reading, as it is the only time in this process when you can relax and read it this way. Take the pressure off yourself as a performer, and pay attention to the beauty, the humanity, the humor, and any universal relevance the script might have to your life or the state of the world. What does the story make you feel? How do you feel yourself emotionally connecting with the characters? Once you get into rehearsals, you will get busy and overwhelmed and may forget this first flush of excitement and observation. But it's the journey that you want to take your audience members on. You'll find that these first impressions will guide you later as you start taking the text apart and getting on your feet.

The world the writer has conjured—the characters, the setting, the situation, the lines—will become the blueprint from which you will build your house (your performance). You will return to those words again and again throughout the rehearsal process. Often in rehearsal, you might hear a director say, "Let's look at the script." Or you might discover you learned a line completely wrong and then, finding the correct words, suddenly realize why that moment never felt right. Never forget that sometimes when you're lost and looking for answers, the answer might already be there in the text, even if it is hidden. Your job as an actor is to uncover these hidden clues as you shape your performance.

It may be true that when you were learning how to act, you may have had some conflicting ideas about how to approach the text (some acting teachers think of the text as the enemy, for example, encouraging you to paraphrase or cross out stage directions). You may have tried different games and exercises to get you to be more present, spontaneous, and improvisational, but now you have to channel those skills of spontaneity and merge them with the writer's words. Or, in the case of devising or physical theater, merge them with the ensemble's vision of the performance as you develop the piece together.

The art of rehearsal is the art of returning to that feeling of the first time. Actors condition themselves in rehearsal to build repeatable performances that feel free enough to unlock that feeling. This journey can feel a long way around, and there are many tasks and activities to do in order to recover that experience. This is why that first reading is so important. It's your introduction to the environment, the characters, the place, the time, and the story, as well as your starting point for your own reactions and interpretations. As an artist, you must figure out what motivates you. Where in the play were you surprised? When did you laugh? Or gasp? Ideally, these same moments are what the audience will experience when they watch your performance.

Exercise 1

Your first task is to commit to a length of uninterrupted time to curl up with the script in a comfortable chair. Feel free to pour yourself some coffee or tea. Read the play as if you were watching it like an audience member. Imagine a theater, a set, the sights, the sounds, the characters in motion. After you have read it, take a moment to jot down your impressions—a line here or there, an image, a smell, words, feelings, memories. Keep your focus on absorbing the world of the play, the characters, the story, and just let it wash over you. You can make some judgments, but you will have much more in-depth work to do later.

STEP 2: READ THE SCRIPT AS AN ACTOR

After you have read the play once all the way through, feel free to take a day or two off, and try not to think about it. Go for a run or do some yoga. Your thoughts and ideas will percolate in the back of your mind. You may find that ideas and images strike you when you are walking down the street to the subway, at the coffee shop getting your latte, or picking up groceries. Too often, we try to rush the process, forcing creative choices as if we are ordering a Big Mac, when really our minds need to rest and relax. Stepping into a new role takes time. Don't force yourself to move too far too fast.

After this break, sit down, and grab a pen or pencil to read the script again. This time you'll be reading not as an audience member but as an actor preparing for a role. You are transitioning from a passive observer into an active and engaged part of the storytelling process. It's time to start thinking of yourself as a collaborator—collaborating first with the writer; then with the director, stage manager, designers, and other actors; and finally with the audience. As you read the script this second time through, you will start doing two things simultaneously: First, you'll start to personalize the story, becoming empathic toward your character as if the events are happening to you; and second, you'll uncover clues about how your character fits into this story. The first goal is focused on your character's unique point of view and could be considered the emotive or impulsive side of your brain (left brain), and the second goal is focused on how to analyze the elements in order to bring that unique point of view to life through behavior and action (right brain). You'll start this process slowly but specifically by taking the play apart, looking at specific elements, and then putting it all back together in rehearsal.

Finding the Large and Small Bits (or Beats)

It's important to break the script down and analyze each element—plot, character, scenes, lines, and so on. Stanislavski was the first actor and teacher to write about how he would break plays down into "bits" (which you may already know as "beats" from your acting class—this small change is due to a language barrier and heavy Russian dialect). His analogy was eating a turkey: You wouldn't try to stuff the whole thing in your mouth in one sitting. You would first cut it up into big bits. You'd cut off a leg first or a large slice of the breast. Then you would take those big bits and cut them up into smaller bits and put those on a plate. That's how you devour your role, as well.[2] You look at the first scene, for example, as a big bit. Then you break that scene down into smaller bits. A scene could have anywhere from three to ten small bits. As an actor, you can start your work by looking at the first bit, such as when Hedda says hello to Judge Brack and tries to make him feel comfortable. Then you work on what happens next in the next bit.

Similarly, let's look at how a painter might create a still life from objects. The painter doesn't dive in with their oils, painting from left to right as if printing from a photocopier. The painter first uses a pencil and drafts a light sketch to see the dimensions of the objects. After looking at the shape and size, she might look only at the negative space, then look at just how the light hits surfaces and the shadows. Then she will consider the color palette. There is a lot of analysis, as well as observation, before any paint even hits the canvas. In the same way, we look at specific elements of the script or character in order to freely paint later. Of course, after several years, the painter might do all this analysis without even thinking. After several years of rehearsing experience, you also might go through these steps without thinking about it. But it's always good to reconsider the fundamentals, even when you have been doing it for years.

Another important aspect to remember is that preparing for your audition is different from preparing for a role. In an audition scenario, you aren't given the luxury of time with the script or any rehearsal. You work quickly on choices, and if you do have the benefit of reading the whole script beforehand, it's usually not a relaxed or in-depth reading. It's not that you aren't making choices or doing analysis, but it's only the rough sketch. It's like a sales pitch. Making good decisions fast is great for auditioning, and many times those decisions will find themselves into your performance (the last thing you want to do is perform the role drastically different from how you auditioned), but to build a role, you want to dive deeper and be even more prepared than with an audition.

For starters, you now have to prepare for all your scenes, not just the short sides. You may have scenes that take place in different days, months, or years. You may have scenes that involve complex stage business, like stage combat or intimate scenes with extreme emotional vulnerability, requiring more preparation. There may even be special skills that you will have to use or learn, such as a physical impediment (like a limp), a dialect, juggling, or playing a musical instrument.

Reading for Clues

For this second reading, in addition to finding the big and small bits (or beats), you'll also start dissecting the words in the lines. Specifically, you'll look at these three things:

1. All the lines other characters say about you
2. Any words that you don't know the definition of or how to pronounce
3. Any words or phrases your character repeats

Notate All the Lines That Other Characters Say about You

As you read, make a list of what characters say about your character, and see what (if any) patterns emerge. This can be illuminating, not only for getting information about how to work on your character, but also in terms of building relationships and understanding how other characters feel about you (we talk more about relationships in chapter 3).

For example, look at the character of John Wick, played by Keanu Reeves in the first movie of this action-packed series of films. If you're not familiar with the story, Wick is a top-notch assassin who retired from an underground organization but then is pulled back into this life after the recent death of his wife. We don't know much about him at the beginning of the movie, but after the first major event, he starts "kicking butt," and the other characters start talking about his combat skills. One character says he's the "bogeyman," and another character adds, "He's the one you call when you want to kill the bogeyman." That's key information about the character that you need to understand.

Another example is with Little Charles in *August: Osage County.* There are various comments made by his mother, Mattie Fae, about how infantile he is: how he can't drive yet (he's thirty-seven years old) and that he will get "eaten alive" if he decides to move to New York City. She later criticizes his piano playing. However, his father, Charlie, says, "You've never let me down." This is all crucial information on the character and the relationships. The actor trap would be to play the role as if all of what Mattie Fae says is true but ignore what his father says. But people are dynamic and are not one thing or the other. You must be attentive to all the clues.

As you write down lines spoken about your character, you might find conflicting statements from different characters, or your character might seem to contradict these statements or disagree with them (or you, the actor, might disagree). This is where your interpretation is important. If your character is described as "fragile" and you get defensive, thinking, "I'm not fragile!" then you're moving from passive observer to active storyteller. You can see how that point of view can blossom and enjoy and embrace the character's point of view as your own.

As human beings, we are complex. We have lots of different thoughts, opinions, and feelings, most of which can't be encapsulated by others. It's up to you to find out if your character is indeed fragile and how that might manifest in your behavior—or if the character is not and why might another character think that. And how might you react to how others treat you? Either way is playable and can be transformed into specific meanings, moments, and behavior. But it's up to you as the interpretive artist to make the decision.

Notate Any Words You Don't Know the Definition of or How to Pronounce

As you read this second time, circle any unfamiliar words, both the definition and pronunciation. After you circle them, make a list, and spend some time after the reading looking them up. It may seem obvious to make a list of words you don't know when it comes to such classical plays as those by Shakespeare (what exactly is a fardel?), but contemporary plays may seem more elusive. If your character is a scientist, they may use words like *phytoplankton* or *biosphere*. You need to know the definitions and what the words mean to you.

We may take for granted that we know the meaning of a word, but when we look at the definition, we find other meanings or usage. For example, Lynn Nottage named her Pulitzer Prize–winning play *Sweat* for a good reason. How many times do different characters use that word, and how do they have different meanings? Some of them escape the sweat of the factory by injury or by moving up, and others take honor in the sweat of their work. One of the character states, "It's no sweat off my back," while another complains about how management doesn't want to get their "diplomas soiled with sweat." In the climactic scene near the end, the character Jason, fueled by anger toward a scabbing worker named Oscar, talks about how the factory can "always find someone to get their hands sweaty." What at first may seem like an innocuous word can suddenly take on great meaning, both political and personal, and be tied to the main conflict of the play and the spine of these characters.

Notate Any Words or Phrases Your Character Repeats

Just like people you know, characters have their own vernacular and vocabulary, and often they repeat words or phrases that define them. You will find clues to your character even in the smallest repetitive phrases or words. For example, Tesman, in Henrik Ibsen's *Hedda Gabler*, has this habit of adding "Eh?" to the ends of his lines. You would think that this small utterance with a question mark wouldn't be much to work with, and it can be easily missed on the printed page, but in the hands of a skilled actor, that little quirk becomes a foundation for a character. If it weren't important, then Ibsen wouldn't have included it. An actor can ask himself many questions about this repeated word: Why does he do it? Is he aware he's doing it? Is it for confirmation? Is he not self-confident? Is it meant to be a comedic bit, or is it simply a character trait? Is it tied to the fact that he is an intellectual, a scholar? And what about the sound that this "Eh?" makes? Is it more nasal or breathier? An actor can spend hours playing around with how this tiny bit of behavior will manifest itself in a performance.

Let's look at an example of reading a play with these three things in mind by taking a close look at Sonya's monologue from Anton Chekhov's *Uncle Vanya*. Similar to Nottage's play *Sweat*, the word *work* takes on many different meanings and is repeated throughout *Uncle Vanya*. Sonya and others are told to work and others are working (or not working) despite or because of Serebryakov. This monologue comes at the end of the play, after Serebryakov and Yelena have left the estate, which Sonya and Vanya continue to take care of by paying the bills (literally paying them in this final scene). Read the monologue through once, just to get a sense of the content and situation. Then read it again, looking for (1) what others say about Sonya, (2) a vocabulary list, and (3) repetitive words and phrases:

> SONYA: What can we do? We must live out our lives. *[A pause]* Yes, we shall live, Uncle Vanya. We shall live all through the endless procession of days ahead of us, and through the long evenings. We shall bear patiently the burdens that fate imposes on us. We shall work without rest for others, both now and when we are old. And when our final hour comes, we shall meet it humbly, and there beyond the grave, we shall say that we have known suffering and tears, that our life was bitter. And God will pity us. Ah, then, dear, dear Uncle, we shall enter on a bright and beautiful life. We shall rejoice and look back upon our grief here. A tender smile—and—we shall rest. I have faith, Uncle, fervent, passionate faith. We shall rest. We shall rest. We shall hear the angels. We shall see heaven shining like a jewel. We shall see evil and all our pain disappear in the great pity that shall enfold the world. Our life will be as peaceful and gentle and sweet as a caress. I have faith; I have faith. *[Wiping away her tears]* My poor, poor Uncle Vanya, you are crying! *[Weeping]* You have never known what it is to be happy, but wait, Uncle Vanya, wait! We shall rest. We shall rest. We shall rest.[3]

As this is just the ending of the play, we don't have all the lines that others say about Sonya. Some include "works alone"; "young"; "what a child"; "has lovely hair" (in response to "Is she beautiful?"); and "She is suffering." But there is a clue when Marina earlier in the play says that Sonya "must work. Everyone must work." Also, Sonya echoes what other people say or might say about her when she says, "And God will pity us." Pity is what she has received from others throughout the entire play.

For a vocabulary list, you may circle and write down these words:

- procession
- burdens
- rejoice

- fervent
- enfold

Those are only a few words that you will want to look up in the dictionary to know exactly what they mean in this context. As for repeated words, some of these are quite obvious. Both *live* and *faith* are said four times. *Life* is said three times. *Rest* is said seven times. *Pity* is used twice. She calls him "poor, poor Uncle" and says, "Wait," twice. Why would she say that? This monologue uses only 221 words, and yet many of the words are repeated, ending with a repeated phrase: "We shall rest." Playwrights know that if they want the audience to understand something or to walk away remembering a particular word or phrase, the best way is repetition. Know that when you come across a repeated word or phrase, those words have extra meaning and importance. As this monologue is the last moment of the play, it bears special importance, so you can find a lot of repetitive words and phrases.

Exercise 2

Read the play again. This time as you read, break the scenes down into large and small bits/beats, and write down everything another character says about your character. Also, make a vocabulary list, words that you don't know the exact definition of, or words that might have several definitions. Third, circle or write in the margins of your script in bold letters any words or phrases that your character repeats. You may even want to use a color-coding system for this, using a different-colored pen or highlighter for these notes (try green for words you don't know and purple for repeated words, for example).

STEP 3: READ THE SCRIPT AS A DETECTIVE

Now you start digging into the tangible stuff that the writer has given you. Read the play all the way through a third time, but this time, think like a detective. Don't worry: We'll use more of your imagination and build on your own interpretations later. For now, let's look at the concrete details that we can build upon. These are called given circumstances, a term and concept introduced more than a hundred years ago by Stanislavski. He thought of the given circumstances not just as what was written on the page but also what the ensemble and the designers would provide, from the size of the set to the sounds and music:

> They mean the plot, the facts, the incidents, the period, the time and place of the action, the way of life, how we as actors and directors understand the play, the contributions we ourselves make, the *mise-en-scene*, the sets and costumes, the props, the stage dressing, the sound effects etc., everything

which is a given for the actors as they rehearse. The given circumstances, just like "If" are suppositions, products of the imagination.[4]

Stanislavski didn't look at writing down given circumstances as "play analysis" but as "creative work on a vast scale," an act of the imagination. Yes, we have to analyze the script, and we can use our analytical brain to make a list of what has been given to us, but this idea of creating a world that we will inhabit is our interpretive role as artists and something we share with the director and designers.

You may not be sure of what will be decided on before rehearsals, so it's important to first take a look at what is given in the script. This will be your springboard for other ideas and will help you fill in the gaps. The script may not give you all the details. That is the joy of acting—you make words into flesh and bone. You have to fill in the gaps with your imagination and choices. You are taking a blueprint, an idea, and constructing a three-dimensional experience.

In his plays, Eugene O'Neill describes the entire room as well as gives you the exact minute of the day and quality of light coming through a window. But some writers are more economical and are more suggestive, if not downright ambiguous. For example, in Sarah Ruhl's play *Eurydice*, which is more poetical and visual, much of the action takes place in the underworld. So what month, day, or season would that be in? Would you even have seasons? Would it feel hot or cold there? Another example is Caryl Churchill's play *A Number*, a play set in the near future about the ethics of cloning, where one character, Salter, speaks with several clones (all played by the same actor), and the only designation of time and place is "where Salter lives." As an actor, you need to first work with what the writer has given you before you start filling in the blanks and making assumptions, like any good detective. With film and TV, writers are especially economical and may only simply state the location.

So, what are the main questions we ask? Think of the "Five Ws" (who, what, where, when, and why). Asking questions should get your curiosity started, and that's what's really important here. You must be curious about every part of this play and ask questions about everything. While some questions may be answered through the design, you need to have a point of view as an artist and an idea of the world you want to create in your imagination. The following are basic questions, some of which we refer to later in this book:

- Who are you? What is your occupation, your age, your personality, your state of being throughout the play? What type of clothes do you wear? What is your level of education? Who are the other characters in this play?

What are your literal relationships (family, friends, colleagues, enemies), and how do you feel about them?
- What happens in this script? What are the major events? What are the actions you perform, to others, with others? What is your role in the action? (We do more work on the events of the script and plot in chapter 2, but start with what happens to your character or what major events affect all characters.)
- Where does this script take place? Do scenes happen outside or inside? What is the environment like, and how do you feel about it? Is it a home or office? Scenes play differently in a mansion rather than in a double-wide trailer or camping by a lake or on a bustling city street. Also, is the location someplace familiar to your character? Is it your home or someone else's? What is your relationship to the location? Emotional or sympathetic attachment?
- When does this story take place? What year, month, or time(s) of day(s)? This should be as specific as possible. Saying that it takes place in summer is only partway there. Saying it takes place at 4:30 p.m. on the Fourth of July in 1932 gives you more to work with in terms of behavior as an actor.
- Why does this story take place in this particular way? Why are these characters here? Why are you here? Why do you do the actions in this play (i.e., what are your motivations, and what's at stake for you)? This will lead further down the road to "what do you want and need?" which is illuminated in a later chapter.

The important thing that we reiterate again and again is that you need to be specific. Specificity leads to clear acting choices, while general and superficial answers lead to generalized acting.

What does that mean? It's the difference between playing the idea of a thing and really "living through it" as if the world is a real place and you are responding to it truthfully.

If you have already taken some acting classes, you may be already familiar with lists of questions for you to develop ideas about your character, such as Uta Hagen's "Six Steps" from her book *A Challenge for the Actor*. We also recommend the wonderful workbook *Acting and Living in Discovery* by Carol Rosenfield.

Exercise 3

Read the play a third time, this time looking for facts or specific given circumstances. Complete the questions listed previously or refer to our "Script Analysis Sheet" (see online materials at http://www.dennisschebetta.com/building-a-performance-book.html).

Chapter Two

Building the Scaffolding

Preparation is the sign of your intention. You can allow your preparedness
to speak for you in rooms you care about.

—Leslie Odom Jr.

THE ACTOR AS STORYTELLER

Actors have always had a purpose in society beyond entertainment. What
began as storytellers around a campfire has grown into more sophisticated
tales and more complex ways of telling them, from such mediums as theater,
film, television, and digital platforms. In ancient Africa, Asia, and Greece,
theater performances were tied to religion and ritual, enriching the sense of
community and legacy. Theater wasn't only a form of entertainment or re-
membrance but also a method of examining issues of state and society. Even
today, performances mirror and reflect the world around us. In this chapter,
we explore the research you can do to discover more about the world of the
play, as well as how to break down the script to understand your function as
a storyteller.

As an actor, you engage in a split identity as you perform. You are tasked
with living in this imaginary world as your character, as if these things are
happening to you. And yet, you must also be conscious and aware that you
are still yourself, a real human being with needs and emotions. For example,
if you really believe you are a razor-wielding serial killer named Sweeney
Todd living in nineteenth-century London, oblivious to the fact that an audience is around you (or the fact that you break out into Sondheim songs when
the mood strikes), then you would be classified as insane. Somewhere in the
back of your mind, you are aware that you are part of the story, making the

story happen, even as you live through it. Because of this, it's important to know as much as possible about the story.

As stated in the last chapter, the script analysis and research you do as an actor is not the same kind that you might do for your literature or history class. You are a storyteller and need to decide what aspects of the story are relevant. What is the story you want to tell? Why did you think this play was important, or why did it resonate with you? And if the play hasn't yet resonated with you, then you need to find a way in. Your job as an actor is to find the value and humanity of the story and connect with it. One way to help you to do that is research.

DO YOUR RESEARCH

The first things to research are the writer and original source material. If it is a well-established script, particularly from the last hundred years, then it's relatively easy to find that information. For example, if you're cast in an August Wilson play, read more of his plays, and pick up a biography to learn about his relationship to blues music, poetry, and the city of Pittsburgh. If it's a director-driven piece that will be devised, then conduct research about the director; methods of the company; and the source material, if any. If you have the opportunity to work with a living playwright, then you may not have a lot of written material about them, but often they attend rehearsals, and you can get to know them and their life to understand their work. As we said in the last chapter, be curious—your curiosity will feed your inspiration.

After you've done research on the writer and context of when the play was written and why, it's time to do research that might be more fun. Explore the world of the script through visual imagery by building an image bank. There are several ways to do this. You could cut and paste into your journal images from newspapers, magazines, and the internet, which beautifully feels child-like and tangible. It also is easier to find those images if you place them next to your comments and notes as you work on your journal. If you have any artistic talent, you could also draw, sketch, or doodle your ideas of what the world might look like and what your character might wear. If you are more digitally driven, a great way to build images is using Pinterest. It's not as tangible, but it is more plentiful, and you may find images that surprise you.

For example, let's say you're playing the role of Jeff in Kenneth Lonergan's play *Lobby Hero*. Jeff is a security guard, but mostly he's an unassuming and unambitious twenty-something who is friendly, talkative, and a bit goofy. He ends up in a moral dilemma regarding the alibi of his supervisor's brother, who may or may not have been involved with a crime. He tangles with an experienced and bull-headed police officer named Bill and develops a crush on Bill's partner, Dawn. The play is set in the "spacious, impersonal lobby of a middle-income apartment building in Manhattan" in New York City. It takes place "at night in mid-November." Those are the specific circumstances of time and place that Lonergan gives you. What needs to be further clarified, of course, is where exactly in Manhattan this play might take place. The Upper West Side is different from the Upper East Side and even more different from Soho or the Financial District. And even then, the East 60s on Madison is different from the East 80s near the Hudson River. These are details that you might not know yet, as they would get discussed and decided in the first few days of rehearsal. But a good actor wants to know what the world might be like for a security guard who spends all night in a lobby in a building in Manhattan. What would that look and feel like? You could collect images of New York apartments. Or you want to make an image bank of activities that Jeff might do to kill the time. Does he do crosswords? Read crime novels? The play takes place in 2001, so you're not likely to have a smartphone (and smartphones haven't been invented yet). And what are his dreams and ambitions? What is his family life like?

One thing to keep in mind as you develop your image bank and ideas of the world of the play is that you have a function different from a scenic designer. Your task of creating the image bank is not so you can create a set but so that you can understand the emotional life of what that environment means to you and so that you develop a relationship with the space. If you've ever had a job you loathed, then you know that just picturing that space in your mind can make your stomach churn. In the same way, if you imagine a place that makes you feel happy, such as the first beach you went to on vacation, then thinking of that space makes you smile. At this stage, we are exploring and planting seeds to build on later when we are on our feet and in rehearsal.

Exercise 1

Read other plays by your playwright, and do research on their life and times to understand better the context and social conditions upon which the play was written.

DIVIDE AND CONQUER WITH PASTO

In John's previous book *Will Power: How to Act Shakespeare in 21 Days*, he introduces the concept of PASTO, an acronym that represents the Aristotelian dramatic play structure found in many Western European plays or movies (the five-act structure).[1] PASTO stands for:

- Preparation
- Attack
- Struggle
- Turn
- Outcome

It is a simple way to think of how stories are structured without getting too bogged down with all the elements of Aristotle and his ideas of how drama functions. For most plays, we write those words down and pinpoint each of those elements in the play. And then we pinpoint those five elements in each scene.

(You may have noticed that we said, "for most plays," instead of "all plays." The five-act structure is a Western European model and not representative of postmodern plays, absurdist plays, or plays from other cultures. Some plays focus more on ritual or revelation and are less plot focused. Some plays may emphasize musicality, language, or physicality. As you work with theatrical writers from after the 1960s, such as Samuel Beckett, María Irene Fornés, and Suzan-Lori Parks, you might find that PASTO doesn't apply. We offer it here as one way of analyzing a text.)

There is a game you might have played in acting class. It's an improvisational ensemble game where everyone stands in a circle, shoulder to shoulder, and you all create a story together. The tricky part is, each actor can only say one word at a time. One actor says a word, then the energy passes to the person next to them, and they add a word, and so on. The goal is to see how quickly you can tell a story without any pauses. It should be like one group mind speaking. It's a great game on so many levels (for starters, it causes you to really listen and not anticipate what will come next), but what is fascinating is that as a group, actors intuitively understand the direction of the story and find an ending that feels resolved.

Stories are central to our core as human beings. We know a good one when we hear it. We may feel a good story has emotional highs and lows or clear events, or it has a beginning, a middle, and an end. Along the way, things happen, or our main characters make things happen. First, someone wants something and she either gets it or doesn't. David Ball, in his book *Backwards and Forwards*, calls that a "major dramatic question."[2] For example, the major dramatic question of *Hamlet* is "Will Hamlet avenge his father's death?" The answer is yes, but he will pay a high price for doing so (including a lot of casualties along the way). Once the question is resolved, the story is over. PASTO is our way of trying to simplify the story to its essence. What is the main question of the play? Once we understand that, we can look at each scene and then more fully understand how our character fits into this piece of machinery.

"That's great," you're thinking, "if you're working on Shakespeare or Ibsen, but what if you have this new play that's only seventy minutes long, has nine scenes, and is basically one long one-act? How do you apply the five-act structure?" Good question! Know that all writers today are conscious of this five-act structure and usually give clues to how it lays out, or they willingly defy the rules. (For screenplays, particularly mainstream Hollywood movies, this five-act structure has been simplified even more into a three-act structure, but the same Aristotelian rules still apply. Indie films may defy this structure, so be aware.) This is also why doing research about the writer is helpful. You can look at Lynn Nottage's plays, like *Intimate Apparel*, *Ruined*, and *Sweat*, and see how they are like well-oiled machines, with one dramatic action causing another to happen, with escalating tension building relentlessly until the climax and resolution of the play. But then you take a play like Mac Wellman's *Murder of Crows*, *Bad Infinity*, or *Harm's Way*, and you'll see a playwright rebelling against the form. His plays are more like collages, with poetic imagery and vivid characters reacting to each other. At first glance, this can seem confusing for an actor, but rest assured that even though he, as a writer, doesn't play by Aristotle's rules, you as an actor still can solve for yourself what rules he is playing by.

One other thing we reiterate is, it's art, not math or science. Interpretation is the name of the game. Using that painter analogy again, what's important is that you're really observing and analyzing as much as you can before you commit paint to canvas. Your breakdown of PASTO might be different from other actors, or even the director. And in rehearsals or on break, you can argue whether Mac Wellman put a turning point in *Harm's Way* or not, but at least you've put thought into it and have made decisions about your character based on this analysis.

So how does this PASTO thing work? Take a look at figure 2.1. You've probably seen this diagram in your English class or play-analysis class, based on the Aristotelian model of dramatic structure. There is line of rising action, a turn, then a descending line, leading to an outcome. Think of each element building on the other. What you want to try to do is encapsulate each element in a sentence.

The first element, preparation, is the opening circumstances of the play. Dennis's old professor and writer/director Davey Marlin-Jones used to say that every ending of a play could be the beginning of a new play. There is an idea of balance being disturbed and then restored. Preparation is the initial balance of the world as presented in the first scene(s). The writer lays out the setting, characters, and world of the play. We may also get hints about the themes and ideas being explored. In *The Government Inspector*, the preparation could be written as, "The mayor has just discovered that a government inspector will be arriving to inspect the town."

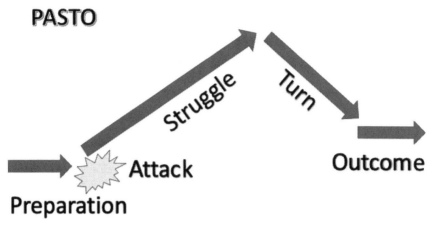

Figure 2.1.   PASTO Source: Dennis Schebetta

The attack in PASTO is the spark that sets off the motion of dramatic action. This is where the major dramatic question might be evident. In a play, there is usually an event that forces the characters into action, setting up their main struggle. In a scene, it may be the moment a character tries to pursue a particular tactic or objective. In *The Government Inspector*, the attack of the play is the moment Khlestakov assumes his mistaken identity and begins fooling the town into thinking he is higher status. The major dramatic question becomes, "Will he get away with it?"

Now you can see how these elements in PASTO are related to each other. If the attack is the spark that sets off the dramatic action, then the struggle is the conflict that occurs throughout the story because of that spark. With modern plays, such as *Lobby Hero*, the conflict can be both internal and external, and the struggle can revolve around the ideas of the play—in this case the moral dilemma that Jeff has to "tell or not tell." As you can see from figure 2.1, the struggle is the escalating line. This means, typically, that each scene gets more and more tense, that the stakes get higher and higher. This is especially important for you as an actor. The seventh scene of the play will likely have higher stakes than that first scene. What you don't want to do is play a scene at the height of struggle as if it's the preparation scene.

The turn (or turning point) is usually the most dramatic moment of the play. In classical plays, it may be the one with the most stage fights or a kiss or a death. Again, think of the elements as linked together. If the struggle is related to the town and Khlestakov, then what is the event that triggers the eventual outcome? Try to think of the turning point as if it's almost a complete change of direction for the characters, a right-angle turn, heading for the resolution. You can also think of this moment as the "point of no return."

There is no way to get back to the beginning balance that we saw in the preparation. All the characters' lives have changed in some way, which will inevitably lead to a new balance.

Outcome is the resolution of all the other elements. Usually the turn leads directly to this outcome. A balance has been restored to the world. It is almost never the same balance that we saw in the beginning of the play. The major dramatic question has been answered, either in the positive or negative, and a new preparation could start us off on a whole new play.

Sometimes the best way to look at a play is backward. Ball's *Backwards and Forwards* asks you to do that very thing. First, look at the last moment or action of the play. What event caused that to happen? And what event caused that to happen? Looking backward gives clarity to how and why the story is told the way it is. So, if you look at the outcome of the play, what are the events that led to that outcome? Was it only the struggle, or did something dramatic happen in between the struggle and the outcome? If so, it was likely the turning point.

In the same way you can divide the play into these five elements, you can also divide each of your scenes into these five elements, as if they are their own little plays. What is the preparation? When does the attack happen? What is your struggle throughout the scene? (What is your own major dramatic question? Does it get answered, and if so, how?) What is the turning point and the outcome? Even if the scene seems short, only a few lines, those elements are there in some way.

With film and television, you may not see the idea of PASTO in your scene. Many scenes are short, only a half page or less. You may have only one line or no lines at all, just walking out of a bar or walking into your apartment and putting your keys away. But trust this: No writer ever puts unnecessary words down on paper. This is especially true for film and television, where the cost to shoot even a few seconds of screen time is extremely high. You can bet that even if it may seem like, "Well, he's only putting his keys on the table," there is a storytelling need for it. Your job is to figure it out and tell that story. And the story of "putting the keys down" needs to be as thought out and detailed as any other element in the script.

TITLE YOUR SCENES

Now that you understand how each event leads to the next, you can see how your character fits into the story. Another tool to help you figure out why your scenes are there is to give them their own titles. Sometimes you can do this before you do PASTO, especially if you're having trouble finding out what the scenes are all about. Then go back and do PASTO after you have titles. As you read and work on the script, your ideas about PASTO and titles might change, and that's okay. Again, it's art, not algebra.

In film and television, there are lots of schedules created in order to keep track of the locations, shooting days, and scenes. With the "strip shooting" schedule, you will see a breakdown of what each shooting day entails. You'll see the scene number, if it's interior or exterior, the location, and the page length. Underneath the location, you'll see a small description of the scene. This is for reference so that you don't have to flip through the entire script to remember what happens in that scene. The titles are anything but poetic, but they're always clear: "Nick confronts Nora" or "Harry breaks up with Sally."

Look at your scenes, and see if you can encapsulate each scene into something short and clear in that same way. What happens in that scene? What happens with you and your character? Be as specific as possible. Writers never write a scene with two people talking for the sake of talking, so avoid titles like, "Dick and Jane talk." Usually, characters talk to get something from the other, so although it can be about relaying information (see later on exposition), it's usually something else. So what are you talking about and why? What changes for your character or in the circumstances at the end of the scene (internally or externally)?

For example, the main event in act 2 of *August: Osage County* is the family dinner scene: Emotional battles are fought, characters argue, secrets are revealed, tempers flare, and all the characters operate on emotional overdrive. It is a pivotal scene, especially for the lead character, Barbara, who basically usurps her mother at the end of the scene in a physical and mental way. But say you're playing the role of Little Charles. He's a bit of a hapless, unemployed, and unambitious black sheep of the family who is in a secret relationship with the character Ivy. For you, the scene may or may not be about the main event of the mother–daughter dynamic (although the consequences of those actions will affect you later). You may just look at when you enter and when you leave and what happens in between and simply title it, "Little Charles almost declares his love for Ivy but chickens out." Taking the idea of a title even further and going beyond being pithy or literal, you could even give it a more poetic or abstract title, like "Silent Love."

As you title scenes, you might struggle with the poetic essence of what you think the scene is about. You may try to look for the right word. At this point, being right is unimportant. You're digging around in creative juices and seeing what you can uncover in the script. The goal is really to uncover your own interpretation. You also may find that in rehearsal, you discover something new about the scene in working with your director or other actors and realize that the title for the scene should change. They say, "Writing is rewriting," and we say, "Acting is recreating." We make a choice, then scratch it out and try something different.

Exercise 2

Divide the play up by writing out PASTO for the story of the full play. Ideally, write out one sentence for each element. After that, look at your scenes, and divide your scenes up into PASTO, as if they are their own little plays. Then, give them each a title.

CATEGORIZE YOUR SCENES

You've gained a lot of crucial information about the play and the scenes and should have a good idea of how this story works. There's one more tool you can use to help you figure out how your scenes can be played. Let's assume that most scenes in a play are tied to the elements of PASTO and so usually move the action forward. Most scenes have an event, even if it is only a small line or moment. Yet you may notice that some scenes seem to have greater importance than others. Some are longer or more intense. Some are funny, while others seem to move slower. All scenes have a purpose, but not all have the same purpose. Some scenes are written to ensure the audience has certain information that may be relevant, while another scene may be for the audience to understand the character, or a scene may be there to give the audience a release in the form of laughter after a serious moment. If you look at a traditional musical, you can think about the different types of moments within scenes, each tied to a song, which may be fun and entertaining or may be "character songs" that reveal character wants.

Think of each scene fitting into one of three categories:

1. Exposition
2. Character development
3. Entertainment

Many times, scenes will be a combination of all three in some way, but usually one category stands more prominently above the rest.

Exposition

If the scene is exposition, you can usually tell by the amount of new information being given to the audience. A good example of a scene relaying information is any Bond or Jason Bourne movie when a character is giving a mission briefing and telling the main hero (and the audience) what they need to know before they take on their mission. Another example, popular with such television shows as *West Wing* or *Ted Lasso*, is the press conference, where a character is answering direct questions. It's important to note, though, that even with scenes that may be heavy on information, your role as the performer is to be specific about the words and how you feel about them.

In other ways that are not so obvious, exposition can come in the form of characters arguing with each other and, in doing so, giving each other (or the audience) certain key pieces of information. For example, the first scene in Theresa Rebeck's play *What We're Up Against* shows two male characters, Stu and Ben, in Stu's office, drinking and talking about a female architect who works at the firm. Stu is the manager of the firm, and Ben is one of the designers. Stu rants about how this female architect tricked him because she put a different name on a design, a design he thought was created by a male employee. The scene may at first appear as if it is merely a misogynistic employer laying down his anger-fueled opinion on the opposite sex, but it actually delivers crucial information to the audience. In less than two minutes of the play, we learn about the main character, Eliza, a female architect, and her struggles at a male-dominated office, particularly with her boss, the opinionated Stu. The theme and ideas of the play are introduced (equality), and most importantly, we learn about the way Eliza tricked Stu, which becomes important information as it lingers over the entire story. This scene also reveals what kind of characters both Stu and Ben are, and although it is entertaining, the information makes it fit more firmly into the "exposition" category.

Good writers make exposition active, so even if it doesn't seem straightforward, think about the scene in relation to the other scenes in the play. On the opposite spectrum, bad writers make exposition awkward and clumsy.

CHARACTER DEVELOPMENT

A scene that emphasizes character development is more complex, revealing something new about the character. It could be an action the character repeats again and again. Audiences may not glean much from the scene that helps them understand the plot, but they will receive clues about why the character does what they do. August Wilson is a master when it comes to creating characters in all his plays. In particular, there is a monologue in his Pulitzer Prize play *Fences*, in which Troy tells an intense and dramatic story about the day he left home as a fourteen-year-old boy after fighting with his father. The story is not essential to the plot but is revelatory to the audience and allows them to feel sympathy for his actions.

Another good example of a moment defining a character is in the play *Jerusalem* by Jez Butterworth. The story of this play centers on Johnny "Rooster" Byron, who lives in a trailer outside a small town in rural England, a town unhappy with his "loose morals" and nightly revelries. In the first scene, we see two characters in suits serve him with an eviction notice. As they read the notice and pin it on his door, his first entrance is off-stage, howling like a dog, then poking his head out of the top of the trailer while wearing a World War II helmet and goggles and barking through a loud-speaker. After the two characters exit, we see Rooster enter from his trailer door, described as "Wiry. Weathered; drinker's mug. . . . Despite a slight limp, he moves with the balance of a dancer, or animal." After a short mono-logue spoken through the loudspeaker, the playwright gives a page of stage directions. Rooster puts on a record, goes to a water trough to splash water on his face, and then plunges his entire head in (in the Broadway production performed by Mark Rylance, he raised his feet off the ground and almost did a handstand above the water). He then picks up an almost-burned-out joint, fishes around in a pint that has become a makeshift ashtray to find a ciga-rette butt he could light again, and fixes himself a drink of vodka and milk. This amount of activity takes several minutes, but the audience immediately gleans a lot about this character from the behavior and actions. The action of this scene is the delivery of the eviction notice, which is important to the plot, but nothing in his daily waking ritual moves the plot forward. The scene is certainly entertaining, as well, but it's really because of what we're learning about the character.

ENTERTAINMENT

When a scene is pure entertainment, you usually know it. We could call this category "just plain fun." A prime example is from *Peter and the Starcatcher*, adapted by Rick Elice from Dave Barry's novel. The play is a prequel of the story of Peter Pan, full of pirates, pixies, fights, and singing. The second act begins with a musical interlude of mermaids (originally played in the Broadway production by the male actors in drag). They sing about the "starstuff" leaking from the large chest and how they used to be fish. While this information about starstuff is important exposition, it's re-peated many other times in the script by other characters. It's also difficult for an audience to understand what that information means, as it is relayed in the form of a music hall drag performance, complete with fish jokes and a big kick-line dance finish. Also, this number must grab the audience's atten-tion immediately after intermission and put them right back into the imagi-native world of the play. This is pure entertainment. It should be fun! As an actor, you don't have to put your primary focus on exposition or character development, although you still have to perform your mermaid part with a clear character point of view and clear articulation of the words. (Otherwise, the jokes don't land!)

Exercise 3

Take each scene and categorize them as (1) exposition, (2) character development, or (3) entertainment.

Chapter Three

Constructing a Shell

Acting is action. The basis of theatre is doing, dynamism.

—Konstantin Stanislavsky[1]

In this chapter, you'll apply the analytical work to conjure up a character you can inhabit. This is a crucial stage. Actors can be brilliant at analyzing a text while sitting at their chairs, but as soon as they start moving around and getting into their bodies, they find it difficult to translate their ideas into behavior. The exercises in this chapter will help get your body to do what your mind imagines!

WHAT'S IN A NAME?

Words have power. The words we use to describe ourselves or others, the words we use to get what we want, or even the absence of words all have power and meaning. For now, let's examine one specific type of word: a name.

Shakespeare asked, "What's in a name?" And Juliet uses this argument to denounce Romeo's surname as their two families are in an ugly feud, claiming that a "rose by any other name would smell as sweet." But is that true in all cases? For example, you might hop aboard a streetcar named "Desire," but we're not sure that a streetcar named "Misery" would have the same enticement.

The power of the meaning of names dates back to ancient times and varies from culture to culture. In the Judeo-Christian bible, God names the first man Adam, after *adama*, or *earth*. The Bible describes how God created Adam out of the dust of the earth, and his relationship to the ground becomes problematic after he eats the apple from the tree of knowledge of good and

27

evil. In this sense, names are meant to carry the essence of that person. The name *Adam*, then, is an extension of his being. A name similar to *Adam* is *George*, which originates with the Greek name *Georgios*, which combines the Greek words of *earth* with *work*, creating a word that may describe a farmer or someone who works the land in some way.

Or take the name *Lucy*, which is derived from the Latin word *lucius*, which means *of light*. This could have different meanings, as it could mean *daylight* or *to illuminate*, but it could also connote *lightness* or *lightheaded*. It may seem like only a coincidence that *Lucy* and *loosey* sound the same, but depending on its use in a comedy or drama, you could see how the meaning may alter your character. By the way, *Luke* is the male version of *Lucy*, and it's no accident that George Lucas named the hero of the *Star Wars* movies that name in order to accent themes of light versus dark. (To really hit that point, Luke wears white, while Darth Vader wears black.)

Think of your own name. Do you know what your name means or where it originates? Were you named after a relative or someone important? Your parents invested meaning into your name, and it may influence part of your personality. In the same way, writers are conscious of the names they give characters, and you should be, too. Edward Albee did not carelessly use the names George and Martha in the play and film *Who's Afraid of Virginia Woolf?* It's a subtle reference to the founding father and first First Lady of our country, George and Martha Washington. To discover why he might do that is part of your job as an actor. It could be because they never conceived any children, an element that becomes important for Albee's play. Even contemporary writers, like Vince Gilligan, who created and wrote *Breaking Bad*, understand the power of names. He purposefully set up an antihero and then named him Mr. White. (Similar to Luke being a "white knight," Gilligan is playing off the idea of light against dark.) He also names the lawyer Saul Goodman (as in "It's all good, man"). As an actor, you have to realize, nothing on that page in front of you is an accident. All choices are carefully considered by the writer, especially your name.

There are times when we hear a name, and it seems obvious about what that name might suggest. Ted Lasso is a prime example, but there's also Feste from *Twelfth Night*, Brick and Big Daddy from *Cat on a Hot Tin Roof*, and Rooster Byron from *Jerusalem*. Some playwrights have names they use more than once in multiple plays. A great example is Tennessee Williams, who loved the name *Sebastian*, which means *venerable*. *Venerable* is defined as *commanding respect or noble character*. St. Sebastian is also a well-known saint, and Williams wrote a poem early in his life about this saint before going on to write the play *Suddenly Last Summer*, which features a dead son named Sebastian.

For example, let's look at the name *Little Charles* from *August: Osage County* by Tracy Letts. Little Charles is the son of Charlie Aiken, who is the brother-in-law of the family matriarch, Violet Weston. One might think that with a name like *Little Charles*, he is young, but in fact, this character is thirty-seven years old. That he is still called Little Charles by the family makes him seem more of a child to them. It seems even more belittling than calling him Charlie Jr. If we look at some of his actions, we see how this name suits him; how the first time he enters, we see him crying like a child and needing to be consoled by his father; or how he is bossed around by his mother, Mattie Fae. For an actor playing this part, you have to figure out what kind of man-child you want to portray.

Let's look at the role of Esther in Lynn Nottage's play *Intimate Apparel*. This play is set in various bedrooms in lower Manhattan in 1905 and revolves around Esther, a Black seamstress who sews intimate apparel (lingerie) for various clients, from rich White women like Mrs. Van Buren to Black prostitutes like Mayme. She lives in a boardinghouse and longs for love and marriage. Nottage has described this character as being based on older members of her family, of women in an "existential crisis" being taken in by charming men. She described the play itself as a "lyrical meditation on one woman's loneliness and desire."[2]

Knowing that Esther is based on real women from Nottage's family history is important, but what is the meaning of her name? In the Book of Esther in the Old Testament, she is the Jewish queen of a Persian king who saves her people from destruction. With a little bit of research, you could discover that *Esther* may be based on the Persian word for *star* or that it comes from the word *Hadassah*, which means *compassion*. *Esther* in the early nineteenth century was a very popular name. President Grover Cleveland named his daughter Esther in 1891 under the belief that it meant *star*. It's probably safe to assume that Esther's mother thought the same thing. However, if we look at some of this character's actions in the play, we may see that many of them are rooted in how much she cares for the people around her and how that feeds the plot. As it's a biblical name, it may give us hints about Esther's parents and upbringing, as well. Did the story of Esther from the Bible have special resonance for her mother? All this information is fuel for your imagination and for your choices in playing the part.

But what if you're playing a part that has no name: for example, the judge in a production of *The Government Inspector*? Even more commonly, you've got this great role in a film, but your part is listed as "waitress." This is where your imagination and creativity can come into play. If no name has been given, it is up to you to create that name for yourself.

Exercise 1

Look up the meaning of your character's name. If your character hasn't been given a name, then decide on one and look it up. You could do this online or with a baby name book from the library. Find out as much as you can about the name: its origins, its meanings, and historical figures who share this name. Also, include any nicknames or pet names that other characters may call you.

WHAT DO YOU NEED?

In the first two chapters, you analyzed the script and examined how your character fits into this story. Now it's time to go deeper, as in what are your deeper needs? According to Mira Rostova, a Russian acting teacher whom John trained with years ago, all human behavior is motivated by five underlying needs:

- Survival
- Love
- Validation
- Happiness
- Winning

Knowing the underlying motives of your character will help you build your performance. It's like the first layer of a painting, which sets the palette and tone of the piece. In the book *Will Power: How to Act Shakespeare in 21 Days*, there is a long description of each of these needs, but we summarize them here.[3]

The Need for Survival

The need to survive is a primal need that applies to life-and-death issues. These include having enough air, water, food, shelter, and money. If someone is threatening your character's life, your character might do anything to survive. For example, in *Jerusalem*, the danger is very real for Rooster, as he may be evicted and is indeed fighting to keep his very lifestyle as well as his place in the world.

The Need for Love (to Love and/or to Be Loved)

The need to love and be loved can be thought of in the classical sense as romantic or familial love. It involves mutuality, sensuality, intimacy, and romance. In plays, this revolves around siblings, parents, and children, as well as sexual and romantic relationships. *Romeo and Juliet* is a prime example of two characters who are bound by their love for each other, and all their actions revolve around that need. Also, you can find this with characters in plays about family, such as *August: Osage County* and August Wilson's *Fences.*

Specifically, let's look at Esther again from *Intimate Apparel.* As Nottage states, Esther is experiencing an existential crisis and is filled with loneliness. Her driving motivation throughout the play is to find someone to love who loves her back. In the first scene in this play, she talks about this very topic with Mrs. Dickson, who runs the boardinghouse. And later, one of the most painful moments of the play is when she asks her husband, George, if he actually loves her.

The Need for Validation

The need for validation means your character wants acknowledgment of worth from others. They want respect, support, or belonging. This need can escalate the more it is thwarted. A prime example would be a character like Tesman in *Hedda Gabler.* You could see how most of his actions and lines are driven by the desire to be acknowledged by his wife, Hedda; by the academic community; and by Brack and Lovberg. He eventually receives validation, but from Thea, not from whom he desires it most.

The Need for Happiness

The need for happiness is common for many characters. As most of us want to be happy or to erase our suffering, it's not surprising that many stories revolve around characters who are unhappy or in pain (spiritual, mental, or emotional). Characters with this need want to relieve that suffering in themselves or in others. You could easily say that this character just wants "to have fun" and wishes everyone could get along. A prime example of a character just wanting to be happy would be Khlestakov from *The Government Inspector.* Another example is Jeff from *Lobby Hero.* Not only does he want to be happy at his job and avoid conflict, but also he is trying to relieve the suffering of his boss, William, who is under duress, as well as trying to make life better for the female cop, Dawn, who is definitely undergoing suffering. In short, he wants to regain harmony in his life.

The Need to Win

The need to win and be at the "top of the heap" is an aggressively competitive motivation. Most of the times in drama, especially in Shakespeare or in action movies, wanting power or wanting to succeed involves killing or other forms of physical violence. These characters struggle to rise above everyone at any cost. These are characters like Macbeth, Richard III, and Walter White from *Breaking Bad.* They are focused and driven to be the best at any cost.

For more subtle variations, we can look at a character like Bill, the police officer from *Lobby Hero*. He truly does want to be the best cop on the force and won't let anyone stand in his way. He plays to win by asserting his power over every other character in the scene.

WHAT ARE YOUR ACTIONS?

You may have heard Sanford Meisner's definition of *acting*: that "acting is living truthfully in imaginary circumstances" and that much of the Meisner-based training is about the "reality of doing."[4] You don't pretend to listen to your partner; you actually listen. You apply the idea that in your life, you have actions you do every day. You go out into the world, and you perform actions—some big, some small. You get up, brush your teeth, get dressed, check your e-mail, text your friend, and go about your day. These are not the actions we're referring to, though. We are talking about the actions you perform, such as when you complain to your roommate about eating your ice cream or when you plead with your boyfriend to not leave you or when you argue with your mother or when you flatter the barista who makes your coffee.

In the same way that living is doing, acting is doing. Acting is not talking. It is not emoting. Characters, just like you and me, are doing things. Characters usually do talk, but all words are rooted in needs, and any emotion comes out of the striving for that need, as well as satisfaction or denial of that need. With theater, words can be plentiful and powerful, but this is not always the case, especially with physical theater or devising. And with other mediums that use images as their primary way of conveying the story, such as film, there are many scenes without any dialogue at all. Because the words are the first things you see when you look at a script, they seem the most important (especially if it's a lot of lines to memorize). But audiences don't come to see you recite words. They want to see you do things, and it's in the way you perform these actions that makes you unique. This is why you can see many versions of an actor playing Hamlet and find each performance enjoyable. Same words, different play. The actions are performed differently by different actors. Part of the joy of accepting a role is thinking about what you get to do. For instance, finding out that you get to do a sword fight or give an intense speech or have some comedic business should inspire you. One of the reasons many of us love acting is because it allows us to do all those actions that we don't get to do in real life. So, when a director asks you, "What are you doing?" they are really asking, "What are your actions?" As we look at our text, we have to start piecing that together. What are your character's doings? Their actions?

Now that we've got some ideas about your inner need, your driving motivation, it's time to think about what you do to get what you want. Let's break our scenes down into smaller playable units or beats (or bits, as mentioned in chapter 1). Before we dive in, remember that nothing at this point is set in stone. Acting is about reacting, working off your fellow actors, and collaborating with the director. You can't perform in a vacuum. While you may make some choices and have ideas in the preplanning stages, be prepared to adjust as soon as you get in that rehearsal room. We're trying to use our conscious brains (our intellect) in order to free our unconscious (our instincts) and access the creative state in performance.

Take a look at your scenes, and break them into these smaller units (or beats). A beat should be thought of as that period of time where you are playing one specific action tied to your objective. These beats could be a sentence, a line, or a line fragment. Think about changes of tone or conversation. Think about the events that are happening in that scene. How does it change from moment to moment? Some scenes have many beats, while others, especially shorter scenes, may have very few. In film and television scripts, you may have a scene with a sentence of action and one or two lines of dialogue. There may only be two or three beats there. Or it may just be one. You need to find the action that your character is playing in order to get what they want at that moment. There is a fine art to not overcomplicating things and trusting your instincts in terms of where the beats are. Also, you may find that it starts to make more sense when you physicalize it. This is technical and precise, but it's also personal.

Actions are best expressed in the form of a transitive verb. This means that they are in the present tense, and the verbs have an inherent receiver. You want to do something to someone else or change behavior in someone else. You want something from this other person. This guideline will keep you away from verbs like *think* or *ponder*, which are internal and not directed toward another character. It also eliminates actions like "I want to feel good." This is an objective (linked to the inner need of happiness) and needs to be translated into an action. In order to feel good, I make jokes, so my action is "to amuse you." In the book *Actions: The Action Thesaurus*, Marina Caldarone and Maggie Lloyd-Williams describe how to test if the verb is transitive or not by placing the words *I* and *you* with it to see if the sentence makes sense.[5] For example, take the words *taunt* and *tease*. You could say, "I tease you," or "I taunt you." If you tried to do this with *think*, as in "I think you," then it doesn't quite work (as it would be more correct to say, "I think with you," or "I think about you," which makes it less active toward the other person).

Actions should not be commonplace. Writers don't write about the everyday but about heightened moments. Therefore, look for verbs that are strong or playable. These don't come from the analytical mind but from the heart or gut. It should give you enough energy to drive you for more than a few minutes. It's in finding a strong playable verb that will elevate your acting and allow you to tap into your instincts. Strong verbs express a character's inner need and also relate to the moment. Here's where many actors get into trouble, mapping out actions like an intellectual activity but then not understanding that they aren't playing the actions or the actions have no meaning or don't resonate with them. This leads to acting from the head, not the heart. We talk about how to avoid that later in rehearsals!

Let's look at the opening line from *Lobby Hero*. It's very late at night in the lobby of this apartment building, and Jeff, the security guard, reads a book as his supervisor, William, enters. William walks in, and Jeff says, "Hey, William." We could just assume that this character is only saying "hello." Ah, but we know that playwrights never write meaningless, everyday conversations. What deeper moment could be happening here? Now, considering the given circumstances, we could surmise that the subtext might be that Jeff is extremely happy to see someone, anyone, because it's late at night, and Jeff is alone and usually enjoys talking, especially with William. He may have been looking forward to William coming by and might even be expecting it. All this could come out in his "hello." The action might be "to greet" or even "to welcome." But if we analyze the given circumstances further and combine that with Jeff's inner need, the need to be happy and keep harmony in himself and others, there's another way to play it.

Given that William enters that scene after hearing about his brother being in trouble, Jeff might see some anxiety or stress in that entrance and then could use that first line to soothe him, to comfort him, or to calm him. Or he could want to give a good impression so that William won't be worried about him on the job, so he may want to impress him. Much of this is going to change and depend on what that actor does playing William, but the process of writing down an action for that moment helps you to understand your character's point of view and relationship to other characters in the play. It is putting forth ideas so that you can try them out in the rehearsal room, instead of coming in with nothing.

In the book *Actions: The Action Thesaurus*, Caldarone and Lloyd-Williams say that "every action has a different flavor in the mouth," and you'll know by instinct when you have found the right one for that moment.[6] They also suggest that you try the action out and say the line to see if it fits. So, for example, if you say the line "Hey, William," try to soothe the other person. Doesn't work? Try a different verb. You could also try speaking the action aloud right before you say the line, putting it in the first person; "I soothe you: Hey, William."

Here's a secret that great actors know: It may seem like there are unlimited actions out there to choose from, but really there are only so many actions that humans do. And many of those actions can also be put into broader categories (see chapter 6). Finding a strong verb is fun because even though *to push* is similar to the action *to shove*, one may resonate with you, while the other doesn't.

Another secret about actions is that they are like a universal acting language. When Dennis was sitting in William Esper's studio in the second year of Meisner training, he said, "There's no action where you could say 'only Italians do that' or 'only French people do that.'" Humans have universal qualities, which is why we can watch movies in another language and still get a sense of an actor's "doings."

Every action has an opposite action, a force working against you. This is not accidental, as in every play there is a form of conflict, and that conflict generally takes the form of opposing forces. Sometimes characters want the same ultimate goal but are going about it in different ways. Too often, actors are good at laying down the actions but forget the obstacle and the conflict. Remember to ask, "What is in your way to achieving the goal?"

Exercise 2

Go through your scenes, and in the margins, write down actions next to your lines. What does your character seem to be doing at first glance? (Remember, this might change once you work off the other actors and collaborate with the director.) Don't just pick any old action from a list of verbs. Say the line, and try different actions with those lines, noticing when they might change from beat to beat. Don't intellectualize this too much. Find an actable verb that feels more from your heart than your head. Using the PASTO breakdown, you should be able to see more clearly how your strategy to get what you want changes.

DEFINE YOUR RELATIONSHIPS

The difficult aspect of defining relationships, when it comes to acting, is that words we choose to label a relationship aren't enough to start making choices about how to play the role. Say the word *mother* to a hundred different people, and you'll get a hundred different responses. Writers often give us the literal relationship, but that's only the beginning for us, and sometimes, it can be a trap. You might understand the literal meaning of *mother*, but how can that help you as an actor? How do you go deeper so that you build your performance from the relationships in the play?

This might be a good time to introduce the idea that there are really two sets of given circumstances. (This is related to the idea of substitution, as well, which we talk about in chapter 5.) Dennis learned about this from Sergio Ostrenko, a Russian theater maker and educator. There are the given circumstances in the play that everyone decides on (what we've already covered in chapter 1—the who, what, where, why, and when). These facts are given to us by the writer or the director. But then there are imaginary given circumstances that we can create for ourselves that no else need ever know about—not our fellow actors, not our director, and especially not the audience. For example, if you got cast as Little Charles in *August: Osage County*, you have to decide how you feel about your parents, Mattie Fae and Charlie. The literal relationship is "mother" and "father." But the way you feel about your mother or father is completely different. If we only work with the first literal definition, then what will happen is we play the generic idea of how we think we should behave toward our mother or father. What we need to do is go deeper and think about how we feel about our mother or father in this scene at this moment. Think about your own mother, and imagine a time when you were having a wonderful conversation. Now, think about another time when you argued with her, perhaps talking about politics. Same person, same literal relationship, but your feelings about her may change.

Notable Meisner-based teacher William Esper told his students, "A relationship is emotional. It's about your feeling towards someone. You have to ask yourself, 'What does this person mean to me? How do I feel toward him?'"[7] For a character like Little Charles, his mother, Mattie Fae, acts anything but motherly toward him (of course, not from her point of view, and she has some serious reasons for the feelings toward Little Charles, revealed later in the play). If anything, he's afraid of her and unable to stand up to her. She's like a prison warden. If the actor playing Little Charles only thinks of her as a mother, then that may not help with his behavior or help with the way he would react to her. But if the actor considers Mattie Fae like a prison warden who could send him into solitary confinement, then he might be able to get some instinctual reactions from that imaginary point of view.

It needs to be specific, not a general idea or general emotional response. We react emotionally to a specific event. If your mother strikes fear in your heart, then there is a reason for that. And it's your job as an actor to use your imagination to figure out what it is. For Little Charles, you could imagine that she embarrasses him all the time and criticizes him about his lack of employment or how he watches too much television. Going deeper, you should be more specific to create an event that you feel would be horrifying: For example, you were playing piano in a music shop, and a very attractive woman started talking to you, but then your mother came over, insulted you by telling this woman you'll never be as good as Elton John or Billy Joel, and hands you a flyer for a job at McDonald's. Perhaps the woman looked at you sadly and walked away. If you embellish this in your imagination, give it time as a daydream, and let it fester in you, then you could see how a humiliating and infuriating event like that would carry emotional meaning that you could use in your scenes. This specificity in your work sharpens your point of view. And the best part is that you don't even have to tell anyone about this imaginary event—it's all yours!

While it's true that in some scripts, you may find out exactly why you feel a certain way about a person and you could use that as your event, the reason the playwright gave you may have little meaning to you as an actor. For instance, in *Hedda Gabler*, Mrs. Elvsted says to Hedda how frightened she was of her in school, how Hedda used to pull her hair and even said she'd burn it off one day. This is wonderful material for you to work with, and it's there for many reasons: It's revealing about both characters, it's funny and foreboding, and it helps convey the story. As an actor, if you're playing Mrs. Elvsted, you have to realize that she's talking about the past, about when they were in school, and she may not be frightened of Hedda in the present scene. Or she may still be frightened, but it's a more mature type of fear, perhaps turned to being intimidated of her. Either way, as an actor playing the part, you have to decide specifically how you view that relationship with Hedda. You could imagine your own set of given circumstances, just for you, that Hedda is part of a cult and is trying to get you to join. Playing the scene with that as your point of view, your behavior will definitely come out as wary and tentative—and the audience will see that behavior and attribute it to your lines and the literal given circumstances.

Exercise 3

It's time to put all this together into an exercise that can aid you in your rehearsal. Create a three-minute nonverbal "étude" of your character. This étude can be abstract or literal, depending on how you want to explore movement and your character's inner life. Make it as simple as you can in terms of action and physical activities. For example, explore getting ready to go out with friends, or create an imaginary circumstance that would coincide with the givens of the play. To help you, choose a piece of music that is about three minutes long, and time out your "étude" to that music. Discover at least five repeatable gestures (each one distinct) that you can use within the étude, and repeat one of them at least three times. You can play with a costume item if you like, and you may want to play with a prop or two. Expect that this work will take you at least an hour of rehearsal but possibly two.

Chapter Four

Brick by Brick

Three Types of Language

Tell me what a person does and I will tell you who they are.

—Uta Hagen[1]

You've done a lot of work, but so far, you've been working alone. We need to prepare you for the demands of rehearsal and being in the room with others. This chapter gives you the tools to start moving and speaking as the character! In this chapter, we explore the three kinds of language (verbal, physical, energy) that your character might use. Building on what we previously constructed, this new work will help finish your foundation.

Before we dive in, take a moment to consider what materials you might use to build your house—some walls might be brick or stone, while others might be wood. The following three types of language are like different materials—not all houses will use them all, but you should know what material is available.

DISCOVERING YOUR VERBAL LANGUAGE

We typically attribute plays with poetic or heightened language as using verbal language as their main tool. Writers like William Shakespeare, Samuel Beckett, Oscar Wilde, Anton Chekhov, Harold Pinter, María Irene Fornés, Sarah Ruhl, or Suzan-Lori Parks rely heavily on verbal language. August Wilson is another playwright whose characters speak with a sense of musicality and poetry. Wilson admits to this (he began a writing career as a poet), and one good example is to look at the play *Seven Guitars*. Wilson uses the metaphor of the guitar for his title and created a musical voice for each of the seven characters. While some authors may emphasize rhythm and visual language, others may highlight wit and rhetoric, such as Tom Stoppard and Theresa Rebeck. But verbal language is a useful and common tool for contemporary writers, as well, from Stephen Adly Guirgis to Nilo Cruz to Katori Hall.

Verbal language can come in different shapes and sizes, so let's look at some examples. If the lines feel like poetry, then they probably are. In a Shakespeare play, it's common to have a line like "But, soft, what light through yonder window breaks? It is the East and Juliet is the sun." And yet, it's not uncommon for his characters to break out of poetic speech and speak in prose, often when something funny is happening (and using physical language instead). But a poetic line by another playwright may just mean that the line needs emphasis in some way.

Some playwrights intentionally write poetic lines, such as Quiara Alegría Hudes (*In the Heights*). In her play, *Elliot, A Soldier's Fugue*, the lyrical voices of the characters should be played as if they were music, which is what the title of the play alludes to. The dialogue is even separated as if it is poetry or lyrics:

GINNY: A room made of cinderblock.
A mattress lies on a cot containing thirty-six springs.
If you lie on the mattress you can feel each of the thirty-six springs.
One at a time.
As you close your eyes.
And try to sleep the full four hours.[2]

In Hudes's play, the lines overlap, there are various styles of music, and time and space are relative to the thoughts and emotions of the characters. This is not fourth-wall realism, and the actors are encouraged to embrace that.

But even if your play is not written like poetry, you may still encounter writers with a definite ear for rhythm. Near the end of the play *Jerusalem* by Jez Butterworth, Johnny has a beautiful monologue after being asked if he'd ever seen a real fairy:

JOHNNY: I've seen a lot of strange things in this wood. I seen a plague of frogs. Of bees. Of bats. I seen a rainbow hit the earth and set fire to the ground. I seen the air go still and all sound stop and a golden stag clear this clearing. Fourteen point antlers of solid gold. I heard an oak tree cry. . . . Elves and fairies, you say. (*Beat.*) Elves and fairies.[3]

A scene that emphasizes verbal language may use some of what you see in that speech. It may use vivid imagery, metaphor, rhythm, and meter. Even though Johnny's speech is written as if it is just another piece of dialogue, you could imagine it as a poem. If you write out just the first five sentences, each on a line, you can begin to sense the rhythm of the poetry inherent in the language:

> I've seen a lot of strange things in this wood.
> I seen a plague of frogs.
> Of bees.
> Of bats.
> I seen a rainbow hit the earth and set fire to the ground.

It may be that a scene with verbal language uses long sentences and polysyllabic words, such as what you might find in Noël Coward or Oscar Wilde. But you also may find poetry in shorter lines with a more staccato rhythm, such as with Caryl Churchill, Will Eno, or Samuel Beckett.

When you look at your scenes, there are a few signposts to alert you to the use of verbal language. Context is important, as well, so you should consider the given circumstances, which is the reason you must know these before taking apart the lines to analyze them for character clues. A character may be speaking a certain way due to the emotional situation, the event that has occurred, or the relationship with the other character(s) in the scene. For instance, people may be usually very talkative, except when they are nervous, so if it's a scene where a man is trying to talk to an attractive woman whom he is in love with, he may stammer. But in another scene, with his friends, he may be boastful and talk endlessly.

First, look at the length of the sentences. Does your character talk in long or short sentences? Does the character use big or small words? You want to start looking for clues to their manner in relating to other characters as well as their level of formal education and street sense. An NYPD officer, like Bill from *Lobby Hero*, may not have a PhD, so he doesn't talk like an academic, but it doesn't mean he isn't smart or has a low level of education, especially when it comes to street sense and relating to other people. He may talk in short sentences and be to the point, but he could still be the smartest person in the room (or at least thinks he is). Using big words and long sentences could mean the character has a feeling of self-importance, loves to hear himself talk, or talks too much. This character might use language to impress everyone. These types of characters may use poetry and quotes or speak in hyperbole. They might even refer to themselves in the third person. (There is an extremely funny character from the sitcom *Seinfeld* named "The Maestro" who did just this!)

If your character has a long speech, then possibly she is having difficulty expressing herself in just the right way. This speech might show how she struggles to articulate her thoughts and be clear, with a need of wanting to be understood (see chapter 9 for more on long speeches). If you've labeled your scene under character development, as in our earlier exercise, then you might find that the long monologue is so that the audience can understand the character's perspective. It may even be poetic, such as the earlier Johnny "Rooster" example.

Many times, when a speech is inserted in a play, the playwright intentionally wants to pause the action to show the characters' thoughts and feelings. August Wilson is a master of these kinds of speeches, notably Troy's speech in *Fences* about the day he stood up to his father and left home at fourteen, when the world got "big" and it took him a "long time to cut it down" so he could handle it.[4] While the speech organically comes out of the conversation about his son's ambitions, it is not connected to the events of the play and could be cut without sacrificing plot. However, if you cut that speech, you'd lose essential facts and emotions of that character, and the audience may not sympathize with his further actions. In looking at the end of that speech, we also see how poetic the words become, especially the use of rhetoric, playing the words of *big* and needing to *cut it down*.

If the character talks in short sentences, then it could mean they speak only what they need to and no more. As before, if your character is a police officer, then the culture will dictate the language used. Professions have their own vernacular and vocabulary. This doesn't mean that all police officers use that language in the same way, though. Short sentences may hint at education, but they can just as easily hint to the emotional life of the character, as well as what's happening in the scene.

Another way to look at the verbal language of your character is to notate the repetition of words and phrases, which we explain in chapter 1. These are often revealing. For instance, can you count how many times Big Daddy says the word *mendacity* throughout *Cat on a Hot Tin Roof*? Or how many times the words *believe* or *hope* come up in the series *Ted Lasso*?

DISCOVERING YOUR PHYSICAL LANGUAGE

Think of your physical language as everything you do physically. It's your body language. It's how you walk, stand, sit, gesture, hold items in your hand, and relate to others in the physical environment.

The most obvious stage directions will be related to the environment itself. If the scene takes place in the large mansion of a Russian mayor in the eighteenth century, you'll move and behave quite differently than if the scene takes place in the lobby of a hotel on the Upper West Side of Manhattan in present day. You will need to think about not just how your character moves in relation to the space or to others but also how your character relates to objects in the room. For instance, if you are cast in the role of Esther in *Intimate Apparel*, then you need to know the way that your body sits to sew those garments, and you should acquaint yourself with that activity. In short, looking first at stage directions can give you clues to understand your physical language. Using those clues, you may then be inspired to add to that information, create from it, and let that form the basis of a character.

If you decide not to pay attention to the stage directions (i.e., only reading your lines of dialogue) or decide to cross them out, then you're deciding to block information or ideas that could inspire you or shape your performance. Some actors are encouraged to immediately cross out all stage directions in their acting edition of their script. This may relate to Uta Hagen's advice to cross out any adjectives and adverbs in a script so that "they can in no way influence you." Actors are not fond of being directed into a choice by the playwright, especially if there is an adverb before a line (such as to say a line "lovingly").[5]

We want to discover our own way of saying the lines and move, sit, stand when our impulse strikes us to avoid being stifled by what the script dictates. This practice of crossing out stage directions may have stemmed from the fact that early acting editions were taken from promptbooks and much of the stage directions were written down by the stage manager from the first production. But this practice of publishing stage management blocking is no longer standard practice in the industry. You can be sure that any play recently produced on Broadway has been published with directions written by the author. The same goes, of course, for all film and TV scripts. And if you are in the hands of a good writer, there will be only the directions needed to convey the idea of the scene. Most playwrights are not as descriptive as Tennessee Williams and Eugene O'Neill. But even if they are, we should look at these directions as part of the story being told. We understand that actors don't want to be restrained in their acting choices, but should we ignore these stage directions completely? Does that mean we can just enter and exit whenever we please?

If we think about the fact that acting is a balancing act between interpretation and creation (as well as between intellect and inspiration), then we realize that many choices are being dictated to us already. It's our job to make all the choices authentic, whether they are given by the author or the director or come from our own crafting. Stage directions and the physical actions in our scripts are another aspect of what the writer has given us. They are clues for behavior and how to play the scene. It's true you may not perform the exact blocking a writer intended. But if the writer has done their job and you've fully explored the given circumstances, then you'll find that your artistic choices won't conflict with that intent. And all stage directions have room for interpretation. For example, Kenneth Lonergan writes in *Lobby Hero* that when we first see Jeff, he's reading a paperback novel. But he doesn't dictate what type of paperback novel. This means you decide. What would Jeff read? Westerns? Crime novels? If you don't make a choice and have strong opinions, then you leave it up to the director or props person, who may not put as much thought into it as you would.

Physical language can also include physical activities that you may perform in the scene. These could be simple activities, such as putting groceries away, setting the table, cleaning, fixing a watch, sewing, or even eating food. The script may already indicate what activity you are doing, and that might be in the stage directions, but sometimes, the activity might just be hinted at. For instance, in *Lobby Hero*, Lonergan gives Jeff a couple activities that he might be doing to pass the time at his job, such as reading a paperback novel or taking a nap. But what else could he doing? He could be doing the crossword puzzle in the paper. He could be trying to learn card tricks. He could be making a list of other jobs he would rather have. The possibilities of other activities to explore are endless. You may not have to actually do these in your scene, or may only do them at the top of a scene for a few moments and then drop them. But this is your opportunity as an actor to bring in choices. As a director, it would fill my heart with immense joy if at our first blocking rehearsal, an actor approached me to say, "I think Jeff would be trying to do a crossword puzzle at the top of this. What do you think?"

You also have to be attentive to lines that call for justification. For instance, if a character says to you, "Sit down," it only makes sense that you're standing at that moment (unless you're going for a joke, that is). You are, therefore, justifying the line. At the beginning of scene 2 of *The Government Inspector*, Khlestakov is dramatically holding a gun to his head, then sees a mirror, and pretends to be James Bond, striking poses—until his servant Osip enters, watches him, and says the line, "Bang." Of course, the next stage direction, in parenthesis, is that Khlestakov "Jumps, shrieks." The gun fires, and plaster falls on Khlestakov's head.[6]

Now, a director could decide to ignore all the stage directions given by the writer or decide to do something completely different (I'm not sure what that would be, as what the writer has given is hilarious and also reveals so much of these characters), but the actor playing Osip still has to justify saying that first line. As an actor, these moments of physical action are what you're looking for. Later in that scene, Osip takes the gun from Khlestakov. You'll have to ask yourself, "How does he take the gun? Is he used to taking a gun away from him?" Osip is a little bit like a babysitter or a stage manager. He knows how to handle this overgrown child. This would affect how he physically interacts with Khlestakov. Therefore, he may grab it like a mother grabbing a dangerous knife from a child, or maybe it's a struggle to get the gun out of his hand, or maybe he takes it out of his hand very carefully and lovingly, soothing him with those words.

It's important to remember that the actions you have started to play with earlier enter into your physicality, as well. You could play different actions for Osip's line, but it's the way the action is performed that defines the character. Like with most things, it's not what you say or do, but how you say and do it. This may sound product oriented, as if you are looking for a result, but at this early point of working on the character, you are still in a playful discovery mode.

Another element that you can start to pay attention to is the use of props. Props can even identify a character (we talk more about props in chapter 5). Who is Indiana Jones without his bullwhip? Or Rey without her lightsaber? What are the items that your character handles, and what is your relationship to each item? We tend to think of a physical object as a "thing," but the truth is, we relate to these objects in a personal way, beyond sentimental items. For instance, you may have an emotional connection to the pen that your grandfather gave you, as it was the last thing he gave you before he died. That makes sense, and I'm sure you've done acting exercises to explore how you relate to a prop. But there is scientific evidence that we have relationships and feelings toward everyday objects, especially our computers, tablets, and smartphones.

Think about the last time you lost your phone. Or the time your computer froze or crashed. As you look at what your character physically does in the scenes, you should make a list of the props that you will come into contact with. Yes, the props person and director will likely decide what that specific prop may be when you get in rehearsal, but it's important for you to start to think about how you handle that prop. This is even more important when it comes to such props as swords, guns, and other weapons. The way a character uses those definitely defines him or her.

DISCOVERING YOUR ENERGY LANGUAGE

Of the three types of language, energy language may be the most difficult to understand and to implement. It takes experience and practice to recognize its use and how to pour the right amount of energy you need into each scene. This isn't to say that in some scenes you use energy and in others you don't; all scenes require your energy as an actor, which includes your focus, concentration, working off your fellow actors, playing actions, and diving into the conflict. But what we're talking about in this chapter is categorizing the emphasis in the types of language used for that scene. And some scenes are elevated beyond verbal and physical into energy.

A scene that involves energy language is a high-intensity scene and requires you to rise to the occasion. When you look at the scene, you must first relate it to the context of the given circumstances. You must understand the key actions and events in the scene, and understanding energy language is understanding what these actions mean at this moment in the story. You know what is at stake for the character and how it relates to the story (all of this building on the research, analysis, and work you've done up to this point). Let's look at this example, from the opening lines of *Peter and the Starcatcher*:

A bare stage. A company of MEN enters with a purpose, the BOY in the middle.

BOY: When I was a boy, I wished I could fly.

PRENTISS: Me too.

SCOTT: So did I!

BOY: Out the window and over the trees—

MOLLY: *(pushing through the men)*—then loop the loop and up to the stars! I dreamed about flying all the time![7]

This prologue introduces the actors and the characters, as well as the many theatrical devices that are used throughout the play. This moment—in fact, the first ten minutes of this play, at least—is one long scene using energy language. It is up to the actors to capture the imagination of the audience immediately and get them interested in the story.

Scenes with energy language are when the playwright, or director, wants heightened energy. It is like the rush of adrenaline before skydiving out of an airplane, a soldier pumping himself up before going into battle, or football players in a ready stance as the ball gets kicked off at the Super Bowl. If you take a look at punctuation, you may notice some exclamation marks; that should tip you off.

To help you understand if the scene uses energy language, ask yourself if this scene is

- a life-or-death situation,
- a dream,
- a fantasy, or
- a nightmare.

A Life-or-Death Situation

As the name suggests, a life-or-death situation involves violence or the threat of death, such as in a scene when Harry Potter battles Voldemort or Romeo fights Tybalt or the final scene of *Breaking Bad*, when Walter White faces off with a gang of neo-Nazis. It could also be a scene where a fireman is trying to rescue a child from a burning building. Although very common in film and TV, you can also encounter life and death on the stage, as well. This could be as simple as the tense scene in Lynn Nottage's *Sweat* near the end of the play, when Oscar is just trying to leave the bar after getting a job at the factory and is being called a scab and the potential fight that might occur.

A Dream

A dream is akin to a character's large sense of vision and purpose. If you look at any sports movie where there is a locker-room speech to the team (usually at halftime when the team is losing), the inspired coach is using this type of energy language, trying to capture the dream of victory. The final episode of the first season of *Ted Lasso* has one of these speeches delivered by Jason Sudeikis, where he counters the argument that "It's the hope that kills you," firing up his soccer players with his speech, "I believe in hope. . . . I believe in belief!"

A Fantasy

A fantasy is slightly different from a dream. It's more about immediate satisfaction and anticipating an upcoming moment. A personal example for you might be the moment you are waiting at a fancy restaurant, on a first date with someone you are excited about. In fact, oftentimes, these moments can be about anticipating romance or a sexual encounter. In the first scene of Nilo Cruz's *Anna in the Tropics*, the three women are waiting at the docks for the arrival of the lector, who will be reading aloud to the workers at a cigar factory. Lectors were like movie stars in those days and were heavily romanticized. For the youngest, Marela, this is a fantasy coming true, a movie star coming to visit. Sometimes a dream may even involve a hint of sensual possibilities or sexuality, thus some anticipation.

A Nightmare

A nightmare is when the worst that could happen is happening in that moment. Also, keep in mind, the scene could start out as a dream and then change into a nightmare. For Hedda Gabler, the final scene is her nightmare scene, where Lovberg has committed suicide in the ugliest way possible (not as she dreamed) and Judge Brack has gained ultimate control over her and her life. Another nightmare can be found in Lynn Nottage's *Intimate Apparel*, when George takes all of Esther's money and she realizes how little he actually cares for her as a wife and a human being.

In all these examples of energy language, they are tied to what is at stake in the scene. You may hear a director ask or give a note about "raising the stakes" (see chapter 14 for more directing notes like these). What this means is that it has to matter if you don't achieve your objective. It can't just "be important"; you specifically know what could happen and what that could mean to you. The stakes and your objective are always tied to the given circumstances and your character. For Hedda, it means loss of freedom and being under someone else's control. That is unbearable to her, and she takes her own life when she loses her objective. For Romeo fighting with Tybalt, the stakes are quite high because he has just married Tybalt's cousin Juliet, so he doesn't want to fight, for her sake. But then he must avenge his friend Mercutio's murder. He also knows that to be caught fighting in the streets may mean punishment by death. That's a lot of stakes!

When a scene or a moment in the play requires energy language, the writer is telling you that a change in energy must happen. That might affect your delivery in terms of volume or pitch. You have to get behind this line with some gusto!

PUTTING THE THREE LANGUAGES INTO PRACTICE

The most important thing to remember about these three types of languages is that it is just another tool for you to open the scene and the lines, to give variety and dynamics to the performance. If you have ever gotten the note from your teacher or director that you often play the same level or the same actions over and over or that the end is very similar to the beginning, then this simple tool could help you make choices with more contrast and variety.

Let's look at this monologue from *The Albatross* by Dennis Schebetta. This speech is near the end of the play when Sofia, a nineteen-year-old first-year student at a small liberal arts college, challenges her professor David. She once considered him her literary idol, and he was the reason she wanted to attend this school, but over the past year of taking his classes, she has seen that he is still recovering from the suicide of his wife and hasn't written anything since. In this scene, he has lashed out at her, jealous of her talent. She finally retaliates against him, letting loose with her honest opinion and putting him in his place:

> SOFIA: I'm going to leave, okay? You're obviously . . . drunk or something. But for the record, I care. I care more than you ever do, or did. You talk to me about . . . You're the one who doesn't care. You walk around like a shadow of a person, mourning your wife. And your wife doesn't exist anymore. She's not real. She's just this idea of happiness you once had. She probably swallowed those pills because she couldn't stand to be around such a hypocrite. I thought I was taking class from, I don't know, some literary giant. I always had this picture of you in my head as this inspiring genius who was enduring the screwed-up cards of life he'd been dealt . . . I thought we understood things or saw things from the same point of view. One day I'd meet you and we'd talk about how this moment changed us, how we captured it in time. But the truth is, I mean, you want honesty, David? Get over it. Your wife killed

herself. Maybe it was your fault, maybe it wasn't. I was twelve when my mom hung herself and I knew how to deal . . . I mean, I was a wreck for years, but I started writing poems and that was my anchor. But you . . . you're stuck. It's like you lost your anchor and you're adrift. I used to think you were someone to look up to, but how can I? How can anyone? You should stop teaching. You've already stopped writing. Just throw in the towel. I'm sorry. It's harsh, but . . . I should just go. I'm sorry.

You might decide that this speech isn't energy language. She isn't about to go into battle, and it doesn't seem like life or death. An actor could choose to play this as if she is consoling David or just setting him straight. However, if we look at the idea of our character living through a nightmare, then doesn't it qualify? The stakes are quite high for her. She has lost faith in her idol and is defending herself against him. She has wanted his praise and approval, and he is telling her she has no talent. Given the power dynamics of teacher and student and the fact that he has been lashing out at her, she may indeed feel as if she is fighting for her life.[8]

Not all of this speech may be energy language. Look at it again. That first line could be energy language, or it could be physical language ("I'm going to leave"), which could be coupled with the physical action of heading toward the door. This could be her way of avoiding the conflict. But then she says, "But," and that stops her. At that moment she could shift from physical to energy language. In the same way, you would play the following lines as verbal language: "I started writing poems and that was my anchor. But you . . . you're stuck. It's like you lost your anchor and you're adrift." That line is rich in imagery, and the audience is going to need to hear it. She is making a point with that language.

The idea of different types of language is so that you can use it as a tool to ensure that you are not playing every moment as the same moment. The stakes must change, just as the given circumstances fluctuate throughout the course of the script and story. There are no hard and fast rules here. You have to decide what the journey of your character is as you go through the scene.

Exercise 1

Look at your scenes, and decide line by line which of the three types of language your character uses: verbal, physical, or energy. Keep in mind, it could start as one and shift to another, or it could use two types, but be as specific as possible, and invest in the scene accordingly.

Part II

BUILDING THE ROLE:
STEPS FOR EARLY REHEARSAL

Chapter Five

Building with Others

All the world's a stage and most of us are desperately unrehearsed.

—Sean O'Casey[1]

If you want to go fast, go alone. If you want to go far, go with others.

—African proverb

This chapter focuses on bringing your ideas and choices into the first rehearsal or table read. This is the moment when all your ideas and choices from reading the script are going to be explored and examined in collaboration with the director, writer, designer, and other actors. This means your work will evolve. You're not throwing it all away, but you are transforming it. The preliminary work is similar to an artist drawing rough sketches that will change in order to make an oil masterpiece on canvas later.

Rehearsal is where the true actor comes alive. Until now, we've been anticipating what might happen for certain choices. But these choices are only rough ideas, ready to be tested out in the rehearsal room. Too many actors become attached to their early homework and forget that their job is to react to other actors and integrate the ideas of the director. As actors, we need to collaborate with our ensemble; this means not just coming into a room together and doing work at the same time. Collaboration means you bring in an idea that sparks another idea, or the director shapes your choice to create a different choice that is even more amazing. Collaboration is at the heart of theatrical creation and also one of the great joys of rehearsal.

Rehearsal is about repetition and building habits, but your goal is to build *good* habits. It is also trial and error, like an experiment. Never forget Edison, who looked at failure quite differently than most normal people. As the story goes, a reporter once asked him how it felt to fail at inventing the lightbulb, and he replied, "I have not failed. I've just found 10,000 ways that will not work." Eventually, he succeeded. Every choice you make, whether it works or not, brings you closer and closer to success. In exchange for throwing away ideas that may not work, you're going to be rewarded by new ideas that will come at you in the moment and by working off the energy and actions of your fellow players.

As we move through the material in this chapter, some of it may seem rudimentary, especially to those who have worked on a production before. We urge you to read through the chapter anyway, as you might learn habits to make your rehearsal more effective. Just as you might have picked up some new ideas on what to look for in your reading of a script, you might discover there are ways to get even more out of your first rehearsal.

FIRST REHEARSAL

The first rehearsal (or table read, if working on film) is always exciting, like the first day of school. Whether you've worked with these actors before or it's a room filled with strangers, most often you have never come together for this particular purpose—to work on this play in these roles at this moment in time.

No production, rehearsal room, director, or group of actors is ever the same. Even with an ensemble company, where the actors work with each other over and over again, that first rehearsal marks the beginning of a new project. And because it's the first day, it often sets the tone for the entire creative process. Actors are immediately relieved when they feel they are in the hands of a good director, one who listens to them, inspires them, trusts them, and is capable and imaginative.

This is the first time everyone is in the room, and you get to hear the script come to life. It's an important reading, but try not to put too much pressure on yourself. Don't feel like this first read-through is an extension of the audition process. Your worst fear may be that the director is going to be filled with regret in casting you and recast the role, but that isn't going to happen.

The most important task for this table read is to relax and listen to your fellow actors. Really listen. Really observe them. The wonderful thing about this reading is that your primary focus is to say the lines and work off your partner(s). You don't have to worry about blocking, movements, props, costumes, lights, the set, or an audience. It sounds simple, but working in that kind of simplicity isn't easy. This doesn't mean reading in a neutral manner. But it doesn't mean pushing or forcing choices. It's called a read-through, but don't let that fool you.

As directors, we're always puzzled when we see actors looking down at their scripts during the first read-through, their noses practically buried in their books. No one makes eye contact. They seem to be barely even talking to each other. Most importantly, they don't seem to be listening and paying attention to each other. It's a way of hiding instead of engaging. It's much safer, so of course it's something inexperienced actors do, completely unaware. When we see this happen, we stop and have the actors start over, reminding them to use each other as much as possible. We may even get the actors on their feet and have them play an acting game or warm up together so that they can have some sense of connection. This same idea of connection with your fellow actors needs to be present even when sitting down with the script.

One important tool for overcoming this is to remember that you don't need to constantly look down at the script. If you've read it as many times as we've asked you to, then you already have a sense of your lines and know where beat changes might be, as well as the circumstances. Even though you don't have the lines memorized, you know more than you realize. And when you need the line, simply look down for it. A good trick is to use your finger or thumb alongside the page and scroll down as you and others talk, so when you need the line, you can scan down to see it. Your goal is to put your focus and attention on the other actors, and you can't do that if you're constantly putting your face in a book. If, by chance, you must take a moment to look down and find a line because you were so intent on another actor or were surprised by a moment, that's okay. No one expects a final performance in the first reading. If we could do that, then we wouldn't need rehearsal.

After this reading, it is likely that there will be discussion, usually led by the director. The director may discuss why this play is important and relevant or the major themes and larger questions. Some directors are more erudite than others. All these discussions are important to unify the vision of the production. Take notes and ask questions, but most of all, listen to the ideas around you.

The discussion often revolves around the given circumstances. The best actors are able to adjust to many directing styles, so it behooves you to listen and find a way to collaborate with your director and the other actors. This is why it's beneficial for you as an actor to already have some clear ideas in your head about the circumstances: so you have an answer when a director asks, "Where were you right before this scene started?" You can reply quickly and specifically, "I was buying a book at the store and running late." Or the director might ask the entire cast, "How much time do we think has passed between scenes three and four? An hour? Two hours?" One actor in the group might say an hour; another might say it feels like three. You might argue that it's closer to two hours because your character has to exit the scene, drive to a town forty miles away to pick up another character, and then drive back another forty miles, and you know all that because you've gotten those clues from the script work you've already done. After some discussion, the director and rest of the cast might still decide that the time gap between those scenes is three hours. So now you know you have to change your idea of how much time has passed and fill it in for your character—what else would they be doing during that time? Rest assured: There will be a lot of logistical and literal questions to be asked in that first reading, and not all will be answered right away.

Now, you might be thinking to yourself, "If the given circumstances and my character needs might be changed on the first day of rehearsal, then why did I bother to start working on that beforehand? Why not just show up and let the director tell me what she thinks it should be? After all, she's the director. The final decision belongs to her, anyway." First, by going through these ideas and choices and using your imagination, you've started to engage in the material actively and creatively, and that will help you when you get into performance. Second, by consciously considering what might be interesting or good choices to feed your work prior to rehearsal, you are contributing to the production. You could be inspiring your director or other actors or giving them ideas to think about (as we stated earlier, collaboration is about sparking new ideas together). This generates creative energy, and that energy will feed off other energy. You want to be a creative giver, not an actor who only receives information.

Finally, it's not the director's job to make your choices for you. In high school or college, that might be the case, as a director is often your teacher, as well. But in the professional world, your job as an actor is to come in with your own choices. It's what you have been hired to do. You need to figure out how you will live this role. If the director wanted to work with puppets, she'd be a puppeteer. In my experience, most directors are far more interested in shaping an actor's ideas into a performance rather than force-feeding choices to an actor. That's not direction; that's dictating. Aside from that, directors have too many other choices to make through the production process. No director is interested in creating and giving choices for all twelve actors in a cast. They say that casting is 90 percent of the job of directing, and it's true. If the director cast you, then she wants your interpretation.

Another minor reason is that there's the possibility you may work with either a nondirector or a bad director. Hey, it happens. Not all directors are geniuses. Like any profession, there are wonderful and brilliant artists out there as well as people who seem to represent the worst in humanity. And there are those who reside somewhere in the middle of that spectrum. You may work with a director whom you don't seem to connect with due to differing personalities or a director who has overcommitted or jobbed in at the last minute and is unprepared. You could be angry, blame the director for lack of direction, and give a poor performance. But the review of your work in the newspaper isn't going to mention how the director can't direct actors. (They usually can't discern the difference between acting and directing choices.) They will look at the work you've done on that stage or on camera. So be prepared to be the best artist in the room. The day will come when you are, whether you want to be or not.

On the opposite side of the spectrum, when you do get the opportunity to work with talented artists and crew, you will find that the level of passion, commitment, and dedication exceeds your own. Working with a director who respects you and your choices is a dream. You bring in your work, and they guide and collaborate with you. Like with many things, the more you invest in a production, the more you get out of it. Professionals are eager to bounce their ideas, energy, and work off each other, discarding choices that don't work and starting again. Professionals do not wait for the first rehearsal to be told what to do. Professionals are working and crafting their part from the minute they get the script. Those people are inspiring to work with and bring everyone's game up. Be that person! Inspire your fellow players!

BALANCING INTELLECT WITH INSTINCT

Here we need to emphasize the importance of the balance between your intellect and your instinct. For many of the exercises you've done so far in this book, you've been exercising your imagination and your intellect. You've analyzed the script and looked for clues and then used your imagination to craft behavior and bring vocal and physical choices to life. And there is instinct involved in that, as well. But in the presence of another actor working opposite you, you must let your instincts guide you. The last thing any audience wants to see is a cold, calculated performance. We want to feel as if all is spontaneous and you're living in the moment, as your character is doing. We also want to see actors working off each other, not playing some part as if in a completely different play.

You have to trust that the work you've done on the part so far is there inside of you. It's not that you're throwing it out the window as you engage in this rehearsal process, but you have to prioritize the choices being made in the room. This is all part of the process. Trust it. As Stanislavski says, we're trying to awaken your subconscious by creating conscious choices. We've been planting seeds so that you can let go of all that intellectual and analytical stuff and work moment to moment.

EXPLORING YOUR INTERACTIONS

In the first reading of the play and in the early rehearsals, something might be obvious to you or was already obvious but now is becoming more real and present. There are certain characters whom you interact with more than others. In some cases, there may be one character who seems to thwart your actions or be an obstacle in some way. Or there is another character whom you confide in and trust as you try to get what you want. It could be your spouse, friend, mother, father, brother, sister, or coworker. Sometimes you don't see that as you read through a play, especially if you're concentrating on the analysis of your circumstances and actions or doing research about the time and place. But it becomes very obvious to you once you get into rehearsal. Suddenly there is this other real person/actor in your face—and they have needs and are performing actions with you or against you.

Remember when we had you make a list of all the things other characters said about you or said directly to you? We asked how you might feel if someone said that to you. That was the first step of making the part personal to you. Now, you must take it deeper. Given what you have learned through your homework and are now learning in rehearsal, you must work with this actor to clearly define the relationship. Most times, your fellow actors will make it easy for you, and you can be open and responsive and react to them as needed. Other times, you may have to use your imagination. You use your imagination through endowing this person with certain attributes. We explore later in this chapter how endowment can help you. For now, simply take note of your key interactions. Most likely, one of these characters will be a focus for you in terms of actions and obstacles, which we also look at in later chapters.

Exercise 1

This exercise is for your first read-through at rehearsal. Put your focus and attention on the other actors, really listening and observing, not having your face in the script. After each scene, when you have a moment, write down basic observations about your interactions. What do you observe? How are things different from what you expected? How did your fellow actors surprise you? What can you use and incorporate into your choices, and how can you modify and adjust other ideas? Who is a character you realize you interact with the most?

COLLABORATING WITH DESIGNERS

In the early phase of rehearsals, there are usually design presentations. Often this occurs on the first day but may be later in that first week, depending on the schedule. This is where the designers (e.g., lighting, scenic, costume, sound, media) present their sketches, images, and schematics for the production. Sometimes they have scale models or fabric samples, as well.

As an actor, this is exciting because now you can start filling in the blanks for those questions you may already have. You may also be awed and inspired by the beauty and ingenuity of your fellow artists. Your job is to listen and be attentive because although it may not seem like everything has to do with you, it's time to start thinking about how all these elements will complete a whole picture. Your character is part of this world, and now you are watching the world being built around you. The design presentations are your chance to start imagining the realities of the playing space and the objects in it.

There are also practical questions and issues to consider. For instance, if your costume involves a long hoop dress and high-heeled shoes, it's going to be important to know how tall each of those steps are or how close two items of furniture are going to be so that you can begin making those physical adjustments before the technical rehearsal. You will also want to know when you can start working with rehearsal skirts or shoes. You'll realize how they can affect your movement (and your character choices), so the sooner the better. There are some theaters where the set is built gradually, and then when an item is completed and safe to walk on, they'll move that unit in. This way actors can begin to play with steps and stairs or other levels. Sometimes, though, you won't begin moving on the set until the first day of your technical rehearsal.

Good directors and stage management crew will do everything they can to help you and remind you about design elements as you rehearse. At some point after the first read-through, you'll start to see lines of multicolored tape on the rehearsal floor, and the stage manager will review what each color represents. Even with this visual aid, you might hear in the first blocking rehearsals something like, "No, you can't go through that wall there," or "You stepped in the fountain." When Dennis was rehearsing in the production of *Peter and the Starcatcher*, there was a circle of green tape near the proscenium arch to represent the giant wooden pole and netting that would later be put there as part of the ship. Every day in rehearsal at least one actor would walk right over that tape without thinking about it, usually on their way off the stage. When the pole was finally built and put onstage for the tech rehearsals, those actors who kept walking through it found themselves tripping over the netting because they ingrained the habit of that movement. But this kind of mistake is easy to avoid. The more you familiarize yourself with your playing space, even in the early stages, the better off you'll be because you can then focus on more important things, like your character and working off the other actors.

The design presentations are also the chance for you to collaborate with your designers. Good designers will not only answer your questions but also ask you about your thoughts on the character. Ultimately, the design is going to be finalized by the designer with the approving eye of the director. However, you should empower yourself to voice your interpretation. For example, just the simple act of telling the designer how your movements for the character are going to accentuate how she is timid and doesn't move well could translate into a costume that helps tell that story.

Other designers are usually eager for input, as well. For example, when Dennis performed as Little Charles in *August: Osage County*, he sat and watched television while the sisters had a scene in another area of the stage. There was no actual television on the set, just a blinking light at the edge of the stage, but there would be ambient sound playing in the background. The sound designer asked what kind of show Little Charles would be watching. Dennis decided it was something like Gordon Ramsay's *Hell's Kitchen* because that would appeal to Little Charles's inner desire to be assertive and powerful like Ramsay. The designer honored that request, finding a soundtrack from an episode of an earlier season. Not only did it help tell the story for the audience, but it also gave Dennis something to do as an actor. Even though the volume was low so as not to disturb the scene with the sisters, he would sit there and listen to the track, trying to figure out what was happening and creating the illusion that he was actually watching a show.

ENDOWMENT

The next part of this chapter will be better understood if you fully understand the idea of endowment. If you've already taken an introductory class, then this concept might already be familiar.

Your job as an actor is to live in the imaginary world that you create, and to do that, you have to endow characteristics toward people and objects. Uta Hagen wrote a whole chapter about endowment in her book *A Challenge for the Actor*, in which she says, "Almost nothing in our character's life is what it is—but we must make it so!"[2] This means that the iced tea in that shot glass must become whiskey if that's what the character is drinking. The necklace your character wears must become a priceless heirloom, even if it's only a piece of cheap glass. The plastic handgun becomes a real weapon. We can endow not just objects but our fellow actors, as well. So even though the actor across from you is not really your mother, you endow her with that relationship and all that entails.

Endowment is simple and something that a four-year-old child understands. They can look at a cardboard box and immediately imagine it's a spaceship. Our advice to you is to keep that same spirit and don't overthink it or make it a complicated process. It's simply using your imagination, the same way you did when you played as kids battling each other with swords made of sticks found in the woods.

When you act, you are in the process of endowing everything you see, hear, touch, taste, and smell. For example, you may be looking out at the audience when you are onstage (or looking into a film production crew with the camera nearby), but in the imaginary world, you are looking out a window at snowy fields. When we do this onstage or on-set, it's not about just trying to imagine those fields. It's also knowing what those fields mean to us. Do the fields of snow make us feel sad, lonely, happy, or contemplative? The audience isn't going to literally see the snowy fields reflected in our eyes. They're going to see our response to what we see, our feelings about it, in the way we interact with that image.

Every relationship you build with every character onstage must be endowed with the meanings you have for them. This is why it's important to know not just the literal relationship but also how you feel about them and want from them at that moment. It's all using your imagination.

Similarly, you have a relationship with your performance space. On some level, you won't forget that you're on a stage performing in front of an audience, but you will have to endow the set with your feelings. For instance, how comfortable are you in the surroundings? If it's your own home, it may give you a feeling of safety. If it's a foreign environment, it should feel different from your home. And your relationship to the space will change depending on who else is in the space. If your home is invaded by a burglar, then your safe space is suddenly threatened. You can also endow the space with a temperature. In *August: Osage County*, the play occurs in the middle of August in Oklahoma (where it gets very hot!), and Violet has shut up the house, so it gets no fresh air and no air conditioning (making it even hotter). For the characters entering that house, it's like stepping into a furnace. You have to endow that set in that way and display that in your behavior (see chapter 9 for more work on playing modifications like temperature).

In the same way, every object and prop should have some meaning for your character. This doesn't necessarily have to be deep, philosophical meaning or make you angry or cry every time you see it, but you should have an idea about how you feel about that specific prop. If you take a sip of water from a bottle of whiskey, the audience should believe that it's whiskey. Of course, some props are more important than others, and a whole story can be built around the way a prop is used. (We talk more about props later.)

As you start to explore the space of your rehearsals, you will need to refer to the given circumstances and the choices you have started to work on. You may have written them down on paper, but now it's time to get on your feet and work it out in rehearsal. You have to activate your imagination and turn that idea into behavior.

CHECK YOUR PROPS

You can be certain that if a writer has given you a prop, it's for a reason. Your job is to make it part of the imaginary world you're building and make it your own in some way. When you are familiarizing yourself with the design elements, your first focus may be on costumes and the set. You should then begin making a list of all the props that you handle and then get your hands on them as soon as you can. Now, this is not always possible due to time constraints or budgets, and often the properties person will provide rehearsal props, which often are not helpful for actors. There's nothing worse than spending weeks working with one prop and then having that be replaced in tech with the real prop, which has a completely different weight, feel, and texture from what you have grown accustomed to. So if you can get your hands on the prop that is actually going to be used in the performance, all the better!

As stated earlier, some characters are defined by a prop: Indiana Jones's bullwhip; Wonder Woman's golden lasso; Walter White's iconic black hat. If you look at your character, what is the one prop that may define him or her? Looking at Hedda Gabler, you might make the choice that her father's pistols are her defining prop. For Tesman, it could be a special pen or quill that he uses for writing his scholarly work. If we look at Jeff in *Lobby Hero*, that prop could be his badge or his pen and sign-in sheet. For Esther in *Intimate Apparel*, it may be her scissors or a set of needles but just as easily could be a piece of satin or silk.

As mentioned earlier in this chapter, you have to consider how you endow each of your props, especially if you have one defining prop. For example, if you were cast as Black Stache in *Peter and the Starcatcher*, you would be given a straight razor as your prop. Now start asking yourself some questions about your relationship to this prop (throwing aside the big side question about whether this is a theatrical nod to the other straight-razor-wielding character Sweeney Todd). First, where did Stache get this straight razor and when? Why does he use that in some of the fights and not a short dagger or sword? Was the blade his father's? Did he buy it in some shop in London or steal it off another pirate?

Making a choice that may yield some kind of sentimental value may help you tap into your character. For example, if you create a choice that Stache's blade used to belong to the first pirate captain that he ever worked for, a pirate that he revered and wanted to become, and when this pirate died, he gave it to him to carry on the legacy of piracy, then that prop has more meaning than merely a tool for fighting (or shaving). Now it represents everything Black Stache stands for. You're going to handle it slightly differently. Second, that prop blade is going to be dulled, so it won't be sharp or dangerous. (It is play-acting after all!) You have to endow that object with properties of danger. This, again, determines how you will handle it onstage. As you rehearse, you should never be without your blade, so that even in your downtime, you can feel it in your hands and make it a part of you. Eventually, the very act of holding that blade with help you tap into the character.

Never underestimate the value of your props. A writer who gives you a prop is giving you a gift. Use that gift wisely. Endow it with meaning, and play with how it can help tell the story of your character in this imaginary world.

Exercise 2

Find a prop that you can use as the defining prop of your character, something you can use as a touchstone to help you tap into the character. If the script and your scene has indicated that you use a prop already (such as Mr. Marks and all his fabric in *Intimate Apparel* or Marela rolling cigars in *Anna in the Tropics*), then you can use that prop if you want. However, feel free to explore other props that may not even be in the scene or play, perhaps a prop you could put in your pocket or keep as a rehearsal tool to be used in the dressing room. This prop could be a lucky rabbit's foot, a stone, a necklace, a watch, or a pen.

Chapter Six

Building Habits

> We are what we repeatedly do. Excellence is not an act, but a habit.
>
> —Will Durant, summarizing Aristotle[1]

> [Stanislavski] said that the actor rehearses to make habits. First, he decides what habits he wants to have, then he rehearses to acquire them, which means conditioning himself by doing it repeatedly until it's a habit. Then the whole performance becomes a habit. In the last phase of rehearsal you make all the habits beautiful.
>
> —William Esper[2]

Rehearsal is for testing out and solidifying your choices and discarding ones that aren't working. As in Esper's quote, you're building habits that will serve you later. You haven't built the performance yet, but you're conditioning yourself to get there. This is a precept we come back to in the next few chapters. An actor isn't supposed to be brilliant immediately. Otherwise, why would you need rehearsal? Even in film and television, few actors are amazing on the first take. Most professional actors are never content to try one choice but will explore many options. Actors love rehearsal because they get to play and experiment. In rehearsal, you dig deeper into the text and move around in the space. You'll make choices about how you feel about other characters and what physical activities you might be doing, as well as defining and refining your actions. All the work you did before that first rehearsal was building a foundation, and now it's time to put scaffolding on top of it.

One idea that novice actors need to overcome is there is only one right way to play a scene. Don't think of "right" or "wrong" but a variety of choices. You need to explore many choices to see the different ways to play a scene and what best serves the goals of the production. These next few chapters, we dig into that rehearsal process and show you how to make changes, firm up your choices, and collaborate with your fellow actors and director.

ARE YOU SURE THAT'S WHAT YOU NEED?

In chapter 3, we look at the idea that all human behavior can be seen as motivated by five basic needs: survival, love, validation, happiness, and winning. These needs are tied to the specific actions of your character. As you work on a scene, you should be making discoveries about your character. Perhaps you feel the basic need works fine. However, you may also realize that perhaps the needs and actions now don't seem to fit with how you are playing the part off other actors or the director's notes. For example, we mentioned earlier how the character of Bill from *Lobby Hero* has the possible need to win. This could be tied to his wanting to be the best cop on the force or to win every argument. But perhaps you find this doesn't work with how you're reacting to your fellow actors. You keep playing it this way but feel it's too aggressive.

Now, two things could be happening. First, it may just be resistance to your own discomfort at playing the part. You may need to commit to the choice and see if you can work through it. Or second, you have worked through it, and it still doesn't feel like it's working as well as it could. So, reevaluate that need. As you rehearse and interact with your fellow actors, you find that you are actually pretending to be more confident than you let on, that much of what you do is bravado as a survival instinct. You could explore the idea that his need might be for validation. He wants everyone to look up to him, especially his new partner, Dawn. Or you could go another direction and explore the possibility that he actually does need to love and be loved (but perhaps going about it in all the wrong ways). When it comes to finding the need for your character, remember that it's not math or science. This is an art, and we must leave room for your interpretation.

YES, BUT HOW ELSE COULD YOU GET THAT?

Realizing you are on the right track in terms of your character's basic need solidifies your actions. In chapter 3, you broke each scene into beats and then wrote in your actions. These actions should be phrased as a transitive verb with a definite and direct target, as in "to amuse her" or "to mock him." You made choices before rehearsals began, so you wrote these based on your early ideas mined from the given circumstances and working on your own.

Although you considered the other character's actions, you now must collaborate with the other actors' choices, which may be quite different from what you anticipated (let's hope!). You may have thought the other character would be weak and you'd be able to "charm her" or "flatter her" to get what you want, but it turns out this actor decides her character is not weak but actually resistant to you and your words (giving you more conflict to work with, yay!). Therefore, you can't merely skate along with charming her—that won't work. You'll have to come up with a stronger action, either a stronger version along the same lines of "to charm" or something entirely different. This latter area is where the real rehearsal begins!

Often actors fall into traps, thinking a line must be said a certain way and stay committed to it no matter what. For example, a line like "I love you" can be a huge trap for an actor, but these words have been said with various types of intention and emotion over the years, so they need not be stereotypically romantic. Rehearsal is our way of eliminating the stereotypes and going deeper.

So what happens when your scene partner surprises you and changes the scene in a way that makes you realize you didn't perform the action you had written down earlier in the process, something completely new and spontaneous? Congratulations! Now, you're really working! Ideally, this should happen a lot. You should be adjusting and reacting spontaneously to your acting partners and letting the scenes come alive. This is the process of testing and retesting what you are doing based on what you want. This constant process of modifying your actions creates a domino effect, as it causes the other actors to react and change their preconceived ideas of how they thought the scene would be done. Together, you create living dramatic moments, and the scene becomes more alive, less static, and less intellectual.

After rehearsal, write down the action you think you are doing and what changed. By labeling it, you give it power and commitment and make it easy to modify again if needed. This way, when a director asks, "What are you doing on that line?" you immediately know what your action is, and the director can then validate the choice or ask you to commit further or change it.

ACTIONS: EIGHT MAJOR CATEGORIES

If writing down actions before rehearsal feels like doing the *New York Times* crossword puzzle and you still don't know what you're doing from moment to moment (but you know it's something), never fear! We are going to give you eight main categories of doings, which all other doings can fall into. As you learned in chapter 3, humans universally do the same things—there are no actions that only Italians do, for example. Although humanity is complex, it's best to start with simplicity and work from there. Here are the eight major categories:

1. To admit
2. To convince or persuade
3. To defy
4. To scold
5. To lament
6. To find out
7. To understand
8. To demonstrate

We're not suggesting that there are only eight actions you can play, of course. Think of these as broad categories, under which many other action verbs might fall under.

1. To Admit

This is a simple and powerful action and can encompass other such actions as "to confess" or "to agree." For example, when the character Thea visits Hedda and Tesman in act 1 of *Hedda Gabler*, she is asked if she is in trouble and says, "Yes, I am. And I don't know another soul in town who can help me." At the end of the play *The Convert* by Danai Gurira, the main character, Jekesai, confesses to Chilford, her priest, about killing her White employers. She actually says those specific words.

2. To Convince or to Persuade

This is an attempt to change someone else's way of thinking or feeling, to get them to agree with your argument or point of view. If we look again at *Hedda Gabler*, we can see that she is a very convincing and persuasive character, and much of what she does in the play has to do with convincing such characters as Thea, Tesman, and Lovberg. Sometimes you don't even need much language to perform an action, as when Hedda hands Lovberg the pistol at the end of act 3 and says, "Here—you use it now."

3. To Defy

"To defy" is almost the opposite of "to admit." You are disagreeing completely and denying anything others put toward you (for more work on playing disagreements and argument, go to chapter 8). A simple action here might be "to argue" but could also be "to stand up to" or "to resist." In some ways, it is contrary and argumentative. In the first scene of *The Government Inspector*, there are many characters playing variations of this verb, such as the mayor shouting, "My wife does not take bribes!"

4. To Scold

This is something that a mother may do to a child or a teacher may do to a naughty student for misbehaving or treating someone badly. It is correcting behavior. Other intentions, such as "to lecture" or "to chastise," fall under this category. Looking at the first few minutes of *The Government Inspector*, you can see the mayor scolding his officials left and right in varying degrees (and intentions).

5. To Lament

"To lament" may seem more of an internal action, but it is directed toward another character. This is not to be confused with mourning or grieving. It is when a character feels things are out of their own control and gives some outward expression, as if they were saying "C'est la vie!" or "That's life!" The character could need sympathy, help, or acknowledgment from the other person. Many of the characters in a Chekhov play are lamenting, such as in *Three Sisters*, when they all lament about going to Moscow. If you ever see the word *well*, it may be a clue that your character is lamenting. *Well* is often another way of saying "That's that!"

There is a moment in *Lobby Hero* later in the play, where Jeff and Dawn are talking, and he says, "Well . . . you missed a really great game today." This lamenting is not just about the game but also refers to his asking her out in a previous scene to watch that game and lamenting that earlier rejection. But you could just as easily take a line like "I'm fine" or "It's okay" and be lamenting your state (understanding that our characters don't always express exactly how they feel or what they want). It all depends on the context. If your character says, "It's fine. I guess I'll just stay in this small town forever and die alone," then they are very likely playing "to lament."

6. To Find Out

This action is all about the search for knowledge. This encompasses such verbs as *interrogating, questioning, investigating, searching, asking,* and *discovering*. If you're playing a detective in a crime drama and it's an interrogation scene, then you can be sure you're probably playing one of those actions in the scene. At the beginning of the second scene of *Anna in the Tropics*, we see Juan Julian enter the cigar factory and be greeted by Cheche, who asks if he is visiting someone. He continues to ask questions, trying to figure out this handsome new stranger. Even though he knows this is the new lector, he wants to gain more information. Later, he plays a different action, "to defy," telling him, "We're not hiring," in order to get him to leave.

7. To Understand

You might at first glance think this is a variation of "to find out," but it has much more to do with how you process the new knowledge. This is not an aggressive digging for information but of seeing what the information means to you. If you were playing a detective in a crime scene and you played "to find out," then you may very well get information, but then you may change to "to understand" to try to put the pieces together, asking, "What does this information mean?" Many actors play this as if they are generally thinking, but to be actively involved in understanding a concept takes your whole mind and body. Think of when you were listening and trying to understand a lecture in your biology or physics class and trying to grasp those big concepts. If you look at Benedict Cumberbatch's work in scenes from the new *Sherlock Holmes* series, he is often trying to understand clues in order to make his deduction. Jeff in *Lobby Hero* is very often playing this verb, especially in the second scene of the first act, when William enters and explains the dilemma with his brother.

8. To Demonstrate

The last category, "to demonstrate," can be larger-than-life expressions or facades that other characters put on to fool people. They are demonstrations of such emotions as anger, delight, scorn, disgust, and surprise. This intention can be used effectively to mask or hide feelings, displaying the subtext, such as when a brownnosing employee compliments a boss on their outfit. In act 1 of *Hedda Gabler*, Hedda grabs Thea after Tesman exits the room and sits her down on the sofa so they could become "best friends again," clearly demonstrating affection, even though she is really more interested in learning about Lovberg. Even after Thea says Hedda used to pull her hair and even said she wanted to burn it, Hedda replies, "Did I? Oh, that was just talk!"

WHAT (OR WHO) IS YOUR OBSTACLE?

Often actors in rehearsal spend so much time working on their need and their actions that they forget about another crucial element: the obstacle. Drama is built on conflict. One easy way to look at conflict is to see it as one force opposing another: I want this, but you want this other thing. It could be as simple as "I want to leave the room, but you want me to stay," or as complex as "I want to avenge my father's murder and kill my uncle, but I don't want to harm my mother, who married my uncle, and my girlfriend wants to marry me, and my uncle wants to have me murdered." Well, you get the idea.

It's not enough for you to plot out your actions as if nothing or no one is opposing you. And in fact, this is a common pitfall if actors only work with actions as an intellectual exercise, putting it all on paper but not testing it and working off their partners. Your actions should be in direct correlation to the other characters but specifically reacting to what the other actors are doing. You should find, hopefully, that lines are coming out completely differently in rehearsal from how you thought you might say them when first reading the play. If your lines are coming out exactly the same as you first imagined, then you're not using your instincts or working off others. You're in your head. This type of acting is not open and spontaneous; you might as well be alone onstage.

We come to the theater to see people interacting with each other, not just saying lines in interesting ways. Working this way is like a downhill skier who gets caught in the grooves of a slalom course. It is building a habit that restricts you rather than habits that enlarge your performance. But being aware of your impulses and acting on them brings spontaneity. As Meisner used to say, "Acting without spontaneity is like soup without salt—stale, flat and totally unprofitable."[3] Add flavor to your acting by responding in the moment, even if it means adjusting earlier homework.

As you block and rework moments, your director will encourage you to go further with your choices or ask you to do something completely different. Most actors are concerned about their blocking and fixated on not bumping into the furniture, but very few are writing down their thoughts about what's happening between those characters in the moment. After each scene you work on, you should be writing down how the scene is changing for you. This could include how the stakes are being raised (what's most important to you) and how it amplifies the conflict or obstacle.

How do you focus on your obstacle? First, identify it. The best way to do this is to go back to your actions. What are you fighting for? Then connect the dots to what is getting in the way of that struggle. Most often, that obstacle is the other character in the scene. If you put your attention on and react to your partner, then you will connect more fully to your actions and why they may need to change.

Exercise 1

Go through your script, and look at the actions you wrote. Keeping in mind what you now know about your character and relationships, as well as how you are working off the other actors in rehearsal, how have any of those actions changed? If they haven't and you're playing the same actions, then try something different. If any actions seem general, then clarify them further using the eight categories of actions.

PUSH AND PULL:
TRANSLATING IDEAS INTO PHYSICALITY

In looking at a scene from the point of view of what the character does, you can extend the idea of actions and physicalize them. To do this, you may want to look at those eight categories and then think of them as breaking down into one of two things: pushing or pulling against the opposing force (the obstacle).

For example, Dennis does an exercise with students where they say, "Go away," while they gently push their partner away. This is a simple physical action connected to a simple physical need. Then they say, "Come with me," by gently grabbing their partner's wrist and pulling them, as if to entice them or lead them somewhere fun. They are diametrically opposed from each other in that respect. The next step in the exercise is to replace the line "Go away" with a line of text from the scene but keep that same physical action of pushing their partner away. If your line of text was "I love you" but you were pushing your partner away, then that would be one way of playing the scene. But if you replaced "Come with me" with the line "I love you" while pulling your partner toward you, then that would be another way of playing the scene. Either choice could be valid, depending on how you are reacting off your partner and the context (the relationship and given circumstances).

If we look at scenes in this simple "pushing/pulling" way, we can see how physical actions can provide insight into psychological needs. Stanislavski references this idea with a simple action like a handshake. It may be only a handshake, and yet, what are the needs of that handshake as per the given circumstances?[4] For instance, if you are shaking the hand of someone who is interviewing you for a job, then you may be nervous and want to impress them. That energy and physicality must go into the act of shaking hands.

If you look at your scene as if your subtext was to push someone away from you ("Go away") or as a scene where you wanted to pull someone toward you ("Come with me"), then how would that change your physicality? As you are dealing with blocking in the space with your fellow actors, do you want to try to control the space or retreat from it?

EXERCISE 2

Write down for each scene where you might be pushing and where you might be pulling. You can use your needs that you have just worked on to help you. You may discover a scene where it shifts from pushing to pulling and back again. The next time you are in rehearsal, consider how you might be able to use that in your behavior and blocking.

SHOULD THE AUDIENCE LISTEN, WATCH, OR WATCH AND LISTEN?

Another way to approach your physicality for a scene is to consider what the author wants the audience to experience. Looking at some of your previous homework, such as how you broke down the play with PASTO and broke scenes down into beats, look at the scene and ask yourself:

• Does the author want the audience to listen?
• Does the author want the audience to watch?
• Does the author want the audience to watch and listen?

Now, you may be thinking to yourself, "Hey, isn't worrying about the audience the director's job?" Yes, which means you're doing a bit of self-directing, and believe it or not, this is not a bad thing. Directors love actors who can direct themselves. It means less work for them! Ultimately, it is the director's decision about where and how the audience will be watching and listening. The acting choices for each category are uniquely different.

Should the Audience Listen?

If it feels like the writer wants the audience to primarily listen to the text, then it would be distracting for the actors to be moving around too much. Actors need to be economical in their movements as they deliver their lines. The most obvious example of a scene that requires the audience to listen is where aural information needs to be conveyed, such as Sherlock Holmes giving his summary of a case. In the first scene of *The Government Inspector*, the characters grapple with the news of a government inspector coming to town. Not only is the audience introduced to all these crooked city officials, but also there are many jokes about how to deal with hiding their immoral behavior. Too much movement in that scene would confuse the audience and possibly step on any laughs. (There is a general rule about not moving when trying to get to a punchline, or it ruins the effect. Watch a stand-up comedian, and notice how still they are when they get to the punchline of a joke.)

Should the Audience Watch?

If the writer wants the audience to watch, then there needs to be more emphasis on physical action and less on spoken text. A farce depends on the movements of characters entering and exiting the scene, as in the riotous play *Noises Off.* There is a moment in *Peter in the Starcatcher* where one of the characters, Black Stache, gets his hand chopped off when he slams a treasure chest shut. In fact, the character repeats the line "ohmigod" several times as he flails about in pain and shock. This moment calls for physical action and is one of the funniest of the show.

Should the Audience Watch and Listen?

Looking at the opening prologue of *Peter and the Starcatcher*, the characters must create a whole world built on the imagination of the audience. In only a few minutes, the audience is introduced not only to many of the characters, like the Lost Boys and Molly, but also a ton of information about stardust and two trunks on two ships. As this information is given, the tone of the playing style is introduced, which involves moving quickly through time and space and how actors change roles. The energy is exciting, and it is important to ensure the audience is both able to hear the important information and able to visualize the settings. Sure, the play could open with the actors sitting still on crates so that the audience could hear only the words and information, but it is the physical information that is just as important (hence, the "watch and listen" aspect of the scene).

GETTING OFF-BOOK

Most actors know that much of the real work begins once the lines are out of the way and they can put all their attention on their partner. Learning lines isn't about rote memorization. It's about connecting to actions. If you've been working through these exercises and doing your homework, then you may find that the lines are already there. Memorization occurs through a process of understanding rather than drilling it in.

Some directors ask actors to memorize their lines before the first rehearsal. Some actors resist, while others thrive on it. As an actor, you must adjust to your director. (Think about it: It's a lot easier for you to adjust to one person than for the director to adjust to ten or more actors.) If you're interested in working in TV or film, it's a requirement to memorize before shooting. You might think memorization kills spontaneity, but it actually can free you up.

At some point, you will be required to be off book for rehearsal. Stage management will then give line notes. This happens until technical or dress rehearsals. Line notes tell you exactly the lines you missed or spoke incorrectly. They're extremely important, and even though it may seem irksome to actors to be corrected because they left out one word, you have to respect the text. Every syllable is there for a reason (see chapter 8 for more on that).

When you get a line note, your first instinct may be, "That can't be right!" Or you might reply, "But I've been saying it that way for two weeks!" (To which, the SM will reply, "Yes, for two weeks you've been saying it wrong.")

Take a look at the line or the moment. When we memorize a line incorrectly or drop a word or two, we usually have a reason. It's tied to a choice that we are making, whether that be an action or that we are trying to be more economical; in other words, we make it more how we might say it. You need to figure out why this character is saying these words at this moment. You may have to rework that moment just a bit to figure it out, but it's worth the time and energy to rewire your brain in a new way. The next run, even if it brings you out of it a bit, make an effort to get that moment correct, and see what happens. It will feel like when you're trying to remember dance steps in the middle of the dance, but then you might discover something that helps you with the character as well as the moment.

Notable actor Bill Nighy once gave an interview in the UK newspaper the *Telegraph*, where he boiled down his advice to new actors:

> [L]earn every word that you have to say backwards, forwards and sideways before you go into a rehearsal room and before you go on a film set. . . . Rehearsal is not the enemy of spontaneity. The idea in the process is you say the lines over and over and over and over and over again until you can give the impression that you've never said them before and it's just occurred to you. That's the gig.[5].

LEARNING LINES: A SIMPLE STRATEGY

An important tip for learning lines is to have a strategy. In the way we broke down our scenes into beats, you should take a similar approach to your lines. This seems obvious when you memorize lines, as you're usually going word by word. And this is typically how actors learn lines; they start with their first scene and go line by line and then move to the next scene. This might work with your acting class or smaller scenes, but when you play a lead or have a lot of lines, it may not be effective. You'll know that first scene really well and have issues with the last scene, which is often the most challenging or most crucial.

A good strategy is to prioritize. Take a look at your breakdown of scenes. Which is going to be the most challenging, either mentally, emotionally, or physically? Where are your large speeches or longer scenes? Which scenes have a lot of physical action (such as any stage combat or dances), physical activities, fast entrances or exits, or props? Which scenes are brief (for you, at least) and only have a few lines of dialogue?

Our advice: Learn the most challenging scene first. You probably already know which scene this is (it might be the one that scares you the most). Maybe it's the most intense or longest scene or your big confession speech. You've probably already put a lot of thought into the scene and have already done some core character work based on the actions in that scene, so learning the lines is really the next logical step. Next, learn the easiest scene. This could be the shortest or that has you doing the least amount of actions. This will build your confidence and help with other scenes.

After you have the most challenging and the easiest scenes out of the way, take another look at your breakdown to prioritize which to tackle next. You could take a look at the rehearsal schedule and prioritize that way (as many actors do). This means that if next week you are working scene 3 on your feet, then you work on that first. This is not a bad idea, of course. But you may have a limited amount of time, and there might be another challenging scene you have to look at first.

You may want to take the second-most challenging scene and begin working on that one so that you have that out of the way. Or you may take a look at what the most fun scene is going to be for you and let that be the motivator. Any scene where you can get that book out of your hand as soon as possible will help further your rehearsal (and impress your director or make your stage manager's job easier).

The goal is to get the book out of your hand as soon as possible. This isn't just so you can handle props or move around easier. This is so you can spend less time in your head *thinking* and more time in the present moment *listening* and responding and actively pursuing your character's needs. Now you may understand why some actors get off book soon as they can. They know the real magic happens when the text is out of the way.

Exercise 3

If you are concerned about getting off book or need to get off book as soon as possible, there are a few ways to do it. The best way is to understand why you are saying your lines (which is the process we are giving you), so all the exercises in the earlier chapters will help you. You can run lines with your fellow cast or find a friend or family member (though they may not be so willing to help all the time). If you are short on time and need to learn right away, get a digital recorder or a smartphone, and make a recording of yourself saying your lines as well as the other character's. The simple act of saying all the lines, including your partner's, which provides cues for you, can be helpful. Once you have that recording, listen to it constantly (in the car, walking around, working out). If you have enough time, you can also make a recording of just the other character's lines and none of yours, so that you can use that to help you learn your cues as well as run your lines.

Chapter Seven

Building Your Character

Yet every role offers an actor the opportunity to improvise, to collaborate and truly co-create with the author and director.

—Michael Chekhov

If you are the kind of actor who feels comfortable with the basics yet yearns to make your characters organic, genuine, and heartbreaking or comedic in such a truthful way that it would make Meryl Streep seethe with envy, then these next few chapters will help you. First, we unlock the idea of "playing status" and how that can change relationships with other actors as well as unlock deeper physical and vocal choices. We also see if your character may be hiding something or outright lying. Telling lies or having a secret can create risk for your character, which raises the stakes and changes the way they interact with others. Finally, we ensure that all your choices are physicalized, so that we aren't just theorizing ideas but also translating them into choices and behavior that can be molded further within the rehearsal room.

WHAT'S YOUR STATUS?

John's previous book *Will Power: How to Act Shakespeare in 21 Days* discusses status as it relates to Shakespearean texts. In Elizabethan England, status was much clearer. There was a "chain of being" among upper and lower classes. Lords and ladies were higher up than farmers and peasants, and everyone was higher up than animals. You might think this worldview is archaic, but if you look closer at our interactions today, you can still observe social standings and class politics.

The armed forces are a great way to look at social status and "chain of command." A general in an army possesses higher status than colonels and every other soldier below them. If you apply that same idea to a corporation, it stands to reason that a CEO will possess higher status than an office assistant. Your first step in looking at status is to look at the obvious status of your character (i.e., the pecking order of any institution, organization, or social group that your character belongs to), which you may have already considered from earlier work in these chapters. But what happens when two people of the same status are in a room together? What if two generals or two CEOs are facing off in a scene? Who has the higher status then? Ah, that's when it gets fun!

The first type of status has more to do with your standing in society, your social status. But there is another type of status that can help you, as explained by Keith Johnstone from his brilliant book *Impro*. Johnstone explains that "every inflection and movement implies a status and no action is due to chance, or motiveless."[2] It's helpful to think of this kind of status as fluid and transformative throughout scenes and interactions. Status is active, it's "something we do, something that changes on a regular basis," something we constantly fight for or withdraw from. Once we realize that status can be raised or lowered, we can start to play around and see how it changes our behavior in the scene (or connects to our actions). You can be low in social status (like a private in the army) and yet play a higher status than a colonel. Johnstone likens it to a seesaw. When one goes up, the other goes down. As actors, you can either raise yourself up to play high status or you can try to lower your scene partner to put them into low status or vice versa.

As Johnstone states, "Audiences enjoy a contrast between the status played and the social status."[3] Charlie Chaplin created the Tramp out of this idea, and many comic actors can be found using this device, from Will Ferrell to Kristen Wiig. Using our chain of command of the armed forces, here's a status example between a general and a private:

GENERAL: Good morning, Private Smith.

PRIVATE SMITH: It's noon, Bob.

GENERAL: My watch must be slow.

PRIVATE SMITH: You should get a Rolex. Mine is as reliable as can be.

As you can see, the text itself tells a story of the general having the higher social status at the beginning of this interaction and possibly playing high status by reminding the private of his pecking order. But then Private Smith immediately knocks down his high status to low by correcting him and calling him by his first name instead of rank, showing a lack of respect. The general keeps that low status by excusing his error of the time, and then Private Smith maintains his high status by bragging about his watch.

Here's another example using the same dialogue, but this time, we have two characters of equal social status:

GENERAL A: Good morning, General Smith.

GENERAL B: It's noon, Bob.

GENERAL A: My watch must be slow.

GENERAL B: You should get a Rolex. Mine is as reliable as can be.

General A's first line is quite neutral, but you could actually play this as low or high status, with respect or disdain. General B's response is to knock down General A to low status by correcting him and calling him by his first name, hence raising himself up. General A could then remain in low status, as he appears to be apologizing or talking about an inferior watch. However, what if General A played that line with an attempt to maintain his high status? It may come out with a subtext like "Are you really correcting me?" General B keeps the high status by bragging about his own watch. In short, both characters could be trying to play high status to each other and trying to knock each other down.

Hint: You may have noticed that we are using active verbs in relation to playing high or low status. That's no accident. Status is related to and can enhance or give dynamics to your previous choices, such as the actions you are playing, or to further define your relationships (see chapter 3).

A good example of status in play is the first scene of *The Government Inspector*, when all the officials of the town are gathered in the mayor's house to discuss this urgent news of this visitor. After the mayor declares that a government inspector is on the way, the officials begin a status game in order to begin covering their own butts, blaming others for issues and declaring knowledge of why the inspector is there. The mayor continually tries to maintain his high status as a leader but keeps getting upended by others.[4]

Near the end of the scene, the mayor's wife, Anna, and his daughter Marya enter, and we see the mayor's status change again in his interactions with them. Even Bobchinsky and Dobchinsky (arguably the lowest status in the scene, both social and in other ways), have a war of status as they fight with each other about who gets to tell the tale of their news that the inspector (Khlestakov) is at the inn.

Whether you realize it or not, you engage in these kinds of status interactions every day. It may not be as obvious or comedic as some of the corrupt and inept officials of *The Government Inspector*, but it's happening when you interact with your teachers or other students, walk down a busy street, order a latte, buy groceries, and talk to your boyfriend or parents (especially your parents, but we get to that in the next section).

The easiest way to think of status is in simple terms of high and low. There are, of course, ranges of status, and you could have as many levels of status as you have characters onstage, but all the characters would be playing either high or low status to each one of the others. Again, looking at the characters in the first scene of *The Government Inspector*, there is social status but also status between the characters as they try to decide the best actions to take.

It is important to note that we are looking at a text that might indicate a particular status for you to play, but it may be that due to the circumstance or relationship, you could play against the text. For instance, you could try to speak the low-status lines as if you are high status and see how that works, creating more subtext and subtlety.

Some of the behavior you might notice in high status includes:

- Holding eye contact with people (making the other person break away from a stare)
- Raising up your head slightly so that you're looking down on others
- Having a relaxed and/or powerful stance (open)
- Moving only when you need to and no more
- Moving clearly and distinctly (purposeful, direct, and confident)
- Speaking clearly, energetically, and articulately

Some of the behavior you might notice in low status includes:

- Breaking eye contact or holding your head down to avoid eye contact
- Blinking too much
- Moving in an unspecific, unclear, or misdirected way (fidgeting with your hands or putting your hands near your face)
- Twitching
- Moving in a timid, unsure, or hesitant way
- Having a closed stance with arms crossed or sitting with legs crossed
- Pausing too much or inserting "er," "uh," or "um"
- Speaking softly or mumbling

Let's look at status interactions from the point of view of the character Dawn from *Lobby Hero*. When she enters her first scene, she plays low status to Bill, the senior police officer who is mentoring her. This stands to reason and is in line with her social status as the probationary officer. In her interactions with Jeff, we can see how her status changes from the first moments as he tries to flirt with her and she demands respect (high status) to when she defends her actions of a violent arrest (low status) or when she discovers it is actually a female escort whom Bill is visiting in 22J (low status). Her status changes with Bill when he reenters the scene. Bill plays low status as he apologizes for lying to her, but now Dawn has the opportunity to play high status with lines like "How stupid do you think I am?" and calls him out as a liar. She does this regardless of her social status and the fact that he is a senior police officer.

Deciding what status to play and when is not an exact science. Remember, this isn't math; it's art. As you play around in your blocking rehearsals, you can play with your status in relationship to other characters. Often, our characters will stay in the same status because that's where we feel more comfortable. For instance, if you're playing Bill from *Lobby Hero*, you may always be playing high status. But if you are to say the line "I'm sorry" to Dawn in a high-status way, that behavior may send the message you don't really care about her, which is one choice. To play the moment with low status, though, you may actually be sorry and need her to forgive you. Neither choice is right or wrong, but it's important that you understand and play with the difference so you know what feels right for you for that production.

When you play with high or low status, you should concentrate on only about two or three specific behaviors to add to your character. It's not about quantity here but quality. For one thing, it's easier to concentrate and incorporate a small number of behavioral traits to what you are already doing. Too many things, and it's like a juggler trying to juggle too many spinning plates. Sooner or later, something will fall and crash on the floor. Also, you have to be mindful of the fact that at the end of the day, you are a storyteller. If you have too many low-status behaviors, for example, you may be so softly spoken, jittery, and timid that you disappear into the scenery. You have to translate your ideas into a performance for an audience. And even if you just did one thing, like avoiding eye contact, that one thing will actually carry a lot of weight, and audience members will feel certain things about your character and not know why.

ARE YOU CHILD, PARENT, OR ADULT?

Another way to consider your status is through the familial roles that we may play. Ever notice how your mother could say one word to you about your outfit, and you'd have an immediate reaction? Or maybe your younger brother throws a tantrum while you're babysitting, and you have to find a way to deal with that meltdown?

University of California Theater Department professor Arthur Wagner shared an insight with John that he gained from the therapeutic techniques of transactional analysis (TA): "When your language changes, your character changes." His basic premise, which he derived from Eric Berne's handbook on transactional analysis, *Games People Play*, is that characters are always adopting one of three possible psychological statuses—parent, child, or adult—in relation to other characters.[5] These roles can shift literally from line to line. In John's book *Will Power*, he talks more about how a parent can dictate or speak in imperatives, whereas a child can be resistant or needy, and adults speak to each other as equals.[6]

If we look at scene 1 in act 2 of *Intimate Apparel*, we can see how a character changes voices within the three psychological roles. Esther and George have just been married, and it's their wedding night, though they hardly know each other. The scene begins with silence, the two of them standing on either side of the bed. Esther finally says, "Don't really feel much different." She tries to relate to him as an adult, as someone who is taking this journey of marriage together equally. George's response is that of a parent, authoritative and clipped, saying, "We ain't need to say nothin' now." Esther then assumes the role of a mother, asking if he would like a bath, but the response from George is another command (which could be parent or adult, as he is asking her to sit near him). It is clear that George wants to initiate the consecration of the marriage, and they do have a few moments of talking to each other as adults, as equals. The scene is a beautiful and heartbreaking scene as Esther reveals intimate details about her family and her love for fabric and sewing. But by the end of their scene, George switches back to the role of parent and reveals very little about himself.

The adult voice doesn't usually last long in a scene. It serves for trading information and for intimate scenes, such as this one. You may look at your scene and find more of a parent or child voice. You may also find that this insight and playing high or low status go hand in hand.

Exercise 1

Find a pack of playing cards, and shuffle them. Pick a card, any card, randomly. Use that card to decide your character's status (so if you pick the four of diamonds, you are low status, but if you pick a ten of spades, you are high status). Choose two or three attributes to concentrate on for that status level (for example, if you are low status, try blinking a lot, looking down, slumping your posture, or speaking less confidently). Walk around and say some of your lines with that status. If you lose some other aspects of your performance, that's okay for now. You're just playing.

Now pick another card. This second card is the status of your scene partner. If you have more than two characters in the scene, pull another card out for each one. Now play through your scene with that status to see how that feels. Do this at least three times, hopefully with an opportunity to play with different ideas of status. Then decide which feels more comfortable as a baseline for your character (are you typically high or low status regardless of who you are interacting with?). Review your script, and mark how and when your status changes in relation to the other characters. If it is helpful, you can even assign status cards to each person for each scene as a way of tracking your status.

ARE YOU LYING?

Does your character always tell the truth? Here's another question: Do *you* personally always tell the truth? A recent study revealed that Americans, on average, tell eleven lies a week.[7] Think about your interactions with others this past week. Did you tell someone that dress looked good on her, even though you thought it made her hips look too big? Did you tell your instructor that your printer ran out of toner and that's why you couldn't hand in your paper? Or did you tell a friend you were going to hang out but then bailed at the last minute, making up an excuse, like you had a headache? We do this all the time: make up little white lies (or what scientists call "prosocial" lies). Most of the time, our lies have low stakes, and we do it to save ourselves from embarrassment or make others feel better, but often our lies can have great meaning or great weight, for good or bad.

Most of us, when we read a script, look at our lines and assume that all those words are spoken truthfully, that our characters are always honest. There are exceptions, of course, especially if we are playing characters who are habitual liars, like Iago (or any salesman, lawyer, politician, etc.). There are, of course, various degrees of liars. A character like Esther in *Intimate Apparel* is quite honest, and yet George is definitely dishonest. But even in her honesty, there are many things that Esther does not say or says in a way that holds things back, especially in scenes with Mrs. Van Buren or Mrs. Dickson. A character like Walter White in the show *Breaking Bad* lives two different lives, so he is not just lying to his wife about where he disappeared to for a few days but also lying by not telling her he's got a secret meth lab.

Looking at your scenes, figure out when you might be telling an outright lie and when you might be, in some ways, omitting the truth. It may even apply to a line that you say about yourself. This may seem counter to the instructions earlier in this book, when you were to look for lines about your character or lines your character says about themselves. Just because a character says she is trustworthy doesn't necessarily mean she actually *is* trustworthy. Once you have identified some lines where you think your character is lying or not telling the whole truth, you can examine why your character may be telling a lie. What is your action? What is the intent on the other person? Sometimes we lie in order to get what we want from someone (flattery, for instance). Other times we lie in order to spare someone's feelings ("Oh no, you were fantastic in that role!").

If you were working on a police procedural television show (*NCIS*, *Law & Order*, *Criminal Minds*), you may be playing a suspect or a witness to a crime, and your entire scene could be filled with deceit, especially if it's your typical interrogation scene. If that's the case, then you may have to decide how good or how bad a liar you may be. There's been a lot of research about what happens to your body when you tell lies, which is what a polygraph measures (such as heart rate, blood pressure, and breathing). But there are also behavioral signs that you may want to incorporate into your scene. You can decide how subtle or overt you want to make it, depending on how good a liar you want to be.

For instance, liars often avoid eye contact when they are not telling the truth. They may fidget or appear nervous. They may also seem sweaty or thirsty, so they may lick their lips as their mouth dries up. Or they may touch their face or twitch. You should try to match the level of behavior with the level of the lie, as well. Small lies have little risk, so you may not show a lot of worry about it while doing it, yet a big lie, like "I didn't sleep with that woman" may carry a lot more risk, and you may end up showing your hand a bit more. Or not. Again, it depends on how good your character is at lying. Iago in *Othello* is a master at lying. However, in *Lobby Hero*, it seems pretty clear from Dawn's point of view that Jeff knows more about what's going on with Williams's brother than he is letting on. A lot of your behavior choices may also depend on your character's physicality and whether you are playing high or low status, as well.

(One thing to think about, when it comes to lying and showing that you're lying, is the medium you're working in and understanding the difference between stage and film. Onstage, your behavior can be much larger so that your actions are read in the back row of a theater. For film, it will pick up every little microexpression. So, if you make the choice to lie on film and want us to see it, it won't take much. One little blink or eye movement, a twitch, a small gesture will carry loads of weight.)

Exercise 2

Scan your script, and look for any lines that you think are definitely lies and not completely truthful. Use a different-colored highlighter (like red or green), and underline those words so the next time you review your script, you know you're telling a lie.

DO YOU HAVE A SECRET?

Along the same lines as telling lies is the idea of secrets. You've already done a lot of work on your character in terms of relationships, actions, basic needs, and status. You may even be one of those actors who loves to write up a fictional biography so that you know everything about this person since they were a little kid. But what are the secrets this character is carrying around throughout your scenes?

Some characters have obvious secrets, such as Khlestakov, who is secretly hiding the fact that (1) he has run out of money and (2) is not really a government inspector. Some characters have suggested secrets, like Hedda's pregnancy. Some characters have secrets that are revealed in the course of the script, such as the middle daughter Ivy and Little Charles in *August: Osage County* being lovers (of course, the bigger secret about those two is revealed later on).

Some characters have secrets that we as the audience are aware of but other characters are not. A good example is Walter White's secrets in *Breaking Bad*, which are many. For starters, he's keeping his drug lab a secret from his family (one of whom, his brother-in-law, is a DEA agent), but he is also keeping his terminal illness a secret from his young partner and former student Jesse. But then he has an even bigger secret that he keeps from Jesse, one that we as viewers know if it is ever revealed, their relationship would be forever changed. (Spoiler alert: Walter watches Jesse's girlfriend overdose and suffocate on her own vomit and decides not to rescue her because he thinks Jesse would be better off without her—talk about a big secret!) There is one episode of *Breaking Bad* (season 3, episode 10, "Fly") when they're making meth in their lab, and Walter and Jesse are desperately trying to kill a fly to decontaminate the area. Walter, who is drugged on sleeping pills, almost confesses what he did. The scene would play totally differently if Bryan Cranston was not aware of the secret he desperately needed to confess as well as what was at stake if it got revealed.

Your character's secrets could be in the script or part of the plot, but even if you can't find a secret that a writer has given you, there's no reason you can't invent one for yourself, one that aids in the playing of the scene. There's no reason to invent any secrets that may confuse the action or the plot or contradict other choices. After all, you don't need to rewrite or try to improve the script, but you can find a secret that may help intensify a relationship or give more stakes to a scene that feels like it could use more dynamics. Many actors might be afraid of doing too much, but remember, the director's job is to pull you back, and they can give a note about doing too much if you are too bold in your choices. Rarely do directors have to give that note to inexperienced actors.

There is a psychological toll in having a secret. Psychologists have done studies and seen that having a secret can be stressful. There's the fear of discovery, the energy expended toward keeping the secret, and shame or guilt.[8] Also, researchers have found that those who have secrets think about them often, especially in relation to the person they are keeping a secret from. One aspect of keeping a secret is that it will always remain an unfulfilled goal;

you are constantly trying not to be found out and may fail at any moment. So how does that relate to your work as an actor?

Your character may be keeping a secret from another character in your scene. This secret can add weight that may help you to solidify the relationship as well as raise the stakes. Depending on the scene, plot, and relationship, it's up to you to decide what secret might be best to play. It could even be a fun or lighthearted secret, like you're planning a surprise birthday party.

Exercise 3

Write down a list of five secrets about your character. These can be simple things like, "He illegally downloads movies," or "She never picks up her dog poop," to more complex things like, "She had an affair with her husband's best friend." Choose secrets that involve other characters as well as what it would cost if the secret is revealed. Choose one of the juiciest secrets, and write it out on an index card. Put that card in your back pocket, and play your scene. You can even glance at it right before entering as a reminder.

Part III

MAKING IT YOUR OWN: STEPS FOR FINAL REHEARSAL

Chapter Eight

Building Dynamics with Textual Clues

> Great dramatic writing is very near to music. It is as organized, as precise and as economical. And music is always inherently dramatic—particularly when it appropriates words and succeeds in making us think at the same time as feel.
>
> —Peter Hall[1]

This chapter is about unlocking deeper clues in the text and building dynamics in your delivery and performance. Wynton Marsalis, noted jazz musician, once said, "Play everything—no matter how trivial or trite it might be—with dynamics and sound and musical expression."[2] Start to think of your words as music, with your own imagination, voice, and body being the instrument.

Composers communicate their ideas of a musical piece with such technical information as notation but still leave space for interpretation. Music notation provides the key, tempo, rhythm, pitch, chords, and melody. Musicians understand these clues immediately. If you think of words as music, you can look at information the composer (a.k.a. the writer) gives you in the way of rhetoric, operative words, and punctuation (basically the writer telling you the rhythm, when to breathe, shift tempo, etc.). Playing with dynamics and musical expression means more than just knowing the notes (or your lines). It's playing with a unique sense of yourself as an interpretive artist.

THIS AGAINST THAT: RHETORICAL DEVICES

There are many ways that composers use music to phrase certain ideas. Think of a song with a call and response to it. A musical phrase is laid out. Then it may repeat. Or it may repeat with a variation. Or it may be completely new, like an argument to what was just said. In the same way, writers use words, not notes, to present ideas. They then build on those ideas or can agree or disagree with an idea, using such tools as repetition and adding another phrase.

Writers use language not only to portray characters in dialogue but also to put ideas into action or to put an argument forward for exploration. The ideas are conveyed through language. Good writers know how to use that language to build those ideas or create conflict, and one of the tools writers use is rhetoric. In dramatic terms, rhetoric is a form of argumentation that takes place between two characters (and sometimes, as is often in the case of Shakespeare, between an actor and the audience). Think of the mathematical formula $1 + 1 = 2$. This plus that equals this other thing. That's a simple way of looking at it. Characters could be using questions and answers, agreements and disagreements, and comparisons and contrasts. Your job is to stand up for your character's point of view and persuade the audience of its rightness. To give an argument a solid foundation, you must know its internal logic. These devices can help you figure out how your lines work in that way.

One thing to remember is that rhetoric is used to build an argument, and at the end of a speech or a scene, you are coming to the point of the argument. There needs to be a dramatic energy, an idea of winning the debate. The next section reveals some technical tools that may seem superficial but will enable you to commit further to your actions and objectives. Characters use rhetoric to get what they want, so the words should be aligned with your character's needs.

Questions and Answers

You probably already know the term *rhetorical question* and how that particular device works. If you have ever said the words, "Do I look like I was born yesterday?" then you have used this form of rhetoric.

Here's a clear example from *Lobby Hero* in act 1, scene 2, when the police officer, Bill, lectures the security guard, Jeff. Jeff has just revealed to Bill's rookie partner, Dawn, that Bill has been lying about his reasons for visiting the building; instead of visiting a friend, he is visiting a call girl. Of course, Dawn is upset by this news for various reasons and confronts him about it. Bill has Dawn wait outside while he sets things straight with Jeff. He asks Jeff to look out the window at Dawn, saying, "Now you listen to me. Look out there. What do you see out there?" He doesn't actually want an answer. He's setting up his argument, which he unveils in a long speech—that although Dawn looks like a cop on the outside, she isn't a real cop yet and would get herself, or someone else, killed if not for Bill, who is there to guide and protect her. His whole speech is a list of ways she could get hurt or needs his help. And it is filled with rhetorical questions along the line of "Who do you think will help these people? Her or me?"[3]

The most obvious place to find these rhetorical questions are in large speeches, but they can be found anywhere. Here's a short example from Cheche in *Anna in the Tropics* in act 2, scene 1, when he says to Santiago, "Have you ever seen the tail of a lizard when it's been cut off? The tail twists and moves from side to side like a worm that's been removed from the soil."[4] He brings up this rhetorical question to give us a metaphor for how he feels about his wife who left him.

Here's another example from Oscar Wilde's *An Ideal Husband*. In act 4, when Lord Goring is trying to convince Lady Chiltern not to allow her husband to give up his political career after nearly escaping public disgrace and ruin at the hands of the antagonist, Mrs. Chevely:

> LORD GORING: Lady Chiltern, why are you playing Mrs. Chevely's cards? . . . Mrs. Chevely made an attempt to ruin your husband. Either to drive him from public life, or to make him adopt a dishonorable position. . . . Why would you do him the wrong Mrs. Chevely tried to do and failed?[5]

Here you can see that Lord Goring is using rhetoric to begin his argument, setting up first the idea of Lady Chiltern against Mrs. Chevely in the first line (which could be paraphrased as "Why are you doing her work for her?"). Then he poses his argument again as an either/or: either this (drive him from public life) or that (make him adopt a dishonorable position). He then finishes with the last line, repeating this idea of putting Lady Chiltern against Mrs. Chevely as well as wrong against right. The entire short passage of a few sentences is filled with rhetoric. A smart actor will recognize this rhetoric in the speech and emphasize certain words in order to make the convincing argument, which in the long run helps achieve the goal of trying to convince Lady Chiltern not to let her husband resign from public office.

Agreements and Disagreements

Another way of looking at your dialogue and the scene is in terms of agreements and disagreements. One way a writer builds dramatic tension is by throwing opposing ideas at each other. This creates conflict. Your job as an actor is to embrace that conflict, either in your wants or in the words and ideas themselves. If you find yourself in a rhetorical argument composed of disagreement, embrace it and commit to it wholeheartedly.

Let's look at this passage from the beginning of act 2 of *Hedda Gabler*, between Judge Brack and Hedda. As you can see, these two characters have similar ideas and interests and are both clever and powerful people in their own right, but they also disagree. This is part of their connection and their own conflict:

Brack: Not a day passed but I have wished that you were home again.

HEDDA: And I have done nothing but wish the same thing. [*Agreement*]

BRACK: You? Really, Mrs. Hedda? And I thought you had been enjoying your tour so much! [*Disagreement*]

HEDDA: Oh yes, you may be sure of that! [*Agreement*]

BRACK: But Tesman's letters spoke of nothing but happiness. [*Disagreement*]

HEDDA: Oh, Tesman! You see, he thinks nothing is so delightful as grubbing in libraries and making copies of old parchments, or whatever you call them. [*Disagreement*]

BRACK: Well, that is his vocation in life—or part of it at any rate. [*Agreement*]

HEDDA: Yes, of course; and no doubt when it's your vocation—. [*Agreement*] But I! Oh, my dear Mr. Brack, how mortally bored I have been. [*Disagreement*][6]

Looking at this exchange, we can easily see when and how they might agree with each other, beginning a line with "Yes," as well as when they introduce a contradictory idea, as in beginning with "But." Not all scripts will make it so easy to spot.

Exercise 1

Decide if and where your character uses either questions and answers or agreement and disagreement. At the end of the scene or speech, write the argument in your own words. How is that argument tied to your basic need as well as your actions (see chapter 3)? To take this step even further, as you are reviewing your lines at home between rehearsals, add the words *yes* or *no* at the beginning of each line to emphasize the argument further and solidify it in your body and voice.

Comparisons and Contrasts

Another device is using comparisons and contrasts in the language. Comparisons put two things side by side, evaluating them. Comparisons are a way for writers to use one subject to illuminate the other (or, as we'll see in a bit, to point out their differences). Again, John F. Kennedy is using a rhetorical argument in the famous line "Ask not what your country can do for you but what you can do for your country," as he was using the comparison between *your country* and *you.*

If we look at the earlier example from *An Ideal Husband,* Lord Goring is comparing and contrasting two types of strategies that Mrs. Chevely was trying to use to ruin Lady Chiltern's husband: "Either to drive him from public life, *or* to make him adopt a dishonorable position." He is putting one thing in one column and another thing in another column, essentially saying, "Either this or that." As an actor, you might find yourself playing *or* as the operative word. What's an operative word you might ask.

Operative Words

As you may have realized, some words carry more weight than others. As we saw in the previous example, the word *or* becomes really important. It's either this *or* that. Think of it this way: All the words are important, but some words are more important than others. The operative word is the most important word in that line. It carries a lot of weight (it's "operating" at a higher level). The weight of the word is sometimes defined by the context (what was just said to you). Other times, the word is connected to the main thrust of the point of an argument, or the word is being used like a fulcrum by the action you are playing.

Think of word importance in a sentence as a scale of 1 to 10. The operative word is number 1, but then this other word is secondary, and then this word is the third-most important, and so on. For instance, we don't think much of using the words *and* or *the*, but a sentence doesn't make sense without them. Writers spend hours agonizing over their scripts and rewrite until each word and phrase sings.

In the line "But I love you," you have four words, and each word could be emphasized as the operative word:

But I love you.
But *I* love you.
But I *love* you.
But I love *you.*

Each choice represents a different meaning and would be aligned with a different action.

How do you know which word should be the operative word? Most times you already do, if you are reacting to how your partner is behaving toward you or what you are reacting to. As stated before, the meaning will come from the context or your action. For instance, if the line being said to you is "Nobody loves me," then your response may be "But *I* love you." Or if a character says to you, "You don't love anybody, do you?" then your response might be, "But I love *you.*" Finally, the line could also be, "I'm sorry I don't want to be with you anymore," and your response could be, "But I *love* you." Watch out that you don't end up in a stale reading of the line, merely articulating your vocal choices by raising pitch or volume. When considering operative words, you must think about what you are reacting to and connect it to your truthful response.

Operative words are extremely important when it comes to comedy. Audiences have to hear and understand the word and the meaning to understand a joke. Nothing will kill a laugh like underemphasizing (or mumbling) a key word. A good example is one of Lord Goring's lines from *An Ideal Husband*: "I love talking about nothing, father. It is the only thing I know anything about." If the actor doesn't emphasize the word *nothing* in that first sentence, then the audience won't get that joke of the next sentence. Also, he is responding to his father, who just gave him a line using the word *nothing*, so the context is giving more weight and meaning to the word *nothing*. Lord Goring repeats that word to throw it right back at him.

If it isn't clear which word is the operative word, then it may very well be the last word in your line or sentence. The previous example references Lord Goring's father, who says, "The thing has gone to the dogs, a lot of damned nobodies talking about nothing." That last word is important, as it sets up a joke for Lord Goring in his next line, and is also the end of the thought. Writers know that the last word carries a lot more weight. Why? Because the energy of a breath is delivered to the end of a thought, and a thought ends with punctuation. This is especially true with heightened language, like Shakespeare or Molière, but every writer uses it. If we look at Bill's line from *Lobby Hero* from earlier in this chapter, he asks the question, "What do you see?" Sure, we could make the operative word either *what* or *you*, but we are really putting all our energy into that rhetorical question, so it makes more sense for us to say the line as, "What do you *see*?"

Exercise 2

This fun little card game requires a deck of cards or two to play. You can even play this game with your scene partner, but it works just as well alone. Although you may have your lines memorized, it may be good to have the script. Sit down (if working with a partner, sit across from them, as if you are playing poker), and hold the stack of cards in your hand. You will read through your speech or scene, and as you do so, choose three different words for each line and then smack down a card for each line. For example, the line may be "I adore political parties. They are the only place left to us where people don't talk politics," and you might choose to throw down a card on *parties*, *people*, and *politics*. As you smack that card down, emphasize the rhythm and intonation of the word; commit to the power of that word. Go through your script, choosing three words for each line or sentence (as appropriate; for example, if the sentence only has two words in it, then both those words are emphasized with cards). After you have done this with three words and cards, then go through it again, choosing only two words to put cards down. Observe how that feels a bit different and how your choices might change. Then do it one final time, this time choosing only one word and one card for each line or sentence of dialogue. Notice how that changes and what words struck you.

DISCLOSURE, DISCOVERY, OR DECISION?

Another way to add dynamics is to decide if the line is one of three things: a disclosure, a discovery, or a decision. A disclosure line delivers information that your character already knows to someone else. It could be in the form of exposition or a simple statement. The context and circumstances can help guide the choice. A discovery line means that you had never known it before and realize it in that moment. It may come as a surprise to you and change your understanding of the world. A discovery can put your character in a vulnerable position because it is a moment where change can happen (even if it is merely a changing of perception). Audiences love when characters are surprised, so it's safe to say audiences lean in and get more invested in the performance with these moments of discovery!

A decision moment is where your character has reached a conclusion about something and decided to do something about it. A character could walk into the scene with a decision moment, or a character could get information or have a discovery and, based on that discovery, decide to do something about it. Going back through your scenes to see when your character decides to pursue the objective is important; you can certainly connect this to your work on the script in the earlier chapters (like chapters 1–3).

As we keep saying, this is all interpretive, so it will depend on your imagination, thoughts, and the given circumstances of the scene or the text. *You* have to make the choice. And it's not solely about the type of line or the way the line is written, though sometimes a particular line will feel more like a decision ("I will have my revenge!") or more like a discovery ("I can't believe she loves me!"). For instance, take the line, "I love you."

Played as a moment of disclosure, it could be very simple. A mother telling her son in the grocery store, "I love you." Simple, matter of fact, "Hey, don't forget." It could also be played even more as a confession or revealing a secret. There are variations. Played as a discovery, it could be during a scene from a rom-com, when the hero actually realizes he can't live without the love of his life and says it to her for the first time as she is about to get in a cab to the airport: "I love you!" That might feel more like a surprise (to both of them), and the character may feel more vulnerable. Played as a decision, it could come out in a scene where two people are vowing to be together, as if saying "I do." It is a moment that says, "Things are going to change."

Let's look at an example from the play *The Albatross*, this time looking at a longer speech from the character of Jack. Jack is a grad student in his twenties and interested in getting to know Sofia, a first-year undergrad. Later in this play, Sofia impresses her professor David and is able to convince him to let her into his graduate workshop. Jack is one of the students in that workshop and has offered to help her out with her analysis of some of the poems they're discussing. Earlier that day in class, they had a small altercation, as Sofia criticized his poem, and he reacted childishly toward her. This excerpt takes place later that day at a coffee shop. Jack is helping her analyze poetry, until he decides to ask her out, offering to cook her dinner. Thinking that he was only helping her for lustful reasons, she gathers her things to leave, and he tries to convince her to stay:

> JACK: Sorry if you got the wrong impression here, but . . . I like you. I think you're beautiful and intelligent and you're really talented. These attributes are rare and attractive, right? Okay, so I'm attracted to you. I don't think that's like, indecent. It doesn't make me some pervert or something. Now, can I just be clear here? I don't want to have sex with you . . . No, shit, that's not what I meant. I mean, I do . . . but not . . . Eventually. Right? Look, I want to hang out with you, get to know you. God, you make me feel so . . . it's infuriating sometimes. I mean, look, I . . . I want to cook you dinner. That's all I want to do. Right now, anyway. I feel bad about what I said in class. I want to make it right. But also, I do want to hear more of your poems and I'd like to share some of mine. So let me cook you dinner, okay? Just let me be a nice guy, not some . . . whatever . . . right? It's just dinner.[7]

(Did you notice the line, "I think you're beautiful and intelligent and you're really talented. These attributes are rare and attractive, right?" That was a rhetorical question.)

Let's break down that speech and examine how we might choose whether the line could be played as discovery, disclosure, or decision:

> JACK: Sorry if you got the wrong impression here, [**Disclosure:** *A simple delivery of information or trying to set the record straight.*] but . . . I like you. I think you're beautiful and intelligent and you're really talented. These attributes are rare and attractive, right? [**Discovery:** *These lines could be part of a big or little discovery. This could be played as if it's the first moment he realizes why he attacked her earlier and why he is interested in her. It could also surprise him. He doesn't know what he is going to say next.*] Okay, so I'm attracted to you. I don't think that's like,

indecent. It doesn't make me some pervert or something. [**Decision:** *He has got the creative argument out and now decides what he wants to do next.*] Now, can I just be clear here? I don't want to have sex with you . . . No, shit, that's not what I meant. I mean, I do . . . but not . . . Eventually. Right? Look, I want to hang out with you, get to know you. God, you make me feel so . . . it's infuriating sometimes. [**Discovery:** *All this could be played as discovery. He is in the moment, responding, not sure what will come out of his mouth. Being in a state of discovery also makes him vulnerable and off-guard.*] I mean, look, I . . . I want to cook you dinner. That's all I want to do. [**Disclosure:** *Another simple statement, trying to get information across to her. This is also tied to his earlier discovery and decision just moments ago.*] Right now anyway. I feel bad about what I said in class. I want to make it right. [**Decision:** *He has decided, not just to her, but also to himself, that this is the way to make it right. He could be trying to convince her or himself, or he could be confessing (all playable actions that could be tied to this decision, as well).*] But also, I do want to hear more of your poems and I'd like to share some of mine. [**Discovery:** *As before, this could come as a surprise to him, something he hasn't thought about before. And he's being honest, with himself and her. This whole idea of a date could be unplanned.*] So let me cook you dinner, okay? Just let me be a nice guy, not some . . . whatever . . . right? It's just dinner. [**Disclosure:** *A simple line, repeating the offer.*]

This is merely one interpretation. There's no reason you couldn't play that last line as a decision moment. And the audience isn't going to be able to tell if you are playing any of these lines as discovery, disclosure, or decision. But they will notice if you're not making any choices at all with the lines or if all the lines seem to be all disclosure or all decision. This is simply another small tool to add dynamics and nuances to what you are doing.

PUNCTUATION AND GRAMMAR

We see punctuation and grammar so often in our scripts that most times we take it for granted, but as stated before, writers are specific about everything. There's a difference between a comma, a semicolon, a period, and an exclamation point. It's like musical notation and should not be ignored.

Some actors write down all their lines in their own handwriting, paying no attention to the punctuation. This is fine as an exercise as a way to personalize the words and make them your own so you don't fall into clichés or line readings, but you ignore the rules of grammar and punctuation at your own risk. Your role as actor is not only to serve your needs to personalize the role but also to convey the thought, intention, and meaning of the text.

Punctuation helps with phrasing so that you can break thoughts down into little thoughts. This phrasing helps with your intentions and actions and when those might shift. It also gives clues of where to breathe and how. You could be shifting gears and trying a new tactic, which is why you ended the sentence at the moment you did. You could be using a comma as a pause, to insert a new idea, a discovery in the moment. Short sentences can provide a different rhythm than longer sentences that are broken up by commas.

Here's a few lines from Dennis's short film *My Date with Adam*. The lead character, Sarah, is frustrated about her dating situation and defending herself to her best friend, Julie. Her new prospective date, Adam, is a man she met online and who seemed to have some odd quirks when they met in person at a coffee shop:

SARAH: Adam is my last hope for a date on my thirtieth birthday. I can't go out of my twenties alone and miserable. You know how hard it is to find a husband after thirty?[8]

The first sentence ends with a period. It's just a statement where the actor defends her choice. Then she switches gears to convince Julie how desperate the situation is and why it means so much to her. Finally, in the third sentence, she uses a question (hey, look, it's another rhetorical device) to drive home her point on the difficulties of finding a good man.

Julie replies with her argument that the "right guy is out there somewhere," and Sarah responds,

SARAH: Where? Tell me! I'm tired of waiting for him to show up! I'm tired of watching other brides in their puffy wedding dresses and silly princess tiaras toast their happiness as they sail off blindly into their "happily ever after." This time *it's my fucking turn*!

These lines begin with stating simple facts, but then we can see how it builds in intensity, emotion, and volume. That exclamation point (and italics for emphasis) is there for a reason. That's the writer suggesting that this character has reached a boiling point. This is a comedic outburst, and the direction is already inherent in the lines, the rhetoric, and the punctuation of the script. Adding to the comedy, Sarah is a wedding planner and currently standing near a pretty bride in a tiara trying on wedding dresses with her bridesmaids, who all turn to look at her in her moment of rage.

So, what should you do with each punctuation? In general, with end stops (like the period, exclamation point, or question mark), you are at the end of a thought. All your energy should rise up and meet the end of that line. Each sentence usually has its own thought and idea (and action), and you commit to it until you have said the entire sentence. Don't drop the energy or the intention before you get to that end of the line. This is especially important with a question or exclamation. With questions, we recognize them by that upward inflection, so if you don't give it that cadence, the audience won't get it. Writers use exclamation points sparingly, so when it's there, commit to the excitement, anger, or energy that it is suggesting.

Think of commas as places to take a quick breath and keep going. You are working through the thought and getting to your end stop, but you're not done yet. Commas are springboards, bouncing you forward. Sometimes it can be a way of putting in a digression, a discovery that happens in the moment, or it can be a small list of things that help you get to the end of your argument and line. It is dangerous to think of commas as a place to pause or think—that's not their purpose. In fact, when it comes to pauses, writers are careful about when they want them, so if they do want a pause, they usually write that in the stage directions. Always assume there are no pauses unless the writer or the director give you one. (For more about pauses and pacing, see chapter 15.)

If you see a parenthesis, which are rare, you should do something different. A parenthesis can be used to make a comment about a thought in a sentence as you are still in that sentence, to make a joke about something, or to add a digression. It may also be a discovery, disclosure, or decision. It's like a little side bar. You can attack these by changing the tempo, pitch, intonation, or tone.

You may also see a colon or semicolon, but these are also rare in modern scripts. The purpose of a semicolon is to link related ideas (independent clauses). Think of a semicolon as a bit like a comma. It's a breath, but it's also an *and*. You are building on a thought with another idea that is similar or proves your argument, still driving toward the end stop. Colons are used to illustrate and expand on an idea or to introduce a list of items or issues. You often will have an idea repeated, but it is more articulate, as if you are revising and redoing your earlier line to make your point.

You may also see an ellipsis (. . .). This usually indicates that the character's thoughts are trailing off. For you, the actor, this is a great clue that you are actively thinking about what you are going to say. You have a couple options here. You can play it as if you don't know how to finish the sentence, as if you are waiting for someone else to finish the sentence, or you are pondering your next move. A good example is from Sofia's monologue from the play *The Albatross*, which we look at in chapter 4:

> SOFIA: I'm going to leave, okay? You're obviously . . . drunk or something. But for the record, I care. I care more than you ever do, or did. You talk to me about . . . You're the one who doesn't care.

The writer doesn't give you clues about why Sofia is trailing off there. Does she want to say, "drunk," or does she want to say something else like, "crazy" or "cruel"? When she says, "You talk to me about," why doesn't she finish? Is it because her mind has already moved on to the next statement, the accusation that he is the one who doesn't care?

The dash (—) is common in contemporary scripts, especially plays, to indicate when a character interrupts or overlaps another character. This is a clue for you as an actor about where your cue word might be and that your character is too anxious or excited to wait for the other character to finish a sentence. It may look like this:

ANNIE: But you didn't teach me how to play the violin like I wanted to—

JAMES: I did teach / you how to play—

ANNIE: No! You didn't teach me / anything!

JAMES: I taught you how to play with your heart!

Here we see that Annie begins her next line with "No!" on James's word *teach*, and then James interrupts Annie when she says her word *me* in the following line.

Each time there is a piece of punctuation, you are able to make a choice and do something different, which may include:

• Change action
• Change direction of the argument
• Shift gears to a lower or higher speed
• Change intonation or pitch
• Fire through
• Slow down
• Breathe or refuel for a new thought

If you want to physically acknowledge the punctuation and put it in your body, a good task is to get up on your feet and make a physical choice each time you come to any punctuation. Start walking in one direction, and as soon as you reach a comma or period, change directions. Play with moving forward and backward. Get the idea of changes into your body. This will also help you with memorization.

THE WAR AGAINST DIS
(DOWNWARD INFLECTION SYNDROME)

Downward inflection is a common issue with actors. John even diagnoses it as "downward inflection syndrome." In standard American dialect, this is a common way of speaking, but it is deadly in performance. It refers to how you drop the end of your line so that the last word is lower in pitch or intention. It could be seen as being noncommittal to a thought, as if your subtext was, "I think this, but maybe I'm wrong." Think of a balloon deflating. That's downward inflection, and when an actor talks like that repetitively, an audience stops listening.

Upward inflection is driving the energy and the thought to the end stop or end of the line. Think of rising action, of a balloon being filled up. A clear example of rising inflection is when you ask a question. The tendency is to punctuate that question mark by sending the energy to the end of the question. Notable voice and speech teacher Patsy Rodenburg once said that downward inflection gives the audience the feeling of depression and pessimism, while upward inflection gives the audience the feeling of optimism and creativity. In *The Actor Speaks: Voice and the Performer*, she elaborates:

> Many theatre people call this dropping inflection and word energy "minor-key speaking." It seems devoid of thought or emotion and far from the major key that passionate acting must strike. From the actor's point of view it is harder work. Every time you drop off or pull back a word or line you have to summon more energy to hoist yourself back onto the text. I will often say to a performer that it is the equivalent of trying to surf: you catch a wave and yet are getting on and off your board mid-wave every few seconds. Not very efficient![9]

Does this mean you should be saying every line like it's a question, with rising inflection? Not at all! It means you must keep the momentum going. Connect this breath/thought with the next. Think about if you were passing a soccer ball to your friend. You would want to make sure the ball makes it not just all the way to where they are, but almost like you are kicking it past them to ensure it will get there and not fall short. You have to adjust your energy depending on whether the distance is five yards or twenty yards away. Now imagine that your words in your line are that ball, and think about not letting the words slowly fall short, in the same way you don't want that ball to slowly roll to your partner; you want the energy of the ball moving to go past your friend so that they can bounce it or catch it with their foot.

Earlier in this chapter, you learned about operative words, and an easy fix for downward inflection is to choose to make the last word in each sentence the operative word. That will give you a "target" for your energy, and you are driving the energy to that specific word.

Exercise 2

As you work on your script, play with the cadence and rhythm by trying it in three different dialects: Italian, Irish, or southern. Each of these dialects has an upward inflection. It doesn't have to be a good dialect either, so don't worry how you sound. This can also be a fun way of reviewing lines. Have fun, and let go of any ideas about character or actions. Just work through the language as an exercise. You may discover new ideas about a character trait as your vocal choices change with the inflection.

Chapter Nine

Interior Fittings: Building Emotional and Verbal Dynamics

If acting were crying, my Aunt Tessie would be a great actress.

—Robert Lewis[1]

Now that we have built the foundation, scaffolding, and brick and mortar of our walls, we look at the wonderful add-ons, customizations, smaller details, and alterations. As with any new building, there are always unforeseen adjustments that need to be made. Building a role is no different.

This chapter examines such challenges as dealing with emotional scenes, long speeches, dense language, physical activities, and physical modifications. Think of these challenges as the fittings you might find in a house, those craftsman-like details that make a house truly unique.

EMOTIONAL DYNAMICS

Emotional scenes come in many different packages: Emotions include anger, sadness, grief, happiness, joy, and frustration. Ideally, all your scenes should have some emotional life to them. After all, we're emotional beings, and the very idea of drama is that we're witnessing the highs and lows of humanity.

For an audience, watching characters cry can be therapeutic. The flip side is that the audience doesn't want to catch an actor trying to force themselves to cry. Audiences are moved by a character doing everything in their power *not* to cry but failing. And then, even as they are breaking down in tears, they are bravely continuing with their actions in the scene.

Before we dive into how to create your emotional life, it's important to remind you that *emoting all by itself is not acting.* Acting is *doing.* All the tools in this book are related to this idea. Emotion is a result of those actions and your investment in what they mean to you. You may have already discovered that the more invested you are in a scene, the more it will cost when you win or lose. Looking at emotion this way, we can focus less on the result ("I have to get angry here" or "I have to cry") to what it is you are doing ("I am lashing out at him" or "I'm saying goodbye forever").

Sooner or later, you'll be handed a role where you see in the stage directions, "He cries." Crying in a scene is demanding; it doesn't matter whether it's happy tears after finally getting a job offer so you can take care of your young son (like Will Smith in *The Pursuit of Happyness*) or a ship captain who has been rescued from a traumatic event and is being medically examined (Tom Hanks in *Captain Phillips*) or a wife feeling betrayed by her husband and trying to get him to see her point of view (Viola Davis in *Fences*). You know, it's the Oscars clip. In other words, when we see those words in our script, "He cries," we psyche ourselves out. We focus on result and not process. Big mistake.

So, what do you do if the scene requires you to cry on cue? First, remember that writers don't sit down and write out a scene solely for the sake of having a character cry. If you have done your homework and know how the scene fits with the rest of the story (see PASTO in chapter 2) as well as the arc of your character, then you already know what you want in the scene (objective), what it means to you, who you are talking to and what they mean to you (relationship), and how you are trying to get what you want (actions). It's the investment in those imaginary circumstances and your action that will help you to achieve emotion. By simply engaging your imagination, you can activate an emotional life. It's also important that your body and your voice is relaxed, free, and open because if it isn't, then any emotion may not release.

The character Little Charles in *August: Osage County* has to cry almost immediately upon entering his first scene in act 2, after his father has picked him up from the bus station. He feels like a failure and that the family hates him, and he is afraid to go inside. As an actor, you can't enter expecting to cry. You have to deal with the given circumstances and use what is front of you. If you know your relationship to your father and what that means to you and imagine that you have just disappointed him on a grand scale and you can see that in his face, then you can let that moment affect you.

However, you may still need to do preparation before you walk into the scene. Emotional preparation is a personal thing for each actor, and you will have to discover the way that works for you (or get yourself to a good teacher to guide you). Larry Silverberg, noted teacher of the Meisner approach, has a simple definition of *emotional preparation*: "It's what you do before you enter, so that when you do enter, you are emotionally alive." [2]

There are two main modes of thought here, but both are really two sides of the same coin, something Uta Hagen calls "substitution," which is part of her idea of "transference."[3] Substitution relates to the idea of relationship that is discussed in chapter 3. If you know what this person means to you—not the literal definition of *relationship* but who this person is to you—then you find a substitute in your own life. Perhaps you are in a scene with your sister, but you are an only child. Then you might consider the relationship you have with your real best friend who is like a sister to you. You would substitute that emotional response for the best friend in the script.

One approach to emotional preparation developed by Sanford Meisner requires engaging the imagination. In this approach, you create a vivid daydream that would result in a similar feeling to what the character may be going through. For example, if you were playing Hamlet and trying to prepare for your first scene, it may be difficult for you to relate to those given circumstances—you're not a prince, your father isn't dead, and your uncle didn't marry your mother. However, if you approach that first scene when he is grieving over his father's death and you decide that he feels betrayed by his mother, then you find a daydream that may have a similar feeling. You may create a fantasy that involves betrayal by your wife, who stole your inheritance and moved the kids to Mexico, letting that daydream get more and more specific until it fuels the emotion within you. This is, of course, a gross simplification of a much more nuanced and complicated process (made clearer in Silverberg's Meisner workbook mentioned previously or in William Esper's book *The Actor's Art and Craft*).

Another approach to emotional preparation is called affective memory and uses your own memories as a substitute for the emotion required for a scene. Stanislavski had experimented with affective memory and then decided it wasn't effective, but noted teacher Lee Strasberg, of the "Method" as we know it in the United States, was a strong advocate for this type of preparation. By using your real-life memories and recalling them in your mind, you essentially reexperience those moments so that they affect you in the present. For instance, if your dog died when you were young and that created grief, then you could call up that memory and use it to help you cry. Affective memory has been used by actors like Al Pacino and Robert De Niro, but it has its difficulties and limitations. First, your memories are limited (whereas your imagination is not), and second, it can fail you if you become inured to that memory.

Both approaches require specificity. If your daydream is a generic daydream without specific details to produce a generic type of anger, then it won't work. The same with affective memory. In order to use your memories, you must recall not just how it made you feel but also the details—the smells, the clothes you were wearing, the objects in a room. You must let those specific images create emotion. No matter what emotional preparation you decide to use, you should always enter a scene with some form of inner life. In other words, never come in empty.

When you do prepare, it is also important to do it in a healthy way. Theater can be therapeutic, but it is not therapy. There is no need to suffer for your art, either psychologically or emotionally. If you have experienced a traumatic event in your life, it is unwise to relive that event so that you can get yourself into tears in a scene. Don't try to use emotional preparation as an excuse to figure out how you feel about your mother's suicide, for example. In the same way, if using daydreams about someone you love causes you to lose complete control of your emotion, so much that you can't even continue to remember your lines, then that may not be the healthiest daydream to use.

Another emotion that triggers a certain response in actors is rage. Some actors are afraid to get angry, echoing the famous refrain from Bruce Banner (the Incredible Hulk): "You won't like me when I get angry." Other actors embrace anger wholeheartedly, jumping at the chance to scream and throw things. But be careful, and don't put your focus on a result or try to show your emotion. Acting is doing, not emoting. When it comes to anger, it is often the most uninteresting and weakest choice to make in terms of what is happening in the scene. But let's face it: Sometimes you know your character is entering full of unbridled anger. Your job is to connect that emotion to the actions, the circumstances, and the relationships. You need to know what you are saying and what it means to you. A lot of times, when a character enters full of anger, it's to "give someone a piece of their mind," a very active thing to do.

But what if you have an emotional or psychological block, and you can't seem to get a single tear or grumpy grimace? In the course of our careers, we may encounter scenes that are easy to tap into and others that cause blocks. According to Rob Roznowski, author of *Roadblocks in Acting*, many of our psychological blocks are self-imposed.[4] This excellent book, written in consultation with psychologists, looks at the way actors throw themselves into roles, essentially inviting vulnerability in front of others, something that most normal people avoid at all costs. Of course, there will be scenes and moments that we will be resistant to. It's human nature.

One final note on emotional preparation; it's to prepare you to enter the scene, as if you are coming from somewhere else. Once you enter, respond to the moment. This may involve letting go of that emotion and reacting to your partner, doing what you have to do to achieve what you want. If the emotional condition finds its way out in crying (or yelling or laughing) or changes from anger to joy, then that's the scene. In some ways, riding atop that emotion can be a little bit like riding a horse; you don't want to grip the reins too tightly, but if the horse takes off running, you don't want to let go!

The more you rehearse your preparation, the more likely you will be able to give a repeatable performance. It is amazing what your mind and body will remember and perform. Please note, that we did say you have to *rehearse your preparation.* Don't wait to be in the room with your fellow actors. Don't leave it up to chance or hope that the mood will strike you when you need it. This is work you can be doing at home between in-person rehearsals.

Exercise 1

Find a quiet place to be alone to do this work. Sit down and close your eyes as you consider the emotional life of your character, particularly the emotions that might arise in an intense scene. As you consider the character's given circumstances, ask yourself how you think those circumstances would make your character feel. Be specific. If it is anger, what kind of anger? If it is joy, what kind of joy? Let the details of the character's situation live in your mind to help you with that specificity.

When you know the feeling, try to imagine a situation that might make you feel that exact way. Perhaps you already have life experience that is similar and can immediately relate it to your character. Or perhaps you would rather use an imaginary scenario, some daydream or fantasy that might make you feel that way. See if there is a metaphor that comes to mind: "It's like if my wife cheated on me with my best friend," or "It's like I just got an audition for Lin Manuel-Miranda." Then let your mind drift and wander as you flesh out those details of the situation. How could you make that feeling increase even more? Don't think about forcing an emotion out of it, but see if anything arises. Keep trying this with different circumstances until you find the preparation that works for you.

VERBAL DYNAMICS

Then there is that moment when you're reading through your script and you see pages of dialogue and it's all you. It's the kind of speech that will make your yellow highlighter dry up just looking at it. Immediately, the stress of learning all those lines seizes you. Or perhaps you're cast in a sci-fi movie as the scientist who has to explain everything happening on the ship. You circle a hundred words you don't know how to pronounce, much less what they mean: artificial intelligence, positronic brain, parallel universe, quasar, terraforming, time-space continuum, force drive—oh my! Or maybe you just got cast in a play by Shakespeare, and you can't tell *thee* from *thou* for the life of you (hint: see John's book *Will Power: How to Act Shakespeare in 21 Days*).

Some scripts are going to require a level of verbal dexterity. Oscar Wilde and Shakespeare may not be anything like *Star Trek* or *Lord of the Rings*, but there's a reason that celebrated classical actors find themselves in leading roles in sci-fi and fantasy movies; they can handle complex language.

(Before Ian McKellen became Gandalf and Patrick Stewart became Captain Picard, they both developed their acting chops at the Royal Shakespeare Theater.)

Let's take a look at the first challenge: long speeches. The following example is one of the many long speeches from act 4 of *An Ideal Husband* by Oscar Wilde (with cuts for clarity):

LORD GORING: Lady Chiltern, why are you playing Mrs. Cheveley's cards? Mrs. Cheveley made an attempt to ruin your husband. Either to drive him from public life, or to make him adopt a dishonorable position. From the latter tragedy you saved him. The former you are now thrusting on him. Why should you do him the wrong Mrs. Cheveley tried to do and failed? . . . Lady Chiltern, allow me. You wrote me a letter last night in which you said you trusted me and wanted my help. Now is the moment when you really want my help, now is the time when you have got to trust me, to trust in my counsel and judgment. You love Robert. Do you want to kill his love for you? What sort of existence will he have if you rob him of the fruits of his ambition, if you take him from the splendor of a great political career, if you close the doors of public life against him, if you condemn him to sterile failure, he who was made for triumph and success? Don't make any terrible mistake, Lady Chiltern.

LADY CHILTERN: But it is my husband himself who wishes to retire from public life. He feels it is his duty. It was he who first said so.

LORD GORING: Rather than lose your love, Robert would do anything, wreck his whole career, as he is on the brink of doing now. He is making for you a terrible sacrifice. Take my advice, Lady Chiltern, and do not accept a sacrifice so great. If you do, you will live to repent it bitterly. Robert has been punished enough.

LADY CHILTERN: We have both been punished. I set him up too high.

LORD GORING: Do not for that reason set him down now too low. If he has fallen from his altar, do not thrust him into the mire. Failure to Robert would be the very mire of shame. Your husband's life is at this moment in your hands, your husband's love is in your hands. Don't mar both for him.[5]

Aside from a few short exchanges from Lady Chiltern, that mouthful of words is all Lord Goring's speech.

The first thing you need to do is break it down into beats, just like you would for a scene. You have to ask, "What is the objective, and what are my actions? (i.e., What am I doing, and why do I keep talking?)" Other than lawyers and teachers, most people don't immediately decide for themselves, "Now I will talk for ten minutes about this." Usually, we start with one statement, which turns into another, and then we think of something else or some other tactic. If you begin the speech with the energy of "and now for my big monologue," you kill the life out of it, and the audience will sense a big speech coming and may tune out. The first step is to ask with specificity, "Why do I keep talking?"

So, why does Lord Goring keep talking? Let's break it down. How many beats would you notate here? Take another read of the text and take a stab at how many you might have. We broke it down into five beats. Did you get five or four? Does it really matter? No—again, this isn't math; it's an interpretive art. Here is how you might title your beats:

1. You're doing him wrong.
2. You want my help or not?
3. Here's why he will hate you for this.
4. Don't you understand that he's doing this for you?
5. It's your choice. Don't let him ruin your life.

In the first beat, he compares Lady Chiltern to Mrs. Cheveley—essentially, saying, "Don't be like her and do him wrong." He then goes on to explain further. In the next beat, he reminds her how she asked for his help and then uses that statement to offer it. He must see that she is open to that help, so he moves on the next beat, which is a new tactic. In this beat, he appeals to her sense of love for her husband and lists all the ways her husband will be destroyed by this action (why he will end up hating her for this). He starts compiling a list:

1. Rob him of the fruits of his ambition
2. Take him from his great political career
3. Close the doors of public life
4. Condemn him to failure

Each item gets worse. He summarizes with "Why would you punish him for doing something in his youth?" and warns her not to make a mistake. Of course, she says she may understand but argues it's her husband's idea. Lord Goring then switches to a new tactic for this fourth beat to convince her that Robert is doing it as a sacrifice and not just any sacrifice: He's doing it for her specifically. That last beat summarizes his points but also lets her know that it's her choice. When we break it down like beats in a scene, we see how one action leads to the next. Lord Goring continues talking because he is changing tactics in his objective to get through to her and realize her mistake. He wants to change her mind.

Even if your long speech doesn't have interjections like this example, you need to figure out why you keep talking. What's going on in the other characters' eyes and faces? There must be a reason you keep talking, so find it. It may even be helpful to give yourself little prompts in the margins of your script, what you think they might say if they could (even if it is just a simple "What do you mean by that?"). The other benefit of breaking up a speech is that you understand its structure. This is also tied to our ideas of rhetoric (see chapter 8). You know how each point adds up to proving your argument, but that argument is tied to an objective; if you're a lawyer, it's to win the case. How do you do it? You convince the jury (your action).

If you're cast in a science-fiction movie and you have speeches filled with jargon, then there are a few ways to make your life easier. As stated in chapter 1, you should've looked up words or phrases that you didn't know the meaning of or didn't understand. It doesn't matter if it's English, French, or Klingon. You need to know what you are saying, what it means, and what it means to you. For example, if it is an actual word or concept like *artificial intelligence*, then you can research that idea on the internet or in actual books from your library or bookstore. You don't need a PhD to understand the concept enough to speak confidently about it in an imaginary situation. For a word that may be created solely for the world of the script, you need to discover what that word means to you. Often, those words are explained in the table read-through or discussions with your director (see chapter 5).

For example, let's say you are cast as the scientist in a sci-fi adventure movie that takes place on the planet Kartek-3. It's not the lead role, but it's important (you get killed off by a slimy space creature). Here's your line:

SCIENTIST: Captain Fryetag, if we jump to hyperspace we risk destabilizing the cindertonium core. I know the Korgs will eventually decode our electromagnetic signal if we don't do something soon, but I cannot risk the lives of this crew because you want to play cowboy. That is not the Kartek code.

On your first read-through, you would be circling a few words: *hyperspace, destabilizing, cindertonium core, Korgs, Kartek code.* Out of those words, *destabilizing* is easy to look up in a dictionary (upsetting the stability or causing unrest), and *hyperspace* you may know from *Star Wars* or *Star Trek* (it's faster than light speed). At the read-through, the director may explain the other words and terms: that cindertonium is an energy source similar to plutonium, the core is a collection of cells like a battery, the Korgs are the alien race invading the planet, and the Kartek code is actually mentioned earlier in the script by the captain ("Honor by one is honor for all; freedom for one is freedom for all").

Those definitions are going to help you on an intellectual level, but your next step is to make it matter to you on a personal level. This is where substitution can be helpful. If you simply think of the ship as if it were a nuclear submarine and that the cindertonium core is like a nuclear reactor, then you can understand and relate to the dangers of what might happen if it is destabilized. So, when you say the words *destabilizing the cindertonium core*, you're really thinking, "It will cause an explosive nuclear reaction and incinerate everyone." In the same way, the Kartek code may be totally alien to you (okay, bad pun, but you get the idea), so you have to substitute it with some credo you can relate to (like perhaps the Marine code, "Semper fi").

By the way, extra points if you noticed in that scientist's lines all the hard *k* sounds: *captain, risk, core, Korgs, decode, cannot, crew, cowboy, Kartek, code*. This is actually a hint that you can really play up those *k* sounds and discover what meaning and emotion might be behind them. Sure, the text isn't Shakespeare, but that doesn't mean you can't play with language as if it is (just ask Patrick Stewart or Ian McKellen).

This is all about personalizing the language and making it your own. One way to do that is to paraphrase the lines. The challenge with paraphrasing is that you can't simply make it an intellectual exercise of just rephrasing words. You have to give the phrases and words personal meanings. Otherwise, it's not so helpful. Sometimes when you find that right phrasing, you find an instinctual intonation and pace that makes the action clear but also illuminates the language. The next step is to apply that intonation and intention to the actual lines.

PHYSICAL ACTIVITIES

Let's define *physical activities* as any task you may be working on in the context of your scene that involves your body. The list of what this could include is about as long as the list of things humans do on a daily basis, from sports to work to hobbies. You could be cast as a seamstress (Lynn Nottage's *Intimate Apparel*), a cigar roller (Nilo Cruz's *Anna in the Tropics*), an origami master (Rajiv Joseph's *Animals Made Out of Paper*), or a boxer (Marco Ramirez's *The Royale*).

The challenge with a physical activity is that you might find it difficult to engage in basic acting fundamentals while also concentrating on that activity (especially if you are unskilled at that activity). Time and again, we see actors doing some activity, like folding laundry, and they stop to look at their scene partner and say the line, then go back to folding, then stop, then say the line. But people don't do that in real life. For example, you might have fixed yourself a bowl of cereal this morning while you were talking to your mom on the phone. Or you were deleting old photos on your phone while warning your roommate not to eat your ice cream again. We can do these things because the physical activity has become second nature. That's what you need to do with the physical activity in your scene. Just because you're doing something that requires focus doesn't mean you can't act and react to your scene partner; be in the moment, and be truthful as your character.

For example, if you were to play Levee in August Wilson's *Ma Rainey's Black Bottom*, you'd research what it means to be a trumpet player in that time period, thinking about how this character started playing this instrument. Levee isn't only a trumpet player; he also considers himself a brilliant musician and composer. He wants to be the next Jelly Roll Morton or at least bigger than Ma Rainey. An actor playing that role should know how to handle a trumpet, from taking it out of its case and cleaning it to putting it together and properly holding it. You may not be tasked with actually playing it, but it's about specificity and details. When Chadwick Boseman played Levee for the film adaptation, he went to who worked on the music for that film, Branford Marsalis, to ask about getting trumpet lessons. He knew that it didn't matter that his playing wasn't going to be used in the film. He wanted to ensure that his fingering looked like he actually knew how to play. Not only that, Boseman used the trumpet in several scenes, not just as a prop, but also as an extension of his character.

It may not be such a specialized activity as playing an instrument. It could be as simple as folding laundry (like the opening scene of *Rabbit Hole* by David Lindsay-Abaire). Tracy Letts, writer of *August: Osage County*, is also an accomplished actor (*Ladybird*) and knows the value of physical activities. Most of the *August: Osage County* involves characters performing physical activities, either getting ready for the big dinner, cleaning up, making a bed, or rolling a joint.

What if you don't have a physical activity in your scene? Could you add one? Of course! Think about what your character could be doing that would help ground your work as well as make sense—and then offer that idea to the director. Any activity that fills you with life and creates the reality of the world will work.

Exercise 2

Think about activities your character might do, either on the job or in their spare time. If your character is at work, what tasks would a typical workday involve? What's on their to-do list? Does your character have a hobby? Does she have a fun recreational activity, like rollerblading or jogging? Your homework is to take an activity and perform it as your character. If your character makes model airplanes, go to a hobby shop as your character to look for your next project. If you go to a library or bookstore, look for a book your character might be interested in. If you go grocery shopping, wear clothes you think your character might wear and pick up your groceries as the character. (You should use some discretion here, of course—if you're playing a criminal, don't actually commit a crime or do anything violent! You will have crossed over from imaginary circumstances to the real world, and that will have real-world consequences!)

PHYSICAL MODIFICATIONS

Physical modifications include any type of modification to your physicality. Think of modifications on a scale from 1 to 10 in terms of complexity. You could change your center of gravity or add bodily discomfort, such as a headache, a hangover, or a broken ankle. Or you could be under the influence of a substance, such as alcohol or drugs. Modifications also include changing your behavior due to different temperatures, such as playing a scene as if it's really hot or really cold.

Although these conditions can seem simple, actor's choices often lead to generalities and cliché. Or they are forgotten completely, especially when the focus is on learning lines, blocking, and playing actions. Let's begin with a condition like a simple headache. Your character enters a scene complaining about the headache. If you look at the given circumstances and your homework (see chapters 1 and 2), you might see why this character has a headache; she could be suffering from migraines, a hangover, or stress. Your first step is to discover what type of headache it is and how severe. This information affects your behavior.

A lot of actors might think, "I've had a headache and know what it is, so I'll just do it," without being specific. What happens is a generic portrayal, usually the actor rubbing their temples (showing us the pain). As we have said and will continue to say, general choices lead to general acting. Be specific. Even with a simple thing like a headache, you can dig deeper and do this truthfully.

Let's start with the symptoms. Obviously, your head hurts. But what happens to your body? Headaches can be caused by issues with the blood vessels, the muscles, and the nerves. They can be centralized or located in larger areas. Do you get a headache in your temple, the back of your head, or the sides? Is there a throbbing or a constant pain? If it's a migraine, the pain can be intense, causing blurred vision, sensitivity to light and sound, and nausea. If it's a headache due to a hangover, you might be dehydrated.

Your task isn't to show us you have a headache. Your task is to display behavior that gives the illusion you are experiencing symptoms of a headache. If your head aches, yes, you might rub your temples. However, you may also rub the back of your neck to relieve the throbbing pressure or tense muscles. You may also flinch if you hear a loud noise. You might rub your eyes if they feel sensitive to light. You only need to work with a few symptoms, but you need to work with specificity.

You also may have a different emotional and psychological life. Not everyone is nice and friendly if they have a throbbing headache. You still need to react truthfully to your scene partners and be in the moment, but it might be through the filter of pain. Maybe a condition like a simple headache isn't all that simple.

Similarly, a hangover can be challenging, as well. Often, actors will play headaches and nothing else. But there are specific symptoms. It's your body's natural response to flushing out too much of a poison (alcohol). And because everyone has a different metabolism and way of dealing with alcohol, each character you play should experience hangovers differently. If you're playing a character experiencing their first ever hangover, it's going to be vastly different than if your character is an experienced drinker with an established morning ritual. For a great example of three actors who are specific with their symptoms, take a look at the scene in the movie *The Hangover.* Bradley Cooper, Zack Galifianakis, and Ed Helms are each very specific with how they grapple with waking up after a very rough night of drinking. (To be clear, the characters were also drugged with a roofie, another element to play with as they try to remember what happened the night before.)

If the character has other modifications, like a broken ankle, back pain, or gunshot wound, you need to be specific about where the pain is located and how it affects you. Also, most importantly, you need to focus on the ways you can alleviate the pain. That's what you're doing—not trying to show us your pain but actively trying to get rid of it, just like you would play any other action.

When it comes to playing the condition of alcohol or drugs, research is important. No, that doesn't mean going out and getting drunk with your friends. The challenge with inebriation and drugs is that it is far too difficult to be aware of what we do when we are intoxicated (or remember it the next day). It's also just plain unhealthy (and possibly illegal).

When Dennis was studying with Meisner teacher William Esper, he would often say, "Every actor should practice working on being blind or being drunk." His reasoning was that for being blind, it was an exercise in listening and working with your other senses. For playing drunk, it is such a common condition in plays that it's good to know how to do it before getting cast in a role where you have to suddenly figure it out. Playing drunk also helps as an exercise in teaching your body to relax in a scene.

Playing any modification is in some ways similar to adding a physical activity. What you are after is the illusion of that condition, not necessarily all the effects. For instance, if you had to play a drunk, you would have to consider how alcohol affects your physical life. You have to decide a few details related to your given circumstances (such as how many drinks your character had), but you also have to decide how it affects you. Alcohol is a depressant that affects your central nervous system, so it relaxes the muscles, which affects your lips and tongue (hence the slurred speech) but also impairs your vision and your balance. If you have had quite a lot of it, it can affect your stomach and create nausea. As you start to work on the physical effects, you need to stay away from the stereotypical idea of these symptoms and concentrate on what you are specifically doing to counter those symptoms.

For instance, to create the illusion that your vision is blurred, you simply need to do the action of trying to see clearly. To create the illusion that you are off balance, you need to make an effort to remain balanced. Add those two specific activities together, and you will start to see a specific behavioral change. The more drunk you want to be, the more you can play with that behavior or add more symptoms, such as trying not to throw up.

In addition, if your character is inebriated, you have to examine the motivation behind it. Would you characterize this character as a social drinker? An alcoholic? Digging deeper into the character, you have to ask what emotional need are they trying to fill? In *Cat on a Hot Tin Roof*, Brick keeps talking about how he drinks until he hears "that click" in his head; he's drinking to numb the pain and the memory of his old pal Skipper. If it is the only time the audience sees this person as inebriated, then what is the particular event or circumstance that led to them being drunk at this particular moment in time? Some people drink to alleviate stress, and others drink to forget their sorrows. Is your character celebrating a promotion? Upset because of a broken heart? Are you in a private setting, where you don't care if someone knows you are drunk, or in a public setting, where you are trying to hide your condition? In the film *Blue Jasmine*, a loose adaptation of *A Streetcar Named Desire*, Cate Blanchett gives a brilliant performance, especially with one scene where she is in a restaurant with two children and is trying to hide how drunk she is—we can see the focus in her eyes coming and going and hear how she is trying to be clear with her speech. It is subtle but effective.

Sometimes alcohol can be like a magnifying glass of inner turmoil or joy, where emotions and thoughts get bigger as the person who is drinking becomes more relaxed through intoxication. Emotions flare up, for good or ill. This is why you often see a drunk man at a bar scream, "I love you, man!" as well as drunk men in bars getting into fights. This magnification of emotion changes your point of view in a scene and the way you might react to other characters around you.

If your character is using some other kind of drug, like marijuana or cocaine (always popular choices in TV and movies), then you need to approach it similar to the strategy with alcohol. You need to first understand what the drug does to you physically and then find out what the emotional needs are of that character and why they take the drug. Marijuana, for example, triggers the release of dopamine in your brain, which is why you feel high. This increase in dopamine heightens your senses—colors seem brighter, sensations of touch seem more vivid, and jokes are funnier to you than they were before. The THC causes your eyes to be red. Your mouth might feel dry, so you might be thirsty. It increases hunger, which is why you get the munchies. Marijuana can also affect the brain, making it difficult to remember facts or form new memories. Once you have that information and research, you can now think about how that affects your behavior. If you take a moment to just imagine your mouth is dry, then you might already be licking your lips or swallowing or trying to get some saliva in there. If you imagine your eyes as red and irritated, then you may blink to alleviate that issue. If your senses are affected, then that means you may react differently to loud sounds or become fascinated by images on a television, or the pattern in someone's shirt.

As stated earlier, you have to connect to the emotional and psychological reasons this character has for taking this drug as well as how much they take. When Jeff Bridges played the Dude in the Coen brothers' film *The Big Lebowski*, he would ask before each scene if his character had smoked up or not and how high he was so that he could play accordingly. He even would rub his eyes to try to get them to be red right before the take.

Each drug has a unique way of working on the body. Cocaine is different from heroin or LSD or ecstasy. Whatever your character is doing, you need to be specific and display that in your behavior to avoid cliché.

One thing to be mindful of when it comes to any condition is that your body and voice must remain relaxed. In real life, when you are in pain, that isn't the case. But with acting, we want the illusion of reality. You can play the conditions without creating stress and tension in your body. Your instrument will be freer, and you are less likely to cause physical stress or damage to your body.

Using a similar approach as earlier, it is important to be specific when it comes to playing temperature. Playing hot and cold is all about the behavioral effects of what that means. Typically, people try to get relief from extreme temperatures. They either cool themselves off when it's hot or warm themselves up when it's cold. Sometimes, cooling your body is as simple as fanning yourself with a magazine, but other times you might think about how humid it is and if your clothes are sticking to you. You have to be specific about where the heat might be for you.

Remember, if a writer puts in the stage directions that it is hot or cold, then it is not random information but important to the story. A good example is the heat in Tracy Lett's *August: Osage County.* Not only is it the height of summer in Oklahoma, but also the home is all shut up. What happens when hot, dry air is kept in a baking-hot home? It becomes the epitome of "stuffy." When characters enter the house, that change in air quality affects them. It isn't actually going to be any different on that set, so as an actor, you have to react in a way that creates the illusion that the air inside is hotter and stale. You would want to try to stay cool. That might mean fanning yourself or undoing a button, but it also may mean you move around just a little bit less. Maybe the heat makes you feel tired.

Now, you might be thinking that this is such a small thing. But this detail is actually an important part of the storytelling device that Letts has created. Letts has given us a physical environment that visually displays how uncomfortable these characters are in this family home. Playing the imaginary world of a hot room is going to connect you to your actions and your relationships in that performance.

Cold temperatures are more difficult because our bodies have a tendency to get stiff and tense when we feel cold. Actors need to learn how to stay physically relaxed and free of tension. Remember, you're not trying to show us you're cold. You are trying to keep warm. So you might stomp your feet, move your arms around, jump up and down. Or you might just put your hands in your pockets and put your chin down to your chest, trying to conserve energy and body heat. Whatever you decide, be specific.

Chapter Ten

Building with Care and Consent
Fights, Extreme Physicality, and Intimacy

Your boundaries are perfect exactly where they are.

—Chelsea Pace[1]

In this chapter, we look at scenes involving armed or unarmed combat, extreme physicality, physical intimacy, and sexual content. When it comes to violence and fight choreography, there are professional standards for stage, film, and television. In the same way, there are now standards for staging intimacy for film, TV, and stage [as these protocols may still be changing, you should see details at the Actors Equity Association (https://www.actors equity.org/) and the Screen Actors Guild (https://www.sagaftra.org/)].

In most cases, a specialist will be brought in, such as a fight director, movement director, or intimacy director. You may see different titles listed on the call sheet for these movement specialists (fight consultant, fight director, stunt coordinator, intimacy director, intimacy coach, etc.). One key difference to understand is that a fight director or intimacy director is a title given for working in the theater. For film and TV, they're called coordinators. You may see other titles, such as violence consultant, movement director, and firearms or weapons specialist. Each title may relate to the specific needs of the production, but the methods and safety protocols will remain the same. Because there are several wonderful books already written about stage combat, we won't go into too much detail. The basic ideas regarding intimacy are just now emerging in the industry (made more prominent by the book *Staging Sex* by Chelsea Pace, with Laura Rikard).[2]

Productions involving violence, intimacy, or both should be choreographed by a specialist. Sometimes theater companies or small independent film projects, especially if they are tight on their budgets or new to producing, will think a scene with a minimal amount of these moments won't need a specialist to choreograph it. Even a scene with a slap or kiss still needs attention, and the actors need to feel that a safe environment has been provided. If anyone asks you to perform any unsafe physical action, you should feel empowered to advocate for yourself. A specialist is much more knowledgeable and can provide the attention needed to these physical moments, so we'd recommend a certified member of the Society of American Fight Directors (SAFD) or the Intimacy Directors and Coordinators (IDC). A fight director or intimacy director is trained to notice the details of how and where things can go wrong but is also outside the power dynamics of the rehearsal room. It can be difficult for actors to speak up when they need adjustments; a specialist can be an advocate when adjustments need to be made.

Even if you aren't in a production right now, a good way to prepare is to take classes and workshops. Train yourself in combat and intimacy in the same way you might work on dialects or Viewpoints. Having these skills will not only heighten the physical life of your character and keep you safer in rehearsal but will also give you experience that could get you considered for more roles. There are many organizations that offer training in major cities, regionally, and even remotely.

BOUNDARIES, CONSENT-BASED PRACTICES, AND SAFETY

Before we dive into what you should expect for working extremely physical scenes, we need to reiterate the idea of safety. As mentioned in the introduction, there has been much conversation about health and safety, partly due to the global pandemic and partly due to equity in the workplaces. Be aware that the director can in all earnestness say to the cast and production team, "This is a safe place." However, just because an authority figure says it is safe doesn't necessarily make it true. And doesn't mean that everyone in the room will immediately feel safe.

When it comes to stage combat, violence, or intimacy, it is always best when expectations are clearly laid out before rehearsals even start. Part of dealing with expectations has to do with being aware of your own and others' boundaries. Consent-based practices are grounded in everyone giving their commitment and enthusiasm.

Consent is something only you can give. A director can't authorize consent from one actor to another. You have to choose to participate and do it wholeheartedly. This isn't a radical idea. You gave consent to audition, to come back for callbacks, to read the play, and when you signed your contract. You gave consent when you walked into the room. Consent, though, is not a blanket condition—just because you consented to a scene with a kiss doesn't mean you consent to an unsafe way of how it may be staged. Consent can be given and taken away.

Consent is about knowing your boundaries. As stated in the introduction, actors often feel that they are powerless to say no, that it will stop rehearsals. But one way of saying no is to offer other ideas or solutions that fit within your boundaries. Of course, if the request is so outside of your boundaries or not something talked about (a director has decided to add a kiss, for example, without any discussion), then you should feel empowered to say, "No, that doesn't work with my boundaries."

The first place where you need to be aware of your boundaries will come when you read the script (either for auditions or when you accept the role). Audition disclosure forms have become more common. These forms mention specific types of activities so you can be clear with the producer and director about your boundaries. They may give a range of activities, from performing or witnessing acts of violence, profanity, sexual intimacy like kissing, sexual assault, text with sexual content, nudity, costume changes, and racial trauma. Some scripts may not have any of these, and some may have a lot. As you read the audition notice or read the script, ask yourself if there is any content you feel crosses your boundaries, and communicate that with the producer or directors. Be clear what you feel you could or couldn't do or if you are unsure and need more information.

Before you accept a role, get clarity on exactly what it is you are being asked to do and what the production plan is for achieving that goal in a safe and healthy manner. It should state in the casting call that all violence or intimacy will be choreographed. Ask about when and how those scenes might be worked on. This is far better than arriving on-set or for rehearsal and being surprised or unprepared.

Once cast, you and your director should talk and review boundaries and expectations because by the time you get into production, you may realize that your expectations about the scene are different from those of the director, the fight director, or the intimacy director. In general, scenes with sexual intimacy will need to be discussed prior to and during the early rehearsals before staging begins. This is mostly because intimacy involves actual bodies touching each other. With fights, safety is maintained by distance, and so conversations can happen later in the process. That doesn't mean conversations about fights won't happen; it just may happen later. Depending on the schedule or budget, you may get some hands-on training specific to the production.

One thing that you, your fellow actors, and the director must understand is that boundaries can change. One day you may be able to perform the fight, but then later that night, you trip and fall on the ice, hurting your wrist. You can now no longer hold your sword and will have to adjust the fight for health and safety. Every director or choreographer should understand that and will likely insert some kind of placeholder or make an adjustment. Similarly, if an event happens or your boundary changes and you're not able to rehearse the kiss, a placeholder or adjustment can also be made for health and safety reasons.

A BRIEF HISTORY OF STAGE COMBAT CHOREOGRAPHY

There are some clear differences between real fighting and theatrical fighting. Real combat can be brutal and short. Sure, a boxing match can last several rounds, but a street fight may be only a few minutes. It doesn't take long for a body to get punched in all the wrong places. Any type of armed combat, such as with knives or swords, will also be short. The reason is simple: A real fight is about making contact with the target and creating as much damage as possible in as little time as possible. As the Cobra Kai dojo from *The Karate Kid* might say, "Strike first, strike hard, no mercy!"

Theatrical fighting is the exact opposite. Your primary goal is to *not* hit your opponent and *not* create any damage (and also to move a bit slower). Real fighting is about really hurting someone. Theatrical fighting is all illusion, but most importantly, it's about storytelling. Every event, even a fight, moves the story forward.

Although theater and film have seen many fights through the ages, it is only in the past fifty years that there has been a choreographer solely focused not just on the story but also on the safety of the combat. In the seventeenth and eighteenth centuries, many of the stage fights involved swords. Theaters would bring in masters of fencing to show a trick or two so the actors would look like they knew what they were doing.[3] By the 1920s, swashbuckling elevated from actors banging swords against each other into the elegance and daring of Errol Flynn as Robin Hood. By the time stuntmen were crawling under stagecoaches, there still wasn't a whole lot of attention put on safety.

In theater, stage combat did not become codified until the 1960s and 1970s, when organizations like the Society of British Fight Directors (now British Academy of Stage and Screen Combat) and the Society of American Fight Directors were formed. Both organizations provide training for actors and choreographers with the goal of promoting safety and furthering the art of fight choreography. They both also provide certification for fight directors and choreographers.

FIGHTING, STAGE COMBAT, AND EXTREME PHYSICALITY

As Dr. Diego Villada, fight director and assistant professor at New College of Florida, said, "There are two ways moments of violence can go—they can be safe or they can be unsafe. We want things to be safe."[4] Here is a short overview of how a fight director or choreographer may go through the process of staging your fight. As you can guess, safety is the priority. After the standard of safety is met, then the choreographer or director will focus on storytelling. Next, they will see what your capabilities are as an actor—your speed, strength, agility, injuries, and boundaries. Then, the choreographer will build moves that help tell the story in the safest way possible using these capabilities. They also want to tell a story that excites the audience and highlights your character.

Here are three intertwined and underlying key ideas to make this process go smoother:

1. Understand boundaries.
2. Communicate and collaborate.
3. Slow down and learn the movements.

Understand Boundaries

We keep talking about boundaries but only because they are that important. If anything should redefine how actors work in the twenty-first century, it is that they are continually evaluating and recognizing their own and others' boundaries. Safety, trust, and respect resides in that agreement.

As you get into rehearsals, be clear with yourself on what you can and cannot do. You don't need to disclose your entire medical history, but you should be clear if you need adjustments due to a bad knee from a sports injury, low flexibility in the shoulder, or a bad back from surgery. The production company will provide you with gloves, a wrist brace, arm pads, or kneepads, if needed. If you're going to be tumbling, rolling, or falling, you want either pads or a soft surface, like an exercise mat.

Look, it's possible you could end up like the comedic actor Bob Odenkirk, who spent more than a year working out with a stunt trainer and getting in shape for the role of a retired hitman in the movie *Nobody*. But that's highly unlikely. You aren't going to suddenly become an expert martial artist in just a few days or weeks. So, don't be a hero. Work with the body you have. Remember, your boundaries are perfect, wherever they are. And a fight choreographer will do magic with that.

Another aspect of boundaries is checking in not only with yourself but also with your acting partner(s). In order to have trust and respect for each other, you have to trust and respect each others' boundaries. So, you have to know them. For that, you have to communicate.

Communicate and Collaborate

There is information that you share with your director or fight director, and there is information that you can share and glean from your fellow actors. Let's start with information you and your partner should share with each other when you begin. This usually comes in the form of a check-in. This check-in needs to happen at the beginning of the session, something simple, such as where you are with your boundaries. How are you able to move today? Anything you need to tell your partner or that your partner needs you to know? As you work on your movements, constantly check in with each other. It may feel like you are being overly cautious, but it's important. Try to keep your question open-ended. If you ask, "Is that okay?" the implied answer is going to be yes, and your partner may feel pressured to agree, even though a slight modification might be better. Get used to asking, "How does this work for you?" And don't forget to listen and be attentive to your partner. If you start getting too close or their blade starts creeping close to your eyeball, then speak up. Accidents are prone to happen when actors ignore small details. Ask any actor who accidently hurt someone onstage; you never forget how bad you feel for that mistake.

You may also want to let the choreographer know if you have any special abilities. Perhaps you have sword or unarmed combat training, or you did ten years of karate. Maybe you can do acrobatics, like flips and falls, or some clown or mime work. All of this could be useful for the choreography.

Another key aspect of the process is that the fight choreographer wants to collaborate with you on the way your character fights, so you may have to give some character information to them. They are experts at fight choreography, and you're the expert on your character. Share with them your interpretation. Show how your character moves and behaves. Going back to some of our earlier chapters, consider why this fight (and event) is happening. Why do you even end up in this fight with this other character? What is your relationship to them? Why is it so important to you to win? What changes for you because of the result of this fight? What makes a fight unique and fun are the details of the character, the little actions that happen in between. For example, would your character laugh after gaining a victory? Would they get more frustrated and angry if they kept getting hit?

Slow Down and Learn the Movements

There is a saying in stage combat: "Learn it slow to do it fast." Your job as an actor is to learn the choreography precisely. There's no room for modifications or error because your safety and the safety of others depend on your accuracy. The choreographer will break down the fight and work through the movements in slow motion. They'll teach you a few moments and have you repeat that until it feels locked in, and then they'll move on to other movements.

After the fight is choreographed, write it down. Writing it down will engage the other intellectual parts of the brain and will help you later as you review the moves. Review it with the fight director or stage manager, if needed, to ensure you have all the correct actions. You'll use these notes when you get home from rehearsal and review the moves on your own. Do them over and over so that you can do it without thinking about it. Although it's difficult to really rehearse the fight on your own, there are parts of the storytelling you can do. The footwork is key. Rehearsing when you step, move back or forth, or spin can help you with remembering the actions of your hands. If there are vocal or physical reactions to rehearse, then work on those. How does it feel for your character when they get hit in the face? What does that mean for them? All the physicality and movement choices that you have been playing with in your character need to be incorporated.

When you rehearse the fight, you may have a fight captain or your choreographer. Generally, stage combat is rehearsed in stages. First, you run through the fight at quarter speed, then see if any questions or issues arise. You can run it slowly as many times as needed. It's a good way to ensure you were rehearsing the correct moves or that your partner remembers it, as well. Then, when all are ready, move up to half speed. Don't forget to communicate and check in with each other. It's amazing how changing speed can change so much in your balance, rhythm, and perception. When ready, run the fight at three-quarter speed. Fights are never run at full speed for one key reason: Actors have a tendency to rush in a performance. If you run it at full speed in rehearsal, you will likely get even faster with your adrenaline, and you will rush the moves, and the timing (and safety) will suffer. SAFD fight master and choreographer David Leong says, "Don't get so excited about fighting that you forget it's a scene. It's about 'I want something from you, and you're in my way.'"[5]

How else might you prepare for your role before rehearsal? As mentioned in chapter 4, part of your preproduction work is to notate any activities or physical actions you might perform. If you read through the script and you know there will be a lot of fights, then you need to figure out how to prepare. While you can't learn any choreography yet, here are a few simple tasks:

• Build awareness and understanding of your body and its mechanics. This is for those of you who have never done any type of physical acting or stage combat. This could be as simple as doing some qigong, tai chi, yoga, or cardio exercises or as complex as exploring movement methodologies like the Laban system, the Michael Chekhov technique, and the Alexander technique.

- Take a stage combat workshop. If you know the scene has unarmed combat or wielding a sword, then take that specific class. You can find regional workshops in most major cities (or even do remote learning). If all else fails, there are plenty of certified instructors who offer private lessons or coaching.
- "Get thee to thy cardio!" If you'll be doing a lot of running around and fighting and speaking, then it is imperative you can catch your breath to speak clearly. Get on the treadmill or a bike, do some kickboxing, or run intervals. Prepare the body and the lungs.
- Work on stretching and agility exercises. Yoga is particularly good for warming up the muscles and providing good stretching. (We recommend this even if you won't be doing any fighting.) Even just ten to fifteen minutes of floor stretching will do wonders for preparing your body as well as your mind.
- Consider what you need to train for, and improvise. Let's say you will be in a production like *Game of Thrones* and were told you'd be carrying a giant axe. You're going to need more hand and arm strength. Pick up something heavy and start swinging it around (not too heavy, though—don't injure yourself). If you will be doing fencing or boxing, then work on your footwork.

It's not so much about becoming an expert before rehearsal. It's about conditioning yourself for the rigors of the role. Not all productions will require intense physical training, but some will. It's better to train the body slowly and early to avoid injuries, just as if you are an athlete in training.

INTIMACY AND SEXUAL CONTENT

The intimacy director (or coordinator) is an emerging but necessary role. The word *intimacy* may be misleading and can often cover a lot of territory. All acting is intimate because it's about being vulnerable and emotionally available. Specifically, *intimacy* in this section refers to physical or sexual intimacy or moments when characters might discuss or witness those actions. This may or may not include nudity or partial nudity. There is intimacy in a handshake or a hug, but an intimacy choreographer will be involved when the intimate moments are more intense or longer duration, such as kissing or other sexual acts.

Due to the power dynamics inherent in the rehearsal room, its problematic having the director stage intimate moments. Actors can be easily coerced or manipulated into making choices out of fear or wanting to please. A qualified expert can be impartial and lead the actors through a safe way to tell the story. In the recent and groundbreaking book *Staging Sex: Best Practices,*

Tools and Techniques for Theatrical Intimacy, Chelsea Pace and Laura Rikard lay out a clear reason codification needs to be realized in the industry:

> Why do so many boundaries get crossed between actors staging intimacy? Because actors kiss. Actually kiss. The contact is real. They physically put their bodies on other people's bodies and share contact that has no obvious separation from reality. Theatre artists haven't had an established technique to rely on that tells us that this is a construction, and choreography, and a craft.[6]

In this highly recommended book, you can find specific tools for you as an actor to cultivate a culture of consent and desexualize the process of intimacy. As they state in the book, "Passion fades. Choreography is forever."[7]

Many practitioners may believe that the rise of intimacy directors and coordinators occurred as a result of the #MeToo movement and #TimesUp. The truth is, the need for this role was seen long before media attention brought awareness to sexual harassment and inequities in the industry. About fifteen years ago, Tonia Sina was getting her MFA in theater pedagogy at Virginia Commonwealth University, studying movement and stage combat with such SAFD fight masters as David Leong. After a personal experience working on a production where she was asked by the director to "figure out" the stage kiss with her scene partner on their own in the hallway, boundaries between real and imaginary were crossed. She knew there was a need for some kind of approach that would help for staging moments of sexual content. At that time, a fight choreographer might step in to serve in this capacity but only when moments of intimacy included sexual violence. Sina saw a gap in the industry, and she wrote the first thesis on this subject. After graduating, she moved to Chicago and developed her techniques, joining forces with Alicia Rodis (Currently, intimacy coordinator at HBO), and in 2015, they formed Intimacy Directors International.[8] Others joined, and they began working in the industry and training others (such as Claire Warden, the first intimacy director to work on Broadway). In 2020, they reformed into the new organization Intimacy Directors and Coordinators (IDC) with the goal of providing consulting services to the industry, comprehensive training for professional actors, and certification. IDC has a foundation that underlies the principles of their work, which they call the "Five Pillars": consent, communication, context, choreography, and closure.[9] In addition to awareness of consent and boundaries, the organization also has an emphasis on trauma-informed approaches, especially as it relates to intense emotional scenes.

Around that same time, Pace was experiencing thoughts and ideas similar to Sina's. She began formulating her ideas when she was a professor teaching young students and seeing their need for boundaries and consent.[10] Pace and Rikard founded Theatrical Intimacy Education (TIE) in 2017. This organization provides educational workshops for students and educators on consent-based practices, intimacy, choreography, and racial equity. On their website and in their training materials, they elaborate on the necessity of these guidelines as well as how actors can use them to advocate for themselves and take agency over their bodies.

You may notice that there are some similar themes to how we approach stage combat. For instance, safety is the priority (not just physical but also mental, emotional, and psychological). In order to maintain safety, each actor must know and be aware of their boundaries. The process is about consent-based practice, which is why consent is one of the pillars. Boundaries and creating an environment where an actor can say no or make alterations or suggestions is paramount.

Communication is important in intimacy work in the same way that it's important for combat. There is a need to check in with your partner and see where their boundaries are each day, as well as your own. This is especially important, as real touch may be involved rather than the distance you might find in stage combat.

Context relates to the needs of the story and how you tell that story through the choreography. The choreographer will want to hear from you about the character's needs and emotional states for the scene. Fundamentally, all intimacy is choreographed (and documented by the stage manager and other actors). It allows for accountability.

Finally and importantly, closure is about how an actor may have to step out of the experience and separate the real from the imaginary. In addition to a check-in at the beginning of the rehearsal, partners are also encouraged to check out, make eye contact, breathe, give a high five, and find some tangible way of separating what just happened from reality.

> In a lot of the intimacy ideology, it is not just about consent but also about desexualizing the experience. As Pace states,When these practices are in place, actors thus far seem more likely to enjoy doing crazy things like taking off their clothes, performing simulated sexual acts, and exploring complex moments of intimacy. The intimacy choreographer can help create a rehearsal room environment that promotes exploration, resulting in whatever it is your production needs. They are not in the room to tell everyone to put their clothes on or to take away all the sex; they just want to "make it less weird."[11]

Working with an intimacy director or coordinator may be a new experience for you, and you may be skeptical. But more and more professional actors are welcoming this role as a way to create an environment of safety, trust, and consent. There's a reason that Maggie Gyllenhaal, as an actor and producer, advocated for them on *The Deuce*. Even Ewan McGregor sang the praises of intimacy coordinators when working on the series *Halston*, relating how awkward and uncomfortable filming sex scenes can be.[12]

Alicia Rodis breaks down what the role of the intimacy coordinator on-set:

> After I discuss with the producer, the director, the showrunner, I then have a conversation with the actors involved and make sure that we're all on the same page. I explain to them that I'm the intimacy coordinator, and that means I'm the liaison. I'm the movement coach and I am an advocate; I'm here for you so that you are always in the loop. It's even small things like making sure the actor knows that for rehearsals, you don't have to take your robe off. Everyone is dealing with so many other things; we have the lights, we have the sound, the camera. Just having one person there for this specific thing has been invaluable. When I'm working with actors, I make sure I read exactly what it is in their nudity or simulated sex rider so that there are no surprises, and I ask them if they've had experiences doing intimacy on set before and what they need.[13]

For theatrical rehearsal, you will likely meet your intimacy choreographer at the table read or early in rehearsal and begin exercises and explorations with your scene partner to build trust and respect and get to know each other's boundaries. The rehearsal schedule should detail exactly when you'll be working on any intimate scenes and may include who will be allowed in the room during the staging. Depending on the early conversations, you may have placeholders for specific actions—for instance, instead of having to kiss your scene partner in every scene, you may just put your hand on their hand as a "marker" and then work the kiss on a later specific date. This is particularly useful for blocking rehearsals, so you can spend a good amount of time working without having to constantly kiss each other over and over.

In the choreography, you will be given tools and techniques that provide language for how and when you might touch. In Pace's book, she calls them "ingredients," which includes such things as types of touch, opening and closing distance, eye contact, sound, shape, visible power shifts, and breath/sound.[14] Another important boundary tool is the use of a "button" word, which is a way of calling out something that isn't working with your boundaries and needs adjustment. As this is an emerging field, your choreographer may use slightly different language or add other tools. This type of language not only desexualizes the process but also creates a way for you to remember and record the choreography for later rehearsals and for the run of the production (as well as for the SM or any other intimacy consultants working on the show).

The choreographing process is similar to the process for stage combat, with some necessary modifications. First, the choreography will be concerned about safety and boundaries. Be clear about what you can and can't do, as well as what you might be open to or have questions about. Check in with your partner before doing any work. The choreographer will work with your body and your ideas about the character to shape the story of this intimate moment. You will learn the moves slowly, just like you would for a fight. You will likely communicate as much as or more than you would for a fight. Some intimate moments may be more of a trigger for some actors who have experienced trauma, so they may need even more sensitivity, time, and space for creation. As you work on the choreography, context and storytelling will shape what needs to be performed.

One important element of intimacy choreography that is different from stage combat is that the choreographer (or director) should never step in to show anyone the moves. Unlike showing someone blocking or stage combat, intimacy is about contact and touching. Trust and safety between partners are built over time and experience, and a director or choreographer stepping in can undermine that in a moment.

How can you prepare for the intimacy work before or between rehearsals? Unfortunately, it's not quite the same as fight choreography. There's little to do before you meet with your partner, as much of the work is based on how you interact. As mentioned, though, part of your preproduction work is to notate any activities or physical actions you might perform, and intimacy would definitely be included. If you read through the script and see stage directions like, "They kiss," then you can start asking questions about the event. One thing you should do is take classes with IDC or TIE (check out their websites). They have regional workshops as well as remote learning opportunities. You could also read the book *Staging Sex*, which outlines the tools and concepts you need for a safe and vibrant process.

Chapter Eleven

Exterior Fittings and Final Touches
The Technical Rehearsal

The readiness is all . . .

—William Shakespeare

Congratulations! You made it to technical rehearsals! The foundation is down, the walls are up, and the wiring and plumbing and fittings are in. Now, it's time to get this house ready for folks to live in. Time to plaster and paint, put some special flooring down, and add last-minute details.

In this chapter, you'll solidify your choices as you transition from the exploration phase into performance. We specifically refer to theatrical productions. (For film, TV, and other media, look at chapter 14.) Much of the focus here is on the lights (yes, that pun was intended), as well as design elements, like scenic, costumes, sound, and media.

The transition into tech is important because not just the nature of the work will change but also your location may change. You will be moving into the performance space. Granted, in some regional theaters and universities, you may enjoy the luxury of rehearsing in the actual performance space. In most major cities, it's too costly to rehearse in the actual theater. You will be in a studio just large enough to have space for the spike tape and your warm bodies.

At this point in the process, whether you have a three- or four-week rehearsal period, you should have had a few run-throughs of the entire performance. One of those was likely a designer run so that the designers could see how they might have to adjust their design to collaborate with the performance. You may also have had a crew run or will at some point during the technical rehearsal stage. This is a run for the crew to know the ins and outs of the shows.

Every director has different strategies for how they prepare the cast for going into technical rehearsals. Some directors are insistent on doing a run of the show every week of rehearsal, or at the very least each act after each week of rehearsal. Some directors love to run the show every day of the week before going into technical rehearsals to set the rhythm and tempo of the full production.

In this chapter we want to build on the work you're doing. It may seem like you can't keep working because the concentration and conversations have shifted from your performance to design and technical elements, but there are still ways you can keep working on your role.

IT'S NOT ABOUT YOU, EXCEPT WHEN IT IS

Be prepared for how the director's concentration will transition more onto design and technical elements. You have spent weeks talking about your character and actions and enjoying this lovely collaboration, and then suddenly it stops. It's like a really great conversation that reaches a climax, and suddenly the person you are talking to sees someone else across the room and runs over there, leaving you feeling a bit adrift. Relax. The director is not bored, angry, or ignoring you. The director has a million other challenges to address, and with opening night approaching, other elements need attention. The director will be incorporating design into the performances you have created.

As each production is unique, so are the technical needs. Some plays, such as Kenneth Lonergan's *Lobby Hero*, are simple one-set affairs, and the lighting and sound cues may be minimal. There aren't even that many costume changes and certainly no quick changes. Other plays, like Lynn Nottage's *Intimate Apparel*, may have several locations and different set pieces that need to move on and off the stage, as well as costume changes. As it's a period piece, those costumes are also going to be an important design element. For large musicals, the technical rehearsals are even longer, as the set pieces may be elaborate, or there may be hundreds of light cues just in the first act alone, not to mention sound design or amplification.

It's important for you to remember that you may have been working on your role for weeks (or longer, depending on how much preparation you did before rehearsals), but the design team and the stage crew have not been in the room. They have not been diving into the play every single day like you and the director have been doing. They are now only realizing their designs in physical space. They want to ensure they modify the design to fit the performance as well as incorporate notes from the director. The stage crew may typically not know the play at all. They won't know who plays whom or what props are needed in each scene until instructed by stage management. In other words, this is their first day of rehearsal, so be kind and patient.

We have a couple of tips for you as you are about to start the new phase of the rehearsal process:

- Get rest. Most often in the schedule, there is a built-in day off before tech because everyone will spend the next several days working in the theater. Take that day off and get some sleep, eat well, and relax. Socialize with friends, and recharge your batteries. You've worked hard the past few weeks, and the body and mind need to reset and get ready for the final push of rehearsals.
- Get your lines and blocking down cold. We know we just advised you to rest and recharge, but be aware that as you go into technical and dress rehearsals, you will likely no longer receive line notes from stage management. Run through your lines before bed. Run your lines in the shower. Run your lines while running. You should know them backward and forward. Trust us: If anything can test you on how well you know your lines, it is technical rehearsal. Don't be the actor slowing down the process because you forgot a line that cues a lighting change.
- Be on time. This goes without saying, and we're sure you have been on time for all rehearsals anyway, right?
- Be ready to wait around. Technical rehearsals are long because it takes time to see the choice, see if it doesn't work, incorporate notes from the director, modify the cue, and then try again. It may take hours to get through the first scene. Unless you are onstage for the duration of the entire play, you may be waiting around in the green room. Although we recommend reviewing your lines, blocking, and notes and making sure you are ready to go, you may also want to bring something else to do to fill your time. Read a play. Sketch. Do a crossword. Knit. Be aware, though: You don't want to get too involved in your activity, and don't wander off. At tech, it could move slowly, but it can also suddenly move very quickly, and you could be called to the stage in a hurry.
- Be ready to work. We know we just said be ready to wait, but the truth is, you have to be ready to do either depending on what is happening at the moment. We can't stress enough that your work as an actor is not done. Just because the director is talking about lights and sound cues doesn't mean that you can't spend time talking about the scene or character relationships with your fellow actors as you wait onstage (unless your speaking will distract ongoing technical conversations). Another aspect of this is professionalism. Too many inexperienced actors find themselves waiting around and then joking around out of boredom. When they are called to work, they aren't ready, and they slow things down. Part of collaboration is coopera-

tion. So work well with everyone on the team (especially those who will help you be well lit or heard).

- Manage your expectations. You should have an open and positive attitude but also know that the art of making theater is all about overcoming several simultaneous obstacles. Some people call it "Hell week," but it really doesn't have to be, and in our experience, when your director, stage manager, and designers are organized and the actors are focused, the technical rehearsal can run smoothly. There is just little time to maneuver when things go wrong. All it takes is one broken light or prop or an unsafe staircase for things to get behind schedule.

- Be prepared and organized for self-care. For the next few days or a week, your schedule is going to be solely concerned with this production. Find ways to minimize the drain on your time and energy. Too often, actors forget about doing simple things, like preparing meals in advance and end up eating fast food (making them lethargic) or not planning for time with friends or family. Get organized. Cook a large pot of chili, or make a bunch of sandwiches the day before tech so you can have them ready to go. Go to the store, and buy some healthy snacks, like fruit and nuts, so you will resist the urge to grab those Cheetos and sodas from the vending machines.

LIGHTS, COSTUMES, SETS, OH MY!

When you enter the theater, the first thing you may encounter is the full set (even though there may still be some last-minute additions to be made). Your stage manager will likely walk you through it and explain if there are any areas still in construction, as well as show you the backstage areas with the props table and the dressing rooms.

There is often time before the start of the technical process for you to explore the space. Do not go directly to the dressing room to socialize and gossip. Put your bag and phone down, and familiarize yourself with the entire set. This means opening and closing doors, sitting on the chairs or couch, opening cupboards, walking up and down steps and stairs, and generally walking around every area of the set. Familiarize yourself in particular with your entrances and exits.

Remember the work you did in chapter 8 with physical language? Now's the time to start working with the actual props and set. If you are in the lobby of an apartment building like Jeff in *Lobby Hero*, you should be looking at where you sit, where your desk or counter is, and if you have a pen and clipboard. This character would be working with these objects every day, so you should be just as familiar with them.

As you mark the space, you might already have questions about how you will get down those stairs while saying your lines without breaking your neck (stairs taped on a rehearsal floor are much easier than actual stairs) or how you might make a particular cross around a table or couch. As an actor, it's your job to try to solve those problems and transition into the next phase. You may run into some major issues with timing of the scene or the blocking as you get into the actual cue to cue, but if you can get ahead of the problem, you will be a director's dream. After you look at the set, you may then get a chance to see your costume, but often the costumes are brought in after the cue to cue. We talk more about costumes later.

TECHNICAL RUN-THROUGHS

We do not dive too deeply into the ins and outs of the cue-to-cue rehearsal or the dress rehearsals, as each theater may have a different approach. Instead, we give some general ideas for how to keep working on your role through the different phases of this last bit of rehearsal.

The first dress rehearsal will elevate the performance one more level. You may have already been walking in your character's shoes or dealing with a rehearsal skirt, but now you will start working with all the elements of your costume. As you spent so much time familiarizing yourself with the set, now is the time to familiarize yourself with your costume, especially if you have more than one costume (as well as any quick costume changes). The weight and feel of fabric can change everything about how you move and behave. Wearing black leather pants, buccaneer boots, a glorious red coat, and a black curly mustache (as Black Stache), for example, will allow you the fun and freedom of incorporating the costume into your movements. If you are playing Esther in *Intimate Apparel*, then the restrictions of those period costumes will also allow you to move around in different ways.

Talk with the costume designer about the costumes, especially the details, like the patterns or types of fabrics, the buttons, and the collars. There are history and choices there and you will get even more information about (as well as develop a relationship with) the costumes. Think about articles of clothing you have in your closet right this minute. You have emotional attachment to them. Your character is no different. What kind of emotional attachment can you build to this costume? How can putting this costume on become a way of stepping into the character? Even looking in the mirror at yourself can help you imagine yourself as this character and embody them further.

As you familiarize yourself with the costume, it's important not to just do that in the dressing room but also to interact and walk around the set. Go through the movements of your blocking, on- and off-stage, up and down stairs, sitting and standing. You want to explore the space, not just so you are familiar as the character, but also for safety. If you have never worn a hoop skirt before, for example, you'll be surprised how hard it can be to get around.

The first dress rehearsal will likely feel a bit rough. Lines that were never an issue will be dropped. Props are going to be misplaced or forgotten. Costumes will get tripped on or hung up on furniture. Even professionals can get flustered by the accumulation of these small hiccups in the performance. You also may find that the energy and focus you used to have for scenes have suddenly disappeared. The emotional monologue you nailed last week feels dry and empty. It's possible that you are able to retain some of the emotional life you had the week before (some actors are unflappable when it comes to transitioning into tech). For a lot of actors, the stress of handling new elements creates a barrier to be overcome.

It may seem like you're taking several steps backward, but trust the process. Your concentration has now gone from the lofty ideals of exploring the humanity and existential crisis of Hamlet to something mundane, such as "I hope I don't trip down those stairs." This is perfectly natural, but also, you can channel that energy into the scene. After all, couldn't Hamlet also worry about tripping down the stairs, in addition to all his other problems? Remember that plays are not about the everyday but about life and death; it doesn't get more high stakes than performing in front of others. So accept that the stress or focus is on these other more pressing matters, and use it as best you can in the scenes.

Your second dress rehearsal will likely go more smoothly. Less lines will be dropped. You will remember your props. Gracious crew will be there to help you as you need it. Everyone—you, the actors, the backstage crew—will have more experience with the rhythms of this production. It's important to remember that every production has its own rhythm, like a symphony. The technical and dress rehearsals are when the whole ensemble (including crew) breathes and moves together in harmony to create this beautiful work of art. You all make this symphony of drama together. But it takes several days of that kind of intense focus to get there.

By the third day of dress rehearsal, you should be feeling more confident in your movements onstage, your relationship to the set, and how you relate to your costume. Once you get past this initial phase of first explorations, it is up to you the actor to integrate all the work you have done.

As you complete these final rehearsals, you will get notes from the director as well as from stage management (some of these notes may be the exact notes you see in chapter 15). Most of the time, you will get technical notes related to your position onstage (finding the light, moving up- or downstage, not upstaging others, etc.). Notes are sometimes received verbally but nowadays may even be through e-mail. Your job is to take the note; look at your script, line, and blocking; and then make the adjustment. That means work on the adjustment several times before you come to the next run of the show.

PREVIEW AUDIENCES

Previews are the final piece of the transition into a performance. Due to the presence of an audience, it's going to feel more like a performance than any rehearsal you've had so far, but remember, it's still a rehearsal. You're still discovering and testing choices. The fun part is that you will discover quite quickly when the show has its highs and lows.

Remember in chapter 1 when we said to write down your first impressions of reading the script all the way through, start to finish? This is where you find out if your initial interpretation of the role is carrying over to this audience. Are they surprised when you got surprised? Laughing at lines you thought were funny? Did they gasp at the big reveal the way you did? You aren't in control of every element, but you should know that your interpretation of the role helped to build that experience for the audience.

One idea you will have to let go of as you perform for the audience is the inside jokes. You might all have had such a good time with that one hilarious scene and felt like your actor friends were doing so much funny stuff, but then you show the scene to the audience, and they don't laugh at all. You might react to that as just a bad audience, but we do get attached to an experience of rehearsal as well as the product itself. Trust that the audience will laugh if it's funny and will cry if it's sad. And if they don't, that will tell you something.

It's actually more dangerous when you do get a laugh in the preview performance. The next rehearsal or performance, you as the actor may then decide to play for laughs, subconsciously knowing that line is funny because it has gotten a laugh before. Or you may get a laugh one night, and then the next night, there is no laugh. You will be puzzled because it seems you did the exact same thing in that moment, so are wondering if you should change it. Don't let one audience reaction from one performance undermine your work. Stay firm in your character choices, your actions, and the notes from your director.

SOLIDIFY YOUR HABITS

In chapter 6, we talk about how rehearsal was about building habits. That doesn't stop, even when the opening is only a few days away. We also look at your actions and evaluate if those are the best tactics for getting what you want. We challenge you to yet again go through your script and contemplate where you see any moments flagging or dropping in energy. That could be a sign that you are unclear or playing a pedestrian action or not considering the obstacles of the stakes.

In every dress rehearsal, you need to fully commit to your choices and evaluate for yourself how they are working. Don't rely solely on your director's eye. Some actors think that just because it's a rehearsal, they don't have to go all out. Some of them want to "save it for the actual show," but the only way the director, the designers, you, and the fellow actors will know for sure if the scenes work is if you play the role at performance level.

TRUST YOUR FOUNDATION

We have said many times that you should trust the script, but in addition, you should trust your own work. You've spent weeks building your foundation and framework for this role. You have worked with the intellectual and imaginative side of your brain. Now it's time for the impulsive and instinctual side to live inside that framework. Sanford Meisner had a great saying about working with text: that the text was like a canoe, and the river was an actor's emotions and thoughts. The canoe will always be a canoe, but the river will change.[2]

On that last evening of the last technical rehearsal, the day before opening, your mind and your emotions will be all over the place. You may feel confident about many moments of the show but anxious about others. You may feel that some scenes are too overplayed and other scenes could use more rehearsal. You may feel that you are only now starting to understand your character and wish you had two more weeks to play around and experiment before showing it to an audience.

As you transition into performance, this is where the real joy begins. You never stop working, even in performance. Yes, you stop rehearsing, but you never stop trying to make every moment feel new and spontaneous for every performance.

No house or any other building ever goes long without needing some work to be done. It's not always a big thing, like a new roof or a leaky faucet, but door hinges that need to be oiled, screws that need to be tightened, or doorknobs that need replacing. As you enjoy the fruits of your labor in these past few weeks of rehearsal, know that you never stop working.

Part IV

OTHER MODELS OF CONSTRUCTION

When There's No Blueprint

Devising, Physical Theater, and Ensemble Plays

The danger is that we will get lost. Plan on it: Count on it.

—Joseph Chaikin[1]

WHAT IS DEVISING?

No doubt you've heard the term *devising* and may even have already worked on some kind of show that involved devising, even if you didn't know it. Devising can sometimes be called many things: ensemble-based, collective, or collaborative creation, total theater, physical theater. Cleveland-based theater-maker Holly Holsinger states, "Anything can be devising. We can make up how to do it. There are so many models now, so when people tell me they devise work, I'm not sure what that means.[2]

Although the word *devising* has become common vernacular in the theater world, the act of creating work through methods of devising has actually been around for a while. You could look back to Viola Spolin in Chicago and her theater games and improvisational methods in the 1920s and '30s as one form of devising. You could also look at Meyerhold's biomechanics in Russia in the 1920s or Grotowski's theater in Poland in the late 1950s and 1960s, or Peter Brook's work in the 1970s with his international company, as well as Jacques Lecoq's training in France. The emergence of devising and ensemble work in the United States has blossomed in the last hundred years, with such companies as the Living Theater, Bread and Puppet, the Open Theater, the Wooster Group, and SITI. Today, you can find several devising companies in major and regional cities, such as Complicité and Frantic Assembly in the United Kingdom. In the United States, there's the Builders Association,

Elevator Repair Service, Lookingglass Theatre, Pig Iron Theatre, Rude Mechanicals, Soujourn Theater, Teatro Luna, and Tectonic Theater, just to name a handful.

As Holsinger states, devising can mean many things. Alison Oddey's book *Devising Theatre: A Practical and Theoretical Handbook* was published in the mid-1990s and defines a devised performance as originating "with the group while making the performance, rather than starting from a play text that someone else has written to be interpreted . . . work that has emerged from and been generated by a group of people working in collaboration."[3] Dierdre Haddon and Jane Milling, authors of *Devising Performance: A Critical History*, simplifies the definition as a "process for creating performance from scratch, by the group, without a pre-existing script."[4] This is an accurate way to look at it, but there are variations within this definition that, for our purposes here, we have to consider. Davis Robinson explains the joy of working on devising after a fruitful workshop, describing the actor's process of "solving and testing out ideas for material, [eating] dinner, [going] back into the studio for a night of improvisation and devising, showing and critiquing work which might get picked up the next day for further development or shelved forever."[5]

Changing definitions and methods makes it difficult for us to dig too deeply into the rehearsal process because, as you'll see in this chapter, when it comes to devising, it's not "The play's the thing" but "The *process* is the thing." Some devising does begin with source material, such as Complicite adapting Bruno Schulz's stories for *Street of Crocodiles* or Frantic Assembly's Scott Graham and Stephen Hogget working on Simon Stephen's adaptation *The Curious Incident of the Dog in the Night-Time.* It is more common, though, that the ensemble are cocreators. In this way, devising theater becomes the most collaborative (and democratic) of theater creation. This does not always mean that the performances are built by committee, though, as often there is a lead collaborator (the director), and there have been many collaborations with authors in the room (such as Caryl Churchill working with Joint Stock Theatre or Jean Claude Van Itallie and the Open Theatre). In short, ask a hundred "devisors" what devising is, and you will likely get a hundred different definitions, as each company defines their own process. This is also why this chapter only touches on some ideas and how you can connect tools from earlier chapters into the work.

For you, the actor, stepping into this process can be an exciting and daunting adventure. Like working on new plays, not every actor will thrive in the world of devising. Building a performance in this way is more about the process. Your house may not even look much like a house when you are done; it may look more like an installation or art project, but it will definitely be eye-catching!

A DIFFERENT PROCESS, YES, BUT SOME SIMILARITIES

As we talk about the devising process, it's good to know that at the end of the day, it is still theater. It is a performance for an audience and involves many skills you already possess. There are some similarities to what you may have done in a script-based rehearsal process as well as differences. Let's first look at how devising theater may differ (please note, these are generalities, and remember that devising can be anything):

- There is creative collaboration or an ensemble-driven process.
- As the ensemble is so vital, the performance usually features the ensemble in equal proportions, unlike a script-based process, which may have a lead, supporting, or other roles.
- Process is valued over product (not that an opening night isn't looming, but explorations continue throughout).
- Creating a script or text is part of the rehearsal process (and may or may not include preliminary text, found text, surveys, input from the ensemble or others).
- Material is generated in rehearsal through the use of exercises, games, prompts, and improvisation by the ensemble.
- There is emphasis on decisions through ensemble involvement (with a possible lead collaborator).
- There is emphasis on physicality, movement, gesture, dance, or even masks or puppets.
- The emphasis is usually not on plot, but story is still important. It may not follow the Aristotelian or Brechtian plot structure; it may not even have any structure at all (could be a series of playlets or vignettes).
- Design elements can often be devised, as well, with designers in the rehearsal room, creating visual ideas with the performers.
- Performance is built around the input and strengths of the ensemble.
- The performance style may not be representational (fourth-wall realism) but presentational (storytelling or involve audience in some way).
- Character roles may allow for actors to play several characters or focus on just one, depending on the scope of the story.
- Performance may involve other forms of entertainment, such as music, dancing, circus acts, and athletics.
- There is a longer rehearsal process to allow for time for development.
- The casting process may include games, exercises, and inquiries into the talents of the performers.
- The process could involve a site-specific or immersive experience (not in a typical theater space).
- The performance may be used for social justice or equity or to bring awareness of current political events.

- There are some similarities that we can focus on:
- The process may or may not have a director (lead collaborator) or dramaturg.
- There may or may not be an author serving as a playwright (also sometimes might be the dramaturg).
- You will likely have text, unless it is a dance theater or silent performance (such as Synetic Theater, a DC-based nonverbal Shakespeare company). The text may or may not be dialogue as you know it but could be prose, poetry, or found text.
- The structure of the performance may still follow an Aristotelian model (PASTO could still apply here).
- Material is created by working with manageable chunks or smaller pieces of the performance (think of this as beats or bits of a different scale).
- The same definition of acting can still apply (for example, "living truthfully in imaginary circumstances"), and you will still have to listen and respond in the moment to your fellow actors or audience.
- You will have research and homework as an actor (on the subject, theme, the character, yourself).
- You will have movement and blocking.
- You will play a character (even if the character is an aspect of yourself).
- Your character will have relationships with other characters (you will have to decide how you feel about each other and what moments mean to you in terms of storytelling, even if not performing fourth-wall realism).
- Your character will have actions and "doings."

The first challenge for you will be to know as much about the company before you begin rehearsals. Do your research. If you are a text-based intellectual who likes to sit around a table and talk about the play, then a movement-based company may not be a good fit. Some companies' mission statements could relate to something specific, such as social justice, or could be as simple as adapting myths or performing verbatim interviews with real people or docu-dramas. Likely, you will have met the director or other members of the ensemble at auditions. Auditions are usually catered to the company or are more exploratory, a chance for you to highlight your strengths. If it is a physical theater company, there may be movement exercises. If the company specializes in viewpoints or moment work, then there may be a short training session as well as ensemble-building games. The more you know about the process and the way they work, the better off you will be. There are many books and articles about these various ways of devising theater. Look up the bios or résumés of the company members, and see where they have trained. An ensemble that has studied Grotowski or Lecoq will be a different experience than if they trained with the SITI company.

Another aspect about ensemble-based or devising is that there is often either a common vocabulary or training among the group (such as Viewpoints), or the vocabulary is built as the rehearsals progress. That vocabulary can be verbal or physical, based on gesture or image, or even musical in terms of space and rhythm. If you are able to learn the common vocabulary of the ensemble before rehearsals begin, all the better. But if there isn't one, be aware that the first few weeks of rehearsal may be focused on how the ensemble operates and communicates. An actor who is eager to start working on the play may feel frustrated by all this focus on process.

Exercise 1

Just as you would for a script (and similar to the exercise in chapter 1), research the company, the director, or ensemble members. What shows have they already created? What is their training and background? Write down methods and vocabulary that you may need to know if you don't already. Follow up with any readings or exercises that might prepare you for the rehearsal process.

WHEN THE ENSEMBLE IS THE AUTHOR

As a performer in a devised piece, you are also an author or cocreator. This means you may literally be writing in the moment. This could take the form of movement or gesture or could be in other improvisational methods of content creation.

When it comes to devising, the act of creation is the most challenging and the most exciting part of the process. It can also be the most intimidating and stressful. If you feel like you are not a writer, never fear. When you work with an ensemble, you will be working within the games, exercises, and prompts given to you. You merely need to remain open, vulnerable, and willing to play.

Building the role is also challenging. Unlike with a script, you have no lines, actions, or a story to start crafting your work. You have to think of the first few weeks of rehearsal as part of that process. You are discovering the story and the character at the same time. You need to be open to your instincts and the guidance of the ensemble or the director as you create the story. This is much different from working with lines and a preplanned plot.

Like any type of writing or improvisation, you may find that only 10 percent of what you do ends up in the actual performance. Some of the work is going to be exploratory. Some of it will enhance your character. Some of it will help find a visual image or gesture that could be repeated somewhere else in the story. You never really know what will be kept or discarded.

It's important for you as the actor not to judge it as good or bad. There are choices and ideas, and it's about how these relate to each other and what story you all want to tell.

THE REHEARSAL PROCESS

The rehearsal process of a devised theatre performance is going to be different from a script-based or traditional process in a few ways. The first is the amount of time devoted to rehearsal. In order to create a show, a devised rehearsal process allows for a longer rehearsal period. This is not always the case, of course. Some companies can work fast and put up a world premiere of a devised performance in only a few weeks. Some can do it in a weekend. Other companies may take several months or even years to fully create the show (with showings of works in progress to the audience in various stages).

In 2008, Dennis directed the devised play *7 Minutes to Midnight* with an ensemble at Bellevue College. The performance used text, movement, and music as the story moves through time and space, highlighting the creation of the atomic bomb and the forming of the Bulletin of Atomic Scientists, as well as a concurrent story of the myth of Kronos. Dennis spent a summer generating material with the ensemble and then went into full rehearsals for six weeks in the fall, shaping the text further. In the process, Dennis leaned heavily on Michael Rohd's *Theatre for Community, Conflict and Dialogue* and his methodology of framing workshop sessions in three phases (warm-up games, bridge activities, and activating material).[6] Dennis uses this format for his individual rehearsals but also for the shape of the entire rehearsal process, breaking the rehearsal down into three overlapping phases: (1) collecting, (2) testing, and (3) shaping. At each point of the rehearsal, he is clear with the ensemble about the function of each game, exercise, or improvisation.

It's best to think of the rehearsal process in these overarching phases, recognizing that they overlap and are also unique to the specific theater company. The first phase (collecting) could also be called a "getting to know you" phase. If it is the first time the ensemble has worked together, then you will spend several days or even a week or two playing ensemble-building games and exercises. These exercises build trust and a common vocabulary. You also are spending these first few weeks collecting ideas and research for the themes and story you will explore.

In the second phase (testing), you are seeing which ideas, prompts, and improvisations will work for the story you want to tell. Sometimes the games and exercises will illuminate what could be developed further but not always. Every theater company will have their own methods (or create their own methods) of generating material. Your character (or characters) will start to formularize and become more specific as you work in the rehearsal room.

You may even have props or design elements to incorporate, and that may spark choices for further exploration. As stated earlier, the company will likely start to see the performance in terms of sections (they may or may not call them beats or bits). You may work on an opening section or scene or a scene that will happen somewhere in the middle. Some companies work with a wall of the studio, where they put up ideas, inspiration, and index cards with scenes as they try to rearrange and structure the performance.

In the third phase (shaping), the ensemble begins to understand what it is they are building and how they can help refine or clarify the story or performance. A dramaturg or director can become very helpful here in making decisions about what to show the audience and in what order. More design elements will be added.

We have mentioned that part of the excitement about devising is that you don't know what you will create or what will happen next. You will probably get lost, and that can be frustrating and discombobulating. The actors working on *7 Minutes to Midnight* kept asking about whether the choice was right or if Dennis, as director, had something specific in mind. Stephen Wangh, who studied with Grotowski, aptly describes that part of the process:

> The central idea of experimental theater is that this process of "stumbling around" is, in fact, an excellent way to proceed. It can lead us to discoveries we might have never made if we had confirmed our explorations to those pathways for which we had maps. . . . It instills in us a willingness to enter each new project with an open mind and with (supremely important) courage to make mistakes.[7]

What the actors began to realize is that some of their "mistakes" end up being choices in the show, choices that surprised the audience and sparked our imagination for other fun ideas.

THE REHEARSAL ROOM AND ENVIRONMENT

A rehearsal studio of an ensemble-driven or devised piece may feel slightly different. If it is a movement-based company, there are actors on the floor, stretching or warming up their bodies before rehearsal even begins (you would be advised to do the same). The environment and the way rehearsals run are often more democratic and nonhierarchical. The director or lead collaborator aims to give over choices in order to empower the actor. If you are the kind of actor who relishes in being told what to do, where to stand, and what to say, then the devising rehearsal may take some getting used to. There is more expected of you in terms of your homework and the work you do in rehearsal. It can be exhilarating but also exhausting (in a good way).

Many theater companies begin each rehearsal with a check-in. You may already be familiar with this from acting class or other productions. It's an opportunity for self-care and reflection, as well as to see what is happening in each ensemble member's life. It may also be a way to see how the world is informing the current work.

Next, the company might engage in warm-up exercises or ensemble-building games. This could evolve into improvisations that are devoted to building material. Or the ensemble may share research and findings. You may be asked to bring in prompts or material (such as a poem, a song, or your written thoughts about a theme, etc.). If there is material already generated, you may take a look at what shape it is in and play around with that. Or you may start working on a new improvisation or a new game that could generate material.

As the rehearsals progress, you will notice that the ensemble takes on a life of its own, finding its own space and rhythm. It is no secret that actors who train and work together at length will develop a bond and shorthand, and that will affect the performance. It is the reason many ensembles work with the same members over several years.

PRESENTATIONAL OR REPRESENTATIONAL PERFORMANCES

Another small challenge for inexperienced actors is that the performance style is often not representational (fourth-wall realism) but presentational. This is not always the case, but as devising theater can be more abstract, more physical, more poetic, or involve non-Western theater-making practices, it is something you should be prepared for and adapt to.

This may not scare you if you have had training in Greek theater, storytelling theater, Black acting methods, or Shakespeare. It simply means that you need to be aware of and accept that the audience is watching you and is an essential part of the performance. As you'll see later, this can be very important for site-specific and immersive work, where the audience could literally be breathing down your neck. But much of devised theater is focused on the actor-audience dynamic, especially in terms of where and how the performance takes place.

SITE-SPECIFIC CHALLENGES

Sometimes a location can inspire a performance, especially when it comes to devising. Who would have thought that *Macbeth* could be transformed into a site-specific and immersive adaptation at a hotel, with scenes in several rooms on several floors, the way it was imagined by Punchdrunk Theatre when they created *Sleep No More*? Or an abandoned warehouse can become an interactive ride through US history, as it did with the National Theatre of the United States' production of *What's That on My Head*?

Your performance might take place in any number of places, such as an alley, a library, a museum, an elevator, a hangar, a beach, a football field, a car, a bus, or a historic house. When you start working on site-specific work, you will start seeing theatrical playing spaces everywhere as you walk around.

When you are working in a traditional theater space, you shape your performance to that space, but when you are working with a specific site, you are letting the space be the impulse and generate ideas for your performance. The benefit of rehearsing in a studio or a traditional theater space is that you are usually in a closed rehearsal. Unless you are in closed space, like an abandoned warehouse or during off hours of a historic site, you are likely rehearsing with the general public around. This can be distracting or discouraging, depending on the interactions. It requires an actor who is flexible and able to concentrate.

One reason that theater companies love working on site-specific performances is that it automatically challenges the audience-actor relationship. The mere act of placing theater outside of the theater building already plays with that dynamic, but the specific spatial relationship of the space can add complexity and depth. We are no longer talking about proscenium or thrust stages. In most site-specific or immersive theater, the audience is in motion, moving in and around the performers or the space. Again, flexibility is crucial. It is somewhat similar to working on a film or TV location (see chapter 14).

Depending on the size of the space, you may have to adjust your performance. If you are performing in an elevator or a car, you are going to feel more like when you perform for a camera (see chapter 14). When you perform in a large warehouse or outside at a pool, you may have to access greater vocal or physical needs. Again, the space shapes the needs of performance.

Chapter Thirteen

New Construction
Rehearsing the New Play

Writing plays is one of the most schizophrenic pastimes on earth. On the one hand you've got to be a rigorous architect, but if you want your plays to breathe you've got to let your characters crash into the very walls you've so carefully designed. It's all about control and surrender—knowing what you're after and then letting the characters take over.

—Tina Howe[1]

In this chapter, we look at rehearsing new material. You use similar tools to build this kind of house, only there are ongoing modifications to the blueprints. Be prepared for the architect (i.e., the writer) to give you changes. This means you may have to take your hammer and smash down all the earlier walls to build new ones. Your character could change from a soft-spoken wallflower to an overt bully in a heartbeat, and you have to be ready to adapt with new, bold choices. Having nothing set in stone and anything possible makes for an exciting process. But not all actors define excitement by building a world on shifting ground. Some actors thrive with new works, and others don't. This chapter helps inform what you are getting into.

The biggest difference with new works, of course, is the presence of the playwright. If actors have never worked with a writer in the room before, it can be intimidating. After actors gain experience with working on new plays, they become more relaxed and view the playwright as just one more collaborator. After all, the play wouldn't be performed without you adding your talents. If the writer in the room makes you nervous, never fear, as we discuss tips for dealing with that in a later section. As you embark on this new work, don't go into it thinking you will help the playwright *fix* the play. If you don't think the play can be staged as is with no changes, then don't do it. It doesn't mean the writer won't make changes or that the play won't find areas that need attention. Your role is to serve the writer, who may still be discovering the story.

What we list here is not a recipe or standardized way of working on new plays. Each new work will have its own process, dictated by the writer, director, or producing entity. This is important when exploring new works, as dramaturg Heather Helinsky states: "Maintaining the same approach to every play, to every project is antithetical to the creation of art. Instead, new play development should be guided by ongoing reflection, and asking: *How is this supporting the playwright?* If you cannot answer this question, then it may be time to review your process."[2]

PLAYWRIGHTS ARE PEOPLE, TOO

To actors who have never experienced new-play development, having a writer sitting there watching as you fumble through their words can be unnerving. It doesn't matter how friendly and supportive the playwright is. Although it's more likely that the writer is wincing at their own words and not your work, you still may take it personally. The challenge of many actors is overcoming fear and anxiety. Either or both can destroy an actor's confidence and undermine the work. Actors start having their inner critic whisper into their subconscious, "I hope this is the way the playwright imagined it."

Here's the thing: Writers are people, too. They have wants, needs, insecurities, flaws, and strengths and are trying to thrive and survive, like you and me. Perhaps you think the creation of a new play is a mystical and magical process, but guess what. They probably think the same thing about your acting process.

In the "Do Your Research" section in chapter 2, we advise you to not just read the play you're working on but to get to know the playwright's other works, as well. Or, at the very least, read about their life and works. With a living writer, you can also do this. An easy internet search may yield the writer's website, news articles, or résumé. Find out what they have written about before, where they're from, or where they've worked.

When you meet the writer in person, at auditions or the first rehearsal, introduce yourself. You don't have to dive right into the play and the character you're working on (although we know you want to), and you don't want to come on like an aggressive fan, either. Ask them questions about their life—you might have colleagues in common. Find some common ground. This small bit of socializing is not only research for your role but also a way of disarming the fear and anxiety of being in the room with them. You won't see them as "the writer" but as part of the collaborative team.

As rehearsals progress, you may then ask more specific research-based questions. Be aware of boundaries, of course. Not all writers want to chat about traumatic experiences or their family lives. Some writers use their imagination and have no idea where the ideas sprang from, while others base their plays on real events. As you chat, you may get helpful information, even if it is just little things, like how a character is based on someone they know or a detail about the environment.

One word of caution: Be aware of the conversations you have if the director isn't present. In rehearsals, your performance notes should come from the director or assistant director. Some directors have a more casual relationship with the playwrights and don't mind when they talk directly to actors, but other directors may not. The purpose of your conversations with the writer is to glean information about the play and character. Do not go up to the writer and ask for notes on your acting. If the writer does give you performance notes, confirm with your director later if they agree or don't. It can be very easy for manipulative actors to try to play the writer against the director as a way of controlling their performance. Don't be that actor.

HOW PLAYS GET BUILT
(FROM READINGS TO WORKSHOPS)

Before we get into the rehearsal process of working on a new script, we should briefly cover a few ways that plays get developed into finished drafts. Let's first dispel the myth that plays are made in isolation by the playwright and then, after weeks or months of toil and sweat, are delivered to a producer, who hires a director for a Broadway premiere. Dreamlike and ideal, yes. Reality? Not quite.

For plays, there could be several routes and directions in the maze known as play development. Every playwright you meet could talk about their route and process of writing a play, and every play you work on could have many different development paths before going into rehearsal. It can start with an idea the writer has or a commission from a theater. The writer could take scenes into a writer's group as she develops the play over months or years. Or the writer could whip it up in a weekend and get a reading the next week. The play may have had an informal reading or been developed in a lab festival or workshop, such as PlayPenn, the Lark, Seven Devils, or the O'Neill Center. The play might go through rewrites after readings or notes from an agent, director, literary manager, or dramaturg. A reading could lead to interest from an artistic director who wants to produce it in the next season but wants to workshop it first. Or the play finally gets an off-Broadway contract and then receives rave reviews and after some more rewrites moves to Broadway.

The main point here is that the writer has been living with this project for months or years before you came along. Although you may offer ideas, the writer has probably already thought of it and tried it several drafts ago. Your job is to come in with ideas of how to perform this role. Let the dramaturg, director, or playwright worry about revisions. This is, of course, a collaboration, and they will want your input, but it's important you recognize your role in the process and be cognizant of when you may be overstepping the boundaries.

Let's briefly review how you might work on a role in different types of readings or performances in the developmental process.

Informal or Casual Reading

This might be a writer calling or e-mailing you to come over and sit around the living room to simply hear the play. There may not be any audience at all, or if so, it may be only a few friends or colleagues. You may get the script in advance or handed the pages as you walk in the door. Some writers belong to a writing group where they share work with others. (If you are an actor new to a major city, ask around and look for these. It's a great way to meet other theater artists as well as hone your acting chops, specifically cold-reading skills.)

In this type of reading, your role is to read the script as written with as much intention and commitment as you can discern from the information given. (We say, "Read the exact words on the page," because it may seem obvious, but you'd be surprised how many actors cannot do this simple task and how irksome it can be to writers.) Don't be confused by the word *reading*. You should bring your performance skills to the character and scenes. It's similar to the reading you might do on the first day of rehearsal (see chapter 5). Listen and respond to the other actors. Make bold choices, but be willing to experiment and modify. Your job is to serve the play and the playwright. Again, you're not there to help the playwright write the play but to help the playwright *hear* the play. (Another solid reason for sticking to the script as written—yes, we will keep repeating this.)

It can be useful for you if can quickly read through the scenes silently to yourself before you read it aloud with the other actors. Take a few minutes and make choices about the character. You don't need to build the entire role here, and no writer expects you to dig deep and do a brilliant performance. (As an actor it's nice not to have that pressure!) Unless the script calls for it, don't add quirks, dialects, or zany character choices. Most times you can read in a character similar to yourself.

Usually the writer will give some kind of context or reference. They may talk about whether it is just a scene or two, a whole work, a first or third draft, and some issues they are exploring. Certain writers may pose questions before or after the reading, asking about character choices, plot devices, or general feedback. If you as the actor are asked about the character, be honest and brief. Being honest doesn't mean being unkind, by the way. Be supportive, and talk first about what you think resonates or what you enjoy about the role. If you can't think of anything positive, then maybe this play is not for you.

Speak in technical terms about what you are wondering about. Do not try to offer suggestions or rewrite the play. Put your thoughts and comments in the form of questions, such as, "Why does she say this line?" or "What is she trying to get from him when she does that at the end of the scene?" They might be questions similar to when you start work on the role in rehearsal. The writer isn't obligated to answer the questions and truthfully may not yet know. But hearing how an experienced actor may build that role is solid information for the writer.

For these informal readings, all the stage directions are usually read aloud so everyone can hear and understand what's happening. Also, depending on how many actors are in the room and number of roles, you could be double or triple cast, which can become quite fun.

Formal Reading (Unrehearsed or Rehearsed)

This type of reading is similar to the informal reading but differs in that it is performed for a more formal audience. It may be open to the public or private, such as a backer's audition (a room full of producers or directors). This type of reading could also involve a director and a dramaturg. The rehearsal process could last for a few days or a week but usually not much longer than that, unless it is a musical. It may only have a short rehearsal the day of the reading or be read cold.

As with the informal reading, you may or may not receive a draft of the script prior to the first rehearsal. You may receive a preliminary draft the week before and then be handed a whole new script the day you walk in. Either way, you should get a three-ring binder that allows for you to easily replace old pages with the rewrites. (Often the binders are provided for you with the scripts by the producer or stage manager.)

These types of readings could either be sitting or standing. You could be holding the script binder or have a music stand. Be prepared for either scenario. If you find yourself holding the script, see if you can hold it with one hand, keeping the other hand free for gestures. Too often, we see inexperienced actors clutching the binder in front of their body, which just closes them off. If you have the script on a music stand, it frees you up tremendously in terms of your physicality. One thing to consider is how you turn pages in your script. Nothing is more distracting or annoying than an actor so caught up in their acting they are oblivious to how they loudly turn a page (usually whipping the page from one side to the other).

As with the informal reading, your job with the character is to listen and respond to your fellow actors, reading it in the same way you would at the first rehearsal of any other performance (see chapter 5). Take your character clues from the script using the same tools you learned from the first few chapters (given circumstances, PASTO, title scenes, actions, etc.). You have limited rehearsal time, so manage expectations of how deep you can go.

This reading may or may not be developmental, so the director may give you a ton of notes or very little. It depends on the goals of the reading. Sometimes the script has been developed, and the institution wants to hear it or share it with subscribers. Other times, the director and playwright are asking questions about certain scenes and characters and trying to see what might need revisions. As an actor involved in the process, simply ask what the level of development is. You can then prepare for rewrites as needed. We discuss the developmental reading later.

As this reading isn't staged, you don't have to worry about blocking. At the most, you may stand up to create an "entrance" to clarify for the audience who is in which scenes. However, not exploring a theatrical space with your body like you would for a full production doesn't mean you can't embody the character. Find your character's center of gravity, and figure out how that character would stand. It will help you with your vocal performance as well as unlock other character choices.

Again, don't be fooled by the word *reading*. You are an actor, not a reader. Keep your eyes up, and look at your fellow actors. The benefit of a reading is that you have the script in hand, so memorizing lines is not an issue. However, you should work on the script with the same attention you would even if you were expected to memorize lines. You want your focus and attention not on the page but on the other actors. You need to listen and work off their behavior so you can react to their choices.

But if you don't have your eyes on the script, how will you know what line to read? Here's a simple trick: Look down at the page for your line, putting your right thumb or finger near the text as a placeholder. As you read the scene, your finger moves down so that the next time you need a line, you quickly look to see what it is, then back up to deliver it. It takes practice and experience, but over time, it becomes second nature. This is something you can practice right now. (It's also helpful for cold reads in auditions.)

As for technical aspects, if you are in a theater, you will have basic lights. It is unlikely you'll have any costume elements or sound design, but again, it could depend on the director and serving the needs of the play. For stage directions, the director and writer will usually confer on what information is essential and should be read aloud. For example, if the convention of entering is established by actors simply standing up and putting their script on a music stand, then the direction "He enters" may be cut. It's all about clarity and finding the rhythm of the scene, marrying the text and performance to work in harmony.

If you are cast to read stage directions, treat this as a performance. Your character serves the function as storyteller. You give important information and must provide the same energy as other performers to keep the speed and clarity consistent. Do not simply read off lines like a grocery list or feel that you are snubbed because you aren't acting. Tell us the story!

Staged Reading

The staged reading is a slightly more elaborate or rehearsed version of the formal reading. As the name implies, staging is involved. The amount of staging will vary. Because these are usually still performed script in hand, the blocking will be minimal, as the director is aiming for clarity in the telling of the story or to help the audience visualize relationships or a sense of location. This reading may involve some amount of costuming or props to suggest design elements, but again, the purpose of the reading is still on story and characters.

Susan Merson, an actor experienced with many new plays, cautions against trying to "act the script," as you don't have the time to create the full performance you would have in a few weeks of rehearsal. This is hard to remember because as you get up on your feet and start exploring the character, it's going to feel more like a blocking rehearsal than a reading. But you don't have the luxury of time and space like you would with a rehearsal process. It's important to remember that when you get to that moment of performance, the audience doesn't want to see you figuring things out the way you would in a blocking rehearsal. They want to see specific and defined choices, listening and reacting to other actors with spontaneity and energy. She elaborates further:

> The main thing to remember is to learn your blocking, not your lines, and read the script. . . . You want to make sure that the externals are apparent. You want to make sure the rhythm of a scene works. You want to make sure the basic character content is revealed. You want to make sure the arc of the scene is there so that the playwright can see whether or not he's got something. Sometimes actors make a script better than it is on the page. For a staged reading, I would suggest—always make it better.[3]

Merson mentions rhythm here, which is crucial when working on new plays. Writers hear their plays more like music. It's not about line readings but a sense of energy and motion. Look at chapters 4 and 8, as the exercises there will help you gather clues about the rhythm of the writer's work.

Even less stage directions will be read aloud with this type of reading, as there is more movement. The director or writer will let you know which directions will be cut from the performance.

Developmental Reading

The developmental reading is, as its name implies, all about developing the ideas and characters. Many of the same ideas and concepts listed previously are going to apply here, as well. The reading could be staged or minimal, open or private, depending on the process and the director. A reading such as this usually has more than just a few days of rehearsals, as the writer, director, and possibly dramaturg are going to spend time talking about the play and trying out different choices. You may get rewrites on a daily basis. You may work a scene that morning, and the writer disappears for a few hours, and then by the afternoon, you have new pages in hand.

If you are given a rewrite of a scene or your whole character changes, go with it. Your ability as an actor to adjust to last-minute revisions and changes will be tested when working on new plays. Do not resist or argue with the director or writer. This may be your biggest challenge as an actor, scrapping all your previous work for something completely new.

Developmental Lab or Workshop

This type of performance is a hybrid: It's not a reading but not quite a full production. You will be staging scenes and may have your lines memorized, but it also may be some book in hand (or a hybrid, depending on the developmental process). There may be a budget for such design elements as costumes or props, but you may only be working with stage blocks as a set. Each producing organization functions differently in terms of how they approach this process. The goal is to start to see how the world of this play could actually function and if the story works. Think of it as the creative team playing around in a sandbox. You might make a sandcastle, but then again, maybe it will look more like a house. Or maybe it will collapse. It's exciting!

Full Production

Then there is the full production. Finally, a play hits the major leagues! A real budget, a real set, a bunch of people working on it. It's in the season at a major regional theater, or it's being produced off-Broadway. It's magic time! We discuss working on this process a little more later.

What is listed previously is, of course, traditional categories of readings that you may come across in your professional career, but as stated earlier, there are many ways plays can be made. In the harsh economic times and realities of getting work up, more and more emerging playwrights and theater artists are creating new models of play development. For instance, the well-known musical *Hedwig and the Angry Inch* was not developed through readings and workshops but by John Cameron Mitchell working on the character by performing songs in downtown New York drag clubs.

BUILDING AN ORIGINAL ROLE
(COLLABORATING WITH DIRECTOR AND PLAYWRIGHT)

There used to be a tradition in the theater where the first day of rehearsal, the playwright would read the play aloud to the director and actors. You might scoff at this, feeling like it's one elaborate line reading, but directors would listen to the writer's particular voice with its rhythm and intonation. It allows everyone to find the music in the play.

Typically, a fully produced production of a new play will have gone through some iteration of any number of the readings or workshops we describe here. You may think that because of all this developmental work, the script is locked, and you shouldn't expect any more rewrites. The truth is, this is rarely the case. You might not experience such major changes as changing location or cutting scenes and characters, but you should expect that the play will evolve as all the production elements come together.

As with any other first rehearsal, you are likely to have a table reading. Many of the same conversations you have about the play and the design discussed in chapter 5 will be present here. The difference, of course, is now you have the writer (and possibly a dramaturg) in the room. They are paying particular attention to the script and analyzing any possible revisions. The stakes here are higher than a reading or workshop because any changes affect not just the director or actors but the design, as well.

You may experience more conversations about the play than other production rehearsals. Oscar Eustis, who shepherded *Angels in America* into fruition and is the artistic direct of the Public Theater, states,

> Some of the most valuable work I've done in play development incorporated discussion with actors not on the level of throughlines and objectives but on the level of "What's this play about?" Almost always, in an extended play development process, we'll have one long session where we just sit and talk about what we think the play's about, why we like it, what it reminds us of. Everybody gets more invested, and it clarifies the thing you always have to go back to, which is, what's the basic theme of the work? You're clarifying it and solidifying it, giving the writer the social context. . . . The function of the actors and the director is to use any way possible to give the playwright the clearest possible vision of the work—warts and all.[4]

As you progress through the rehearsal process, you may have some of the same challenges as with any other play. The difference might be that instead of trying to make it work, the director or the writer might try to solve the problem with a rewrite. Some actors are too quick to blame the text when it might be because the actors need more time. Just because a line doesn't make sense to you in the first week of rehearsal doesn't mean that it won't make sense to you three weeks later, after you have a better understanding of the relationships and the character's needs. This is part of trusting the process.

As you work through the blocking, you can use all the exercises from chapters 5 through 10. Examine and reexamine your actions and obstacles, define your relationships, explore your three types of language, know your status relationships, and think about times you are dishonest or keeping secrets. You particularly want to pay attention to textual clues, so look at the techniques about rhetoric and punctuation in chapter 8. Treat the words with the same respect and discipline as you would Shakespeare or any other "tested" work.

In some rare cases, depending on the director or writer, you may be asked to participate in some exploratory exercises, such as improvisation. Some directors are renowned for their use of improvisation, and indeed, entire plays can be built and written using this technique (such as Caryl Churchill's work with Joint Stock Theater). If you have been doing the exercises in this book, then you should feel comfortable exploring your character through improvisation with text or movement other than with only lines.

You may be asked to improvise the event that occurred right before a scene in a play or some other past event that is important to the characters. Because you've done your homework and explored these events and what these other characters mean to you, it should not be difficult to imagine your character in that scenario. Usually, a good director will set up the improvisation and give you the clear parameters.

Keep in mind that these improvisations are usually exploratory and for everyone to have a greater understanding of this unwritten event. It's not necessarily to build material or to give a performance. So be open and play. However, don't be surprised if some of your words end up in a rewrite. Writers are sponges and will incorporate any good idea.

As stated before, you are going to notice that all the acting notes come from the director, assistant director, or stage manager. Typically, the writer will observe and take notes, occasionally conferring with the director about a particular scene, moment, or line. This is not about hierarchy but more for clarity. Getting notes from different sources can often lead to confusion.

If you do get contrasting notes from the director and the writer, it's best to chat with both and let them discuss it together. If a dramaturg is present, they can facilitate disagreements about the script. There can sometimes be ugly battles between the writer and director, especially if the collaboration is new or if their working styles don't mesh. You don't want to be caught in the middle of that.

WORKING WITH REWRITES

Other than the challenge of dealing with fear and anxiety due to the presence of the writer in the room, the other big challenge is adjusting to revisions in the text. As an actor, you must commit to specific and bold choices, but also don't get too attached. You may be reticent about making specific choices, thinking it may all change anyway. Don't be. The writer and director must see you perform with 100 percent conviction to know how the scene is playing. Also, don't judge it as worse or better. See the change as a new direction, and commit to that 100 percent. The only way to know if a choice won't work is to play it at that level.

The largest complaint from writers and directors who specialize in new works is working with actors who refuse to try new things and who are not open or willing to be flexible. Their number one quality that these directors and writers look for in an actor is their ability to adjust to rewrites. This ranks above even the ability to take direction, although they often overlap. Other qualities they looked for are enthusiasm, energy, ability to make choices quickly, commitment to choices, preparation, curiosity, and reading the script as written and not paraphrasing. (See, we told you we'd mention this multiple times.) All this ranks well above talent or training, though that is important, as well.[5] If the idea of spending several weeks in rehearsal building your role and then having it all come crashing down and having to rebuild the role from a completely different angle in even less time sounds frustrating to you, then maybe new-play development is not for you.

Here's an example from one of Dennis's plays, *Love's Labors Won or Benvolio Is Alive and Well and Living in the Bahamas*, a comedic sequel of sorts to Shakespeare's *Romeo and Juliet*, which was directed by Scott C. Embler at Vital Theater in New York City. As expected, this play references many of Shakespeare's plays and characters, such as *Hamlet* and *Twelfth Night*, but the main plot involves Benvolio (whom you might remember as Romeo's cousin) fleeing the violence and bloodshed of Verona with Rosaline (she's the woman Romeo coos about before he meets Juliet). They end up at a seaside villa looking to buy boat tickets to the Bahamas (hence the title). The plot thickens when the ghost of Romeo appears and warns Benvolio about the evil and selfish nature of Rosaline. Going into rehearsals, Dennis knew that the scenes with Romeo were fizzling and lifeless, and the character had to change. The production cast a good actor as Romeo, someone who looked like your typical lovesick actor/model. He was perfectly capable of doing the part as written before rehearsals began. However, after the first week of rehearsal, Romeo's character was rewritten as a vain and bombastic poet who loved to hear himself talk. Every single one of Romeo's lines was rewritten to fit this new direction. You might think this is a rare exception, but it's actually a small revision. Entire scenes can be cut or rewritten. That ten-minute monologue you agonized over, memorizing and staging it so every beat is clear and succinct—cut and replaced with a one-line quip.

Revisions are not a commentary on your work as an actor. If anything, it's because you are doing solid work that a writer or dramaturg can see how the play can be made clearer. Writers could be responding to ideas from the director or dramaturg or responding to the "music" they hear or don't hear. As Suzan-Lori Parks says, "It's about hearing the voices you've heard in your head for years and making sure they're coming through. . . . A writer knows." She elaborates to explain that rehearsal is like the full-color version of her black-and-white stick figures.[6]

In general, here is advice for working on new plays, especially as you embrace revisions:

- Respect the words. Say the lines as written, and don't paraphrase. Treat each line as if it took months to decide on just those words (because it probably did).
- Be prepared. Don't forget that even though this is an untested play, it's still your job to bring your acting tools into the room. Do your research and preparation, and work on your role with the clues given in the text. Don't try to overcompensate for lack of clues, but don't be lazy, either. Make specific choices!
- Be flexible. You may get direction in total contrast to how you originally prepared. Trust the director. With new-play development, the only constant is change.
- Be open to getting lost. Unlike a role that others have explored, no one knows how to play this part (not even the writer). Be prepared to make some choices that just won't work as well as choices that will. You are creating the path as you walk it. That's exciting but also a little scary. You might get lost, but trust that the director will put you back on the map.
- Trust the rhythm/music. Treat text and punctuation like music notes. Lean into operative words and rhetoric, and find not only the heartbeat for the scene but also the ebbs and flows of the play.
- Trust your impulses. Don't forget what *you* bring to the process—your unique ability to work off your instincts. Be open and aware of those spontaneous moments that make the scene come alive. You are serving not just the playwright but also the truth of the given circumstances.
- Trust the process. If it seems like the scene or character isn't working, trust that (a) it will get fleshed out with rehearsal, (b) the writer and director will see that something needs attention, or (c) the scene will be performed in all its glory and maybe the writer will see needs for revision months later. It's not your responsibility to ensure there is a fully fledged play at the end of this process.

- Be playful, and have a sense of humor. It is, after all, a play. It's easy to get lost in the seriousness of the task or to have unnecessary expectations. Everyone wants to work on the next *Hamilton*, but even *Hamilton* didn't start out as a breakout Broadway show. You should enjoy the process and the people you are working with as much as the play itself.

Chapter Fourteen

The Fast Build

Rehearsing Film, TV, and Other Media

Movie acting is more like rehearsing because you're shooting rehearsal and accidents are great stuff.

—Christopher Walken

We've spent most of this book assuming you have the luxury of a long rehearsal period. In this chapter, we explore acting for the camera (film, television, or the web), where rehearsal time is minimal to nonexistent. There are a lot of reasons for this, the primary one being financial. Film and television employ a large amount of people, sometimes hundreds, and it costs a lot to pay and feed them. This also affects scheduling requirements, as it's difficult to get everyone available. For example, a TV star cast in the lead of a movie may only be available for a certain time frame, making any rehearsal impossible. For smaller parts, such as an under-five (this means your role has less than five lines), you will likely receive no rehearsal other than being told where your marks are and to set up the lighting or camera movements.

Given this, it may seem odd to even devote a chapter on rehearsing for screen acting. However, just because rehearsal time is shorter doesn't mean you can't use techniques from earlier chapters for your preproduction preparation or when you arrive on-set. It's important to remember, though, that with camera acting, there is a danger of rehearsing the life out of the performance. The beauty of screen acting is that you have to employ some of the techniques you might use in a rehearsal for stage as part of your performance. With film, you have the luxury of doing several takes, of pushing your performance to the limits, or of working even more simply from take to take. Christopher Walken's quote at the start of this chapter mentions the importance of spontaneity, how those first inspirational moments in rehearsal become magic on-screen.

There are various books on acting for the camera, which we refer to, but if you haven't done any on-camera work at all, the best thing you can do is get into a class to learn the terminology and techniques. It's also extremely easy to set up a home studio with a simple ring light and your smartphone. You can work on sides and scenes on your own and review the film to see what works on camera and what doesn't.

But let's fast-forward to where you have aced that audition and scored the role in a film or television shoot. As with theater performance styles and types of plays, there are many categories and genres of film and television, so it's important for you to do the fundamental work we mention in earlier chapters (specifically chapters 1–4). Read the script first as an audience, but this time, really try to imagine how you think it might look on-screen. Think about the pacing, tone, and even genre (Is it a sitcom, a procedural crime show, or a drama?). Every show has a unique style, whether it's *Schitt's Creek*, *Stranger Things*, or *This Is Us.* And knowing the work of the film director can be helpful, as well. Chloe Zhao's style (director of *Nomadland*) is different from Edgar Wright's (*Scott Pilgrim*, *Baby Driver*), and both are different from Ava DuVernay's (*Selma*, *When They See Us*).

With a film script, you may be dealing with a scene that is only a half page. For film, a long scene is typically only two or three pages. One of the key differences between film and theater is that film is "moving pictures," and as we all have heard, a picture speaks a thousand words. Film is shot at twenty-four frames per second (24 fps; and due to digital technology, some are even going up to 60 fps). That's a lot of information and storytelling that happens in a very short amount of time. Every image, word, and moment has a specific meaning. Your character may not even have dialogue, but as we've shown earlier, acting is not talking. Acting is doing. What do you want in this scene, and how do you get it or not? What's your obstacle? What is your relationship to the others in the scene?

Some film actors may approach the work in a breezy manner, not wanting to kill spontaneity by overpreparing, so they don't do much more than a simple glance at their lines. But as we (and Bill Nighy) state in chapter 6, this isn't necessary. Rehearsal doesn't kill spontaneity but enriches your choices. That's why you read the script and make choices before the table read. There are certainly celebrities who can get away with never having the script before the first table read. But often this is because of their hectic schedule. They also may have the experience of working much faster in a shorter time. Don't let this practice be your guide.

Assignment 1

If you haven't already done so, take a look at the first few chapters of this book. Before the table read, you should have read the script as an audience, as an actor, and as a detective. Do any research about your character or the show itself (watch some episodes to get a feel for the tone of the show). Then break the script into beats (PASTO), and categorize each scene. Define your actions and your relationships to the other characters in your scene.

THE TABLE READ

Typically, with television or film scripts, there will be a scheduled table read prior to shooting. It's important to know that not every director or production will have a table read. Some directors love table reads, and others want to start shooting immediately. Some directors want a table read simply to know that all the actors have read the entire script at least once.

For the actor, the table read is similar to a stage production's first rehearsal (see chapter 5). You will likely have already met the director and possibly the producer. This table read may be your first meeting with the first AD. The first AD is like the director's second-in-command. He or she commands the schedule, runs the set, and gets everything and everyone moving on time. This person, unless otherwise specified, is your go-to person on anything logistical. So be nice and keep them close. The table read is also when you may meet fellow actors, if you haven't met them already. There may also be other producers; executive producers; and such key personnel as the directors of photography (DP), sound, costumes, and makeup.

One particular aspect of a screenplay or teleplay that an actor will notice is that with scripts written for the screen, there are more directions and action than dialogue. Plays are usually built on verbal language, so a reading feels more active for the actor. A reading of a film script is like talking about a blueprint of a building. All the artists are working to turn that script into a series of images that will ultimately become the film. There will be moments when you may feel your mind wandering, waiting to speak, but if you listen and put your focus on the script or other actors, you can get a better sense of what story is being told and how you can best serve that vision in your performance.

In chapter 5, we mention how endowment plays a part in building the imaginary world. For screen acting, endowment is equally important. The advantage with screen acting is that the medium usually is realism. You'll be on location or a set that looks exactly like it should. You don't have to imagine you're in an ER or police station. You don't have to imagine a knife or gun is real (assuming that the film is not relying on CGI and green screen, a whole other acting challenge). This means you can give your attention to and use your surroundings. The aspect that will require you to use endowment is in the relationships to other characters. You may be required to play an intimate scene with an actor who is playing your wife of ten years, and yet, you just met her. Professional actors are able to be vulnerable, invest in emotional circumstances, and create that believable relationship quickly. As your rehearsal for screen acting is short or nonexistent, this means you don't have time to get to know the other actors. Therefore, you must use every available moment in the rehearsal to notate everything about them you can use or not and to endow the relationship with specific meaning.

Assignment 2

This assignment is for your first table read, if you have one. You must put your focus and attention on the other actors, really listening and observing, not having your face in your script. After each scene, when you have a moment, write down observations. What do you see? How is it different from what you expected? How are your fellow actors surprising you? What can you use and incorporate?

ON-SET REHEARSAL

Here's a quick and dirty breakdown of a typical routine for a rehearsal and shoot for a television or movie. After you arrive and check in, you'll assemble with the director and the DP. You may be handed sides for the day, which are very similar to sides you get at auditions. These are the pages being filmed that day. If you aren't handed any, ask for them. Check that these pages are the same! Often, rewrites can happen the night before, and you want to ensure you have the most updated script. (Don't throw away any previous script that may have your notes on it about your character or intentions. You may still want to refer to that preparatory work if needed.)

Jenna Fischer, actor from *The Office* and author of the book *The Actor's Life*, tells a harrowing tale of memorizing an entire speech prior to shooting day, only to learn that the speech had to be rewritten for legal reasons. She also talks about how not just a script but also schedules can change, so actors have to be prepared and adjust. But after learning that lesson, she now says, "I make sure I have my whole role prepared from day one and I read every script and every set of sides each morning so I'm ready for anything."[1]

You will go through the script with your fellow actors. This is simply to get the content of the scene. It's usually just actors with the director and the DP. This is where you work out blocking and get direction. There is no need for you to give a final performance. Use it as a way of connecting to the other actors and the space. This is also a way for everyone to begin the conversation of how shots will be set up. The director will work through the scene again and solidify blocking. Typically, the director or the first AD has ideas of your starting marks and where you will end up. Some directors have everything planned out and may even refer to storyboards. There will be a run-through to flesh it out. This should still be very simple for now. Then they will call other crew members to watch a rehearsal and talk about lighting and camera choices. After a few rehearsals, the director may give some adjustments.

This small amount of rehearsal is crucial. As Ben Kingsley once said, "Rehearsal is like walking the track before racing around it." You have to invest some energy and intention into what you're doing so the director and the DP know what to expect, but you don't want to give it all away. This is also a good time to ask any technical questions or follow-up questions from the table read (particularly if it has to do with spatial relationships between characters, such as, "Would I put my arm around him here or keep my distance?"). This is not the time to ask deep questions about the character's back story or motivation unless it's directly related to this scene and any action or blocking involved.

For a two- to three-page scene, all the above may take only thirty minutes. This is not much time, so it's necessary for you to make strong choices and make them quickly. After this short rehearsal, they will clear the set and set up lights and cameras to plan the shots. As an actor, you can head to makeup and costume. It could take anywhere from forty minutes to a few hours for setup, depending on the size of the crew.

Once your blocking is set, you need to remember it. This is what the director and the DP will plan to shoot. Write it down in your script so that you can review it in your dressing room or refer to it right before shooting the scene. This is why even though you're off-book before stepping on-set, you should bring your script with you. For starters, research has shown that you will remember things more clearly if you write them down, but also you can refer to your notes in the script and run through it as you wait (and there will be plenty of waiting).

When the DP finishes the setup, you are called back to set to shoot the scene. If there was a stand-in on, that person would have already been used to adjust lighting on your face and ensure you were in focus for the first shot. If not, they may take some time to pull focus for your first mark, as well as any travel or other marks you might have. Some directors may have you do a quick rehearsal to see if you remember the blocking or need to ease into it, while other directors may immediately start with a take.

Sometimes a production will use more than one camera, which is becoming more common, but often it may only be one. This means the camera may be on you for the scene, and then they have to set up the shot for a reverse angle on the other actor. Typically, the master is shot first, which is a wide angle and encompasses the entire space and captures all movements. From this master, they then start finding different angles so that the scene can be put together for a final edit. For one scene, a camera could be moved several times, depending on how many shots are on the director's shot list. This includes wide shots, medium shots, and close-ups.

If a director requests another take, it doesn't necessarily mean your performance was the issue, unless the director specifically gives you a note. A failed take could be because the camera was out of focus or the sound mixer heard noises in the background or the art director realized a poster was falling off a wall. There are a million things that can go wrong, which is why you as the actor need to be consistent and on your marks.

ADJUSTING TO DIRECTOR NOTES

Most film directors learn a lot about the craft of making movies in film school but not the ability to communicate clearly with actors. Some directors already have good instincts when it comes to working with actors, while some may have been actors themselves, so they know the terminology or techniques. Others realize they lack these necessary skills, so in their desire to learn more, they take an acting class. This is not singular to film directors, either, as some stage directors can be equally unaware or esoteric.

If you are working with inexperienced directors, be prepared for the way your director may give notes. Be prepared, also, for directors who never give you any notes. Sometimes this is because you are doing your job, and there is nothing to comment on, but sometimes it's because the director doesn't know what note to give or that the performance you want to give is not there.

Directing notes can range from unhelpful to erudite. If you ask the director a question, be as specific as possible. For instance, you might ask the director, "Why am I walking to the window?" The director might reply, "At this moment, you are symbolizing the futility of mankind seeking redemption." While a phrase like that may make perfect sense to a director setting up the shot, it doesn't help you as an actor. You can't play a symbol of mankind, and the mere physical act of walking to the window may not hold redemption for you. You could try to rephrase the question, "What am I looking for out the window?" or "What do I see out the window?" to see if that may elicit a more helpful response. Sometimes, you just want a simple reason, like you're looking to see what the weather is like so you know if you need a coat or not. Or you're looking to see if another character is outside waiting for you.

As actors, you need to craft your own justifications for simple actions. Don't rely on the director to do your job for you. If they give you direction, do it, and find the reason afterward. But if you have a moment that seems contradictory to your interpretation of the role, then the rehearsal of that scene is the time to bring that up. If it comes up as you get notes in the scene, then work with it then, but be cognizant that time is ticking and everyone wants to stay on schedule. You have to manage each acting moment. If you feel a moment is crucial to your character and you want to give your best performance to make the best film possible, then everyone will be able to get onboard with you. But don't be the actor who has to hold up the shooting day because of small moments that may end up on the cutting-room floor anyway.

SAME BUT DIFFERENT:
REPEATING PERFORMANCES FOR CONTINUITY

Another big challenge for actors when it comes to film and TV is that actors have to build a repeatable performance. It's true that actors have to do that with stage work, as well, but they have several weeks to develop that repeatable performance and the luxury of performing everything in linear order. With film, you have less rehearsal time and must do it for different camera shots and angles, sometimes starting and stopping in different places. You also may be shooting the final scene of the film on the first day and then shooting a scene from the middle of the movie the next day. Michael Caine's book *Acting in Film* has many examples and tips for how to achieve a repeatable performance, so we don't spend much time on it here. He covers everything from how and when to smoke a cigarette, when to take a drink, and even exactly how many steps you take to get from one mark to another.[2]

In addition to having a repeatable performance, you as an actor must know the scene backward and forward. You may be asked to start the scene in the middle or only do the last few lines. You may be asked to only do one line for a close-up. This is just due to the nature of filmic storytelling. This is why doing your homework is so important. You need to know what each moment means and how it fits into the arc of the scene as well as the whole script and make decisions accordingly.

Exercise 3

Look at how you broke the script into beats and actions. Be specific about each moment you have. Although you may not have been on-set or rehearsed it yet, get on your feet, and explore how your character moves and talks (or sits). Work out each moment you can. Then make another copy of the script, and get some scissors. Cut up your script into different pieces, and move the moments of the scene around. Play a game of "Wild Card," where you pick up one of the pieces of the scene and only perform that moment. Repeat that moment, and try it a few different ways. Pick another piece. After you have worked on the scene again, run the whole scene in its entirety, and reflect on how it felt different.

LOCATION! LOCATION! LOCATION!

Location shoots brings many benefits as well as drawbacks. The main benefit is that you don't have to use your imagination. You are actually in that space and can use the reality of the world to feed your choices. This makes your job of finding a relationship to the space much easier than creating it from your imagination. For example, if the setting is a hospital room and you're playing the doctor, you'll be shooting in an actual hospital room and may feel that this familiar workplace is your comfort zone, while if you're playing the patient, you may feel nervous by the surroundings.

As an actor, you should familiarize yourself with the location as soon as possible. This typically happens for the on-set rehearsal, but depending on your role and your relationship to the space, you may be able to ask the director about finding more time in the space. This gets tricky, as you don't want to be in the way when they set up for shots, so find time when that area is not being used. If your role necessitates that you know the space intimately, then you need to be able to move around it almost with your eyes closed. If you're playing a bartender, then you should know where every type of liquor or glasses are and be able to move around as if you've been doing it for years. If it's your office, then you should know exactly where the phone is or grab a pen without looking. Familiarize yourself with everything around you before the shoot as well as between takes.

One drawback with shooting on location is that there are elements out of everyone's control. Exterior locations are subject to changes in sunlight, as well as to rain or heavy wind. Sound is also an issue. Planes, trains, or automobiles can be problematic on location. Another drawback can be bystanders. There is something magical about a movie set, and if you're on location, you will likely draw an audience. It doesn't matter if it's a crowded city or quiet suburb; be prepared for random strangers to be watching you work. They may even take photos, especially if you are doing a scene with a celebrity. Usually, the production assistants or security are able to keep them at a distance, but it's still distracting. Be flexible, and adapt to your surroundings. Use it as best you can, and let it help you create the scene in the moment.

I HAVE TO CRY ON CUE
(AND OTHER SCREEN-ACTING CHALLENGES)

The amazing thing about camera acting is that you can create an intimacy between you and the viewer in a way you can't onstage. You can pull the viewer right up close to your eyes and let the viewer feel like they are inside your mind and know your thoughts. This is especially useful for emotional and intense scenes. Take a look at Viola Davis as Rose in the movie *Fences*, when she declares to her husband, Troy, that she's had dreams for the past eighteen years just like he has: "I been standing with you!" That scene was shot from several angles—a master, a medium close-up, and over-the-shoulders from Troy's and Rose's points of view. But it is her close-up where we witness the authentic and powerful performance from this master actor of stage and film.

An emotional scene like this is never easy to film for the actors or for the director. It is a lot of pressure to deliver the authentic and gritty performance that everyone dreams about. Usually, these scenes are not the first on the schedule. A director will work with the first AD to find a day in the schedule when the actors and crew have familiarity and have developed a solid routine so that they will be able to spend as much time as needed to find the emotional truth of the scene. It also usually isn't too late in the shooting schedule, either, because the director may anticipate problems arising if the shoot falls behind schedule and they have to rush the shot. However, because much about what decides things is monetary, it may be the first scene if it was the only time the location was available.

Before the day of shooting, you not only need to prepare with the script, your character, the actions, and the relationships to other characters, but you also need to strategize your emotional preparation. If you're not familiar with emotional preparation, there are several schools of thought on how best to prepare. Strasberg felt that sense memory could release emotions (e.g., using the memory of your dog dying to help you form tears). Another train of thought, like Meisner or Adler, is to use your imagination to coax the emotions out of you. This includes daydreaming or creating a "what if" scenario in your head to prepare. In some cases, you may be able to immediately connect to the moment, and the mere power of the suggestion of the words and actions will help you find your emotional truth (see chapter 9).

Regardless of how you prepare, you will still need to save some emotional life for the actual shooting of the scene. Find yourself a quiet or secluded area where you can do the emotional preparation you need to do. When you arrive on-set, you are going to have a dozen crew members and a microphone in your face, but you will still need to maintain that raw emotional vulnerability.

When shooting your scene, use your partner as much as possible, and react to what they give you. Never forget that emoting is not acting. Viola Davis is amazing as Rose not because she is in tears but because she is fighting for her marriage, trying to make her husband understand what he has done to her. If anything, she is trying not to cry, but it's happening anyway.

Chapter Fifteen

Moving In

Common Notes from Directors

Consider the public. Never fear it nor despise it. Coax it, charm it, interest it, stimulate it, shock it now and then if you must, make it laugh, make it cry, but above all never, never, never bore the living hell out of it.

—Noël Coward[1]

Audience is like a great beast which the actor must tame into silence.

—Thomas Dekker[2]

Over the years, we have repeated the same notes again and again in our final rehearsals. We say them so often that we assume all actors know what the note means and how to adjust. This chapter is a list of common notes, what they mean, and how you can translate that note into an adjustment.

In final dress rehearsals, notes sessions are either immediately following the run, right before rehearsal the next day, or (as is more common now) through an e-mail from the director or assistant director. It is imperative that you write down those notes so that you remember to incorporate them in the next run-through. Research shows that writing something down helps you remember it better, but also you are able to review your notes later that evening when you get home as well as before the next rehearsal. Too often, actors don't write their notes down, and the director ends up repeating the same note. This wastes time.

When receiving notes, a simple "Thank you" or "Got it" is all that is needed. If you need clarification on the exact moment or specifics of the note, that's okay, but a notes session is not the time to get into a discussion or argument about what happened and why you did it that way. If there was a safety or timing issue that needs to be directed toward the stage manager, that may be another issue. Keep in mind during the final rehearsals that time to spend on the details is getting shorter and shorter.

There is some truth to the common directing note "Louder, faster, funnier." Audiences are savvy. Don't get fooled into thinking you have to slow down for them. They want to see the play performed in the same spirit and energy as a basketball game. This is why directors are always concerned about pace, volume, and staging but especially so when it comes to final rehearsals. The director will be paying attention to whether the music of the text is coming out, whether they can hear and understand you, and whether those pretty stage pictures you have worked on are fully realized. This is the time to eliminate unnecessary pauses, for example. Or simplify movement and physicality. You may even hear a director talk about how they want to "shave five minutes off the first act" and wonder what a difference five minutes can make. But it does. Pacing is key. So, let's dig in. They may seem nitpicky, but they are directly related to your earlier choices.

"I DON'T KNOW WHAT YOU ARE DOING" OR "I DON'T KNOW WHAT YOU WANT"

Probably the biggest note you may get from a director will be, "What are you doing in that moment?" When a director asks that, she wants to know what action you are playing or what your objective is for the beat or scene. Your answer should not be, "I'm walking in the door and saying this line." The director knows the lines and stage directions. The director is asking, "What are you trying to get from the other character?" This is a red flag that whatever you think you're doing needs clarity and specificity. Either that, or you need to upgrade your action. It could also be that you can't see the forest for the trees; in other words, you have been focusing so much on the fine details of the performance that you have forgotten the foundational work that you did earlier in rehearsals.

Go back through the exercises in either chapter 3 or chapter 6. Are you really playing those actions? Are you playing the same action over and over again? How do your actions change in the scene in reaction to what other actors are doing?

"RAISE THE STAKES"

This is similar to the previous note and could be related to your objective or actions. "What's at stake" means, "What do you have to lose here if you fail?" It's not enough to think about what you are doing and why. You have to understand specifically what it means to you. Often actors play a scene as if they have already won (because they read the script and know the outcome). Your character doesn't know what will happen. What happens if you don't get what you want? What happens in the scene when you realize that you may be losing or winning?

Now that you have worked on this script for so long, you may be taking for granted that you'll achieve or lose at your objective. If the worst thing that will happen is you will be a bit annoyed, then the stakes are not high enough. As stated before, writers tell stories of life and death and high stakes. Look back at some of the work you did in chapters 1 and 2, and think about the consequences of the event in the scene.

"PICK UP YOUR CUES" OR "GO FASTER"

If you get this note, you might think you have to talk faster, but that's not actually what the director wants (unless you're playing an auctioneer). What they usually mean is that there are small pauses between lines, little bits of air that are slowing down the pace of the scene. One simple reason these pauses exist is that as actors, we make an effort not to step on someone else's line. At this point in the process, that shouldn't be an issue.

Picking up your cues is an easy fix. It's really about listening and picking up your impulse. Go back to your script and figure out what you are listening and responding to specifically. What is in that line before yours (or what is it that the other character does) that makes you speak? Are you responding to a cue word or to the behavior of your partner?

If you haven't figured that out, that's part of the problem. If you have, then perhaps you can adjust and react to something else, something earlier. Sometimes, it may mean you have rehearsed the line but you aren't actually listening and responding to your partner truthfully and in the moment. You're only talking because the script says you have to, not because your character needs to. Impulse is also tied to your breath. If you find that impulse comes earlier, the breath will come earlier, and you will be able to speak immediately when you need to.

"NO PAUSES"

Director Davey Marlin-Jones once gave this note to Dennis: "There's one pause in this play, and it's not yours." What he was saying was, "There's no need to pause unless you are told to." Nowadays, contemporary writers will write a pause in the stage directions. Harold Pinter is notorious for this. But if the writer hasn't inserted a direction to pause at that moment, don't add one for the sake of adding one.

Often, when learning a long speech, an actor will insert pauses when a line is dropped, and then that rhythm gets ingrained through repetition. Related to this note, you must be aware of internal pauses or pauses between your lines. Now is the time to take out all those unnecessary pauses—unless it is earned (see the next note). Think of this as trying to hide all the nails and glue and other ways you constructed the house. You want it to look polished and seamless.

Director John Michael Diresta tells his actors in rehearsals, "Every time you pause, a kitten dies." And then at the end of the run, he will tell them how many kittens they killed. Gruesome, yes, but effective. Don't kill any kittens! Keep it moving!

"EARN YOUR PAUSES"

This is similar to the previous note about picking up your cues. You need to move the pace along with intention and speed until the moment when you can slow down. Lauren Gunderson (author of many plays and films and, for a few years in a row, the most produced playwright in the United States) says, "Pace is structural not aesthetic: if the rest of the scene clips along, the break of that pace will tell the audience this moment is important."[2]

Your character may have a pause before a moment of discovery, disclosure, or decision, but you can only call that out as special if you have been charging along at an urgent pace.

"MORE ENERGY" (VOCAL, PHYSICAL, OR OTHERWISE)

You may get this note at the end of the rehearsal process, especially after a long week of technical rehearsals. It may be stress and strain of moving from the rehearsal studio into the theater space or dealing with costumes, makeup, and lights. Or perhaps, it's the second dress rehearsal, and you didn't sleep well the night before or didn't eat enough. (Remember to keep yourself healthy: Eat well, get sleep, and manage self-care.)

Believe us, your director will notice if you phone it in. The wind may be out of your sail, but this is the time when you row. You must dig in deep and find the energy. Your job is to play this role at the same intensity every time. Audiences don't want to see a character half-trying. They paid full price for their tickets, and they want full commitment from their actors.

This note is also related to the previous notes—playing your objective or raising the stakes. You should always enter or exit a scene as if you have purpose (objective) and commit fully to your actions. You can also focus on what's at stake for your character—what will happen if you don't get what you want?

Another way to combat this is to ensure you warm up before the performance. Energize your voice and body, and get them stimulated for the show. Physical activity and exercise can get the blood pumping. If all else fails, drink some coffee or tea before the next run. And get some sleep!

"DON'T DROP THE ENDS OF LINES"

A director may give this note specifically or say that they are losing parts of your line. If the part of the line they don't hear is near the end, then you're probably dropping the energy and creating a downward inflection. You need to connect the thought and intention all the way through to the very last word of the line or to the end stop or both (refer to chapter 8).

"DON'T UPSTAGE"

If you get this note, it means some other actor had the audience's attention and you stole it by doing something. It's important to remember that movement steals focus. Even a simple movement like scratching your nose can take focus.

It's an easy fix. Listen to your other actors, and focus on your objective for the scene. Go back to what your character wants. Are they listening to the dialogue? Do they perhaps want to react but just don't say anything at this moment? What can you use from your fellow actors? Acting is not only saying lines. It is being present, listening, and working off your fellow actors.

What if you are in the background, and you are supposed to be moving around? Like bussing tables or playing a poker game? As long as the movement is consistent and repetitive, the audience won't pay attention, much like people do at a busy café. When you are in the background or not the central focus of that moment, think of yourself as an accompanying musician, not the soloist. You want to lay down a backing track that will highlight the performer who needs to be heard at that moment.

"TAKE THE FOCUS"

This is the opposite of upstaging. There may be moments when there are a lot of actors onstage and the director needs you to take focus immediately. One clear way to take focus is to move. Movement always steals focus (see the previous note). This movement can come in a reaction to what just happened or some dialogue, such as a facial expression change or a larger movement, like changing the gesture of your body or even a cross downstage. Yes, your speaking will take some focus, but the audience's eyes may be uncertain of where that voice is coming from unless they see you move at the same time. Again, as with any note, justify it. Why would your character move at this moment? What are the stakes, and what is your action? (See chapter 6.)

"I THINK THE OPERATIVE WORD IS . . ."

This is a simple but technical note. The director wants you to emphasize a word. Be aware. They may not use the phrase *operative word* and may say, "stress this word." Other times, some directors will give a line reading. This means, they will tell you exactly how they want the line to sound (some actors and directors abhor this, but it still happens).

Go back to the section "Operative Words" in chapter 8 so that you can justify stressing this word. Does it have to do with anything a character said to you in the line before? Is it important information that another character needs to know? Don't just change your vocal quality, as that will lead to general acting. Be specific with why you say that line with more emphasis.

(By the way, if a director does give you line readings, just listen for the intonation and ask which words they want stressed. Be patient and adjust. Do not get offended. Some directors are frustrated actors, and some just don't know how to communicate. Your job, as with all directing notes, is to translate the note into an adjustment.)

"FIND YOUR LIGHT"

The joy of technical rehearsals is that you discover where the more playable areas of the stage are located. Some areas are going to be hotter than others. To ensure the light is on your face, you need to feel (and see) where the light hits your face. You may have hit this spot during the technical rehearsals but are somehow straying out of the light due to your focus and attention being elsewhere (probably absorbed in an acting moment).

Finding your light is easy when that's all you're doing and have time to look up or ask the lighting director if you are in the right spot. But being able to hit that mark every time can be harder. Here's a little trick. Once you have learned your mark, look around. Is there something on the set, like the edge of a rug, a piece of furniture, or a mark on the wall, that you can use to gauge how you can get to that spot when you need to? Choose something that will be in your line of sight when you need it. Now all you have to do is aim for the spot. And then feel the light on your face.

"CHEAT OUT MORE"

This is also a simple note on your staging or position of your body. To cheat out means to adjust your body so that the audience can see more of you. An easy way to do this is to stand with the upstage leg slightly up and pivot with your hips so that more of your torso is revealed.

Sitting a table can be more problematic. If you are sitting, your natural inclination is to face opposite the person on the other side of the table. But if you are able to adjust your body slightly so that your shoulders face out, then you can still use your neck and head to look at your acting partner. And then you can move your face toward the audience to cheat out when you need to, paying particular attention to how and when you may want to make eye contact.

"DON'T PLAY FOR LAUGHS"

In dress rehearsals, you may discover that some of your lines are funny. This is especially true with comedic plays. The sure sign of this is when stage crew or ushers chuckle and guffaw at your performance in previews. It may only be one person, but it doesn't matter. This bit of feedback may encourage you to play that line up even more, to try to play it as a joke. As soon as you do that, the audience will see you pushing for comedy, trying to get a laugh.

If a director gives this note, it's a reminder that comedy comes from the truth and humanity of the characters. You must keep your eye on the action and stay in the moment, responding truthfully to your partner. Go back to chapter 6, and reconnect with your actions.

Conclusion

Moving On

Only those who will risk going too far can possibly find out how far one can go.

—T. S. Eliot[1]

Congratulations! It's opening night! You're finally able to share all the glorious work you've been doing for weeks with an audience. If you've worked through these exercises and gotten on your feet in and out of the rehearsal room, then you have embodied your choices. Now the true test of your playing will be apparent for the audience. You can learn so much about your work from their reactions.

Your performance is now like a house that needs to settle. If you know anything about houses, the weight of the structure will cause pressure on the foundation or on the soil. Moisture in the wood might dry out, or bricks will shift. Sometimes gaps might appear. It's all part of the final process. That's where you are now: You're settling in as you perform a role, letting everything sink into the foundation of your work in rehearsal. Enjoy this part of the process and live in the moment. You earned it.

It may feel like your work has come to an end, but every ending is a beginning. Just because you're settling doesn't mean you have to settle. As you live through the events and actions of this character in performance, you'll discover an elegance, grace, and beauty while you make the habits you have developed truly your own. You may make minor modifications and improvements in the run, keeping spontaneity as you work off your fellow actors. The rough parts you thought weren't ready for opening will be sanded down to a polished smoothness. You know that there's always some aspect of the performance that can be improved.

The tools and techniques in this book allow you to adapt your process for any future roles. Some roles will be challenging, and some you may not even think you're right for, but take any part you can, even if only for the learning experience it can provide about your process. Eventually you'll find yourself playing the exact part you need to at exactly the right time.

Each production and character you step into will change you in some way; it may change your knowledge and perception of the world and maybe even inform you as you go about your days. When he played Mr. Rogers for the film *A Beautiful Day in the Neighborhood*, Tom Hanks talked about how the experience made him a kinder and more generous person. Let's hope that the role you work on also will work on you in the same positive way.

Remember that each performance requires different tools. What works today may not work next year. But now you have the tools to build from whatever blueprint you have been given, and when you get stuck, you can dip back into this book. Go try and fail and learn. There is no substitute for experience.

The success of your acting career is not dependent on building only one performance. You will build many over the years, each one a chance to go deeper into your craft. As you grow, your process may grow with it, and many of the tools or concepts in this book that seemed challenging or difficult to grasp will eventually seem easy.

As you continue to act over the years, realize that new challenges and difficulties will be right around the corner. If acting were easy, everyone would be doing it. You are revealing your soul to the world, opening up, and investing in imaginary circumstances in a vulnerable emotional state. It can be a scary but thrilling place to be. When you feel unmoored, trust your work. Trust your process. You have the tools to meet any future challenges.

Break a leg!

Notes

INTRODUCTION

1. Silverberg, Larry. *True Acting: A Path to Aliveness, Freedom, Passion, and Vitality.* Milwaukee, Limelight, 2002, p. 68.

2. For purposes of clarity, we use the pronoun *we* to reflect both John's and Dennis's points of view and refer by name to specific examples.

3. Diep Tran, "10 Out of 12: How the Other Half Techs," *American Theater*, June 2015.

4. Miguel Flores, R. Christopher Maxwell, John Meredith, Alexander Murphy, Quinn O'Connor, Phyllis Smith, and Chris Waters, "Hold Please: Addressing Urgency and Other White Supremacist Standards in Stage Management," HowlRound, October 15, 2020, https:// howlround.com/hold-please.

5. Alison E. Robb, "Exploring Psychological Wellbeing in a Sample of Australian Actors," *Australian Psychologist* 53, no. 1 (2018), https://doi.org/10.1111/ap.12221.

6. "'Post-Dramatic' Stress: Negotiating Vulnerability for Performance," Mark Cariston Seton, 2006 Conference of the Australasian Association for Drama, Theatre and Performance Studies, University of Sydney, July 4–7, 2006.

7. Chelsea Pace, with Laura Rikard, *Staging Sex: Best Practices, Tools and Techniques for Theatrical Intimacy* (New York: Routledge, 2020), 9.

8. Pace and Rikard, *Staging Sex*, 10.

9. Keith Johnstone, *Impro: Improvisation and the Theatre* (New York: Theatre Arts Books, 1981), 95.

10. Konstantin Stanislavski, *An Actor's Work*, trans. and ed. Jean Benedetti (New York: Routledge, 2008).

1. READING THE BLUEPRINT

1. Lecoq, Jacques with Jean-Gabriel Carasso and Jean-Claude Lallias. Trans. David Bradby. The Moving Body. New York: Routledge, 2001. p. 21.

2. Konstantin Stanislavski, *An Actor's Work*, trans. and ed. Jean Benedetti (New York: Routledge, 2008), 136.

3. Anton Chekhov, *Uncle Vanya*, 1898, https://www.gutenberg.org/files/1756/1756-h/1756-h.htm.

4. Stanislavski, *Actor's Work*, 53.

2. BUILDING THE SCAFFOLDING

1. John Basil, with Stephanie Gunning, *Will Power: How to Act Shakespeare in 21 Days* (New York: Applause Books, 2006), 317.
2. David Ball, *Backwards and Forwards: A Technical Manual for Reading Plays* (Carbondale: Southern Illinois University Press, 1983).

3. CONSTRUCTING A SHELL

1. Stanislavsky, Konstantin. An Actor's Work. Translated by Jean Benedetti. New York: Routledge, 2008. p. 40
2. Jason Zinoman, "Lynn Nottage Enters Her Flippant Period," *New York Times*, June 13, 2004.
3. John Basil with Stephanie Gunning, *Will Power: How to Act Shakespeare in 21 Days* (New York: Applause Books, 2006).
4. Sanford Meisner and Dennis Longwell, *Sanford Meisner on Acting* (New York: Random House, 1987), 17.
5. Marina Caldarone and Maggie Lloyd-Williams, *Actions: The Actor's Thesaurus* (London: Nick Hern Books, 2004), xvii.
6. Caldarone and Lloyd-Williams, *Actions*, xix.
7. William Esper and Damon Dimarco, *The Actor's Art and Craft* (New York: Anchor Books, 2008), 223.

4. BRICK BY BRICK

1. Hagen, Uta. *A Challenge for the Actor* (New York: Scribner, 1991), 288.
2. Quiara Alegría Hudes, *Elliot, A Soldier's Fugue* (New York: TCG, 2012), 7.
3. Jez Butterworth, *Jerusalem* (London: Nick Hern Books, 2009), 102.
4. August Wilson, *Fences* (New York: Penguin, 1986), 53.
5. Uta Hagen, *A Challenge for the Actor* (New York: Scribner, 1991), 117.
6. Nicolai Gogol, *The Government Inspector*, adapted by Jeffrey Hatcher (New York: Dramatists Play Service, 2009), 18.
7. Rick Elice, *Peter and the Starcatcher*, acting ed. (New York: Disney Editions, 2014), 3.
8. Dennis Schebetta. *The Albatross* (unpublished).

5. BUILDING WITH OTHERS

1. Sloan, Gary. *In Rehearsal*, p. 239.
2. Uta Hagen, *A Challenge for the Actor* (New York: Scribner, 1991), 175.

6. BUILDING HABITS

1. Durant, Will. *The Story of Philosophy: The Lives and Opinions of the World's Greatest Philosophers* (New York: Simon & Schuster, 1961) p. 98.
2. "Interview with William Esper" https://esperstudio.com/an-interview-with-william-esper/.

3. William Esper and Damon DiMarco, *The Actors' Art and Craft* (New York: Anchor Books, 2008), 86.

4. Konstantin Stanislavski, *An Actor Prepares*, 146.

5. Hannah Furness, "It Has Become Fashionable for Actors Not to Learn Their Lines, Bill Nighy Complains," *Telegraph*, October 5, 2017, http://www.telegraph.co.uk/news/2017/10/15/has-become-fashionable-actors-not-learn-lines-bill-nighy-complains/

7. BUILDING YOUR CHARACTER

1. Chekhov, Michael. *To the Actor on the Technique of Acting.* New York: Routledge, 2002. p. 36.

2. Keith Johnstone, *Impro: Improvisation and the Theatre* (London: Methuen, 1981), 33.

3. Johnstone, *Impro*, 36.

4. Nicolai Gogol, *The Government Inspector*, adapted by Jeffrey Hatcher (New York: Dramatists Play Service, 2009), 8.

5. Eric Berne, *Games People Play: The Basic Handbook of Transactional Analysis* (New York: Ballantine, 1964), 25.

6. John Basil, with Stephanie Gunning, *Will Power: How to Act Shakespeare in 21 Days* (New York: Applause Books, 2006), 239–40.

7. Anita E. Kelly, "Lying Less Linked to Better Health, New Research Finds," American Psychological Association, August 2012, https://www.apa.org/news/press/releases/2012/08/lying-less.aspx.

8. Michael Slepian, "Why the Secrets You Keep Are Hurting You," *Scientific American*, February 5, 2019, https://www.scientificamerican.com/article/why-the-secrets-you-keep-are-hurting-you/.

8. BUILDING DYNAMICS WITH TEXTUAL CLUES

1. Hall, Peter. *Exposed by the Mask*. New York, Theatre Communications Group, 2000. p. 100

2. *Tackling the Monster: Marsalis on Practice*. Sony Classical, 1995 (https://www.youtube.com/watch?v=T2ch-2Z-JW4).

3. Lonergan, Kenneth. *Lobby Hero*. New York, Dramatists Play Service, Inc., 2002. p. 36.

4. Cruz, Nilo. *Anna in the Tropics*. New York, Dramatists Play Service, Inc., 2003. p. 44

5. Oscar Wilde, *The Ideal Husband* (London: Methuen, 1893), https://www.gutenberg.org/files/885/885-h/885-h.htm.

6. Henrik Ibsen, *Hedda Gabler*, trans. Edmund Gosse and William Archer (1906), https://www.gutenberg.org/files/4093/4093-h/4093-h.htm.

7. Schebetta, Dennis. *The Albatross* (unpublished).

8. Schebetta, Dennis. *The Albatross* (unpublished).

9. Patsy Rodenburg, *The Actor Speaks: Voice and the Performer* (New York: Methuen, 1997), 64.

9. INTERIOR FITTINGS

1. Esper & Dimarco, *Actor's Art & Craft*, p. 211.

2. Larry Silverberg, *The Sanford Meisner Approach: Workbook Two: Emotional Freedom*, (Hanover, NH: Smith & Kraus, 1997), 7.

3. Uta Hagen, *A Challenge for the Actor* (New York: Scribner, 1991), 62.

4. Rob Roznowski, *Roadblocks in Acting* (London: Palgrave, 2017), 52–53.

5. Oscar Wilde, *The Ideal Husband* (London: Methuen, 1893), https://www.gutenberg.org/files/885/885-h/885-h.htm.

10. BUILDING WITH CARE AND CONSENT

1. Chelsea Pace, with Laura Rikard, *Staging Sex: Best Practices, Tools and Techniques for Theatrical Intimacy* (New York: Routledge, 2020), p. 15.

2. Chelsea Pace, with Laura Rikard, *Staging Sex: Best Practices, Tools and Techniques for Theatrical Intimacy* (New York: Routledge, 2020).

3. Brian LeTraunik, *A History of Contemporary Stage Combat* (Routledge: New York, 2020), 3.

4. Diego Villada, interview with the author, May 20, 2021.

5. Gary Sloan, *In Rehearsal* (New York: Routledge, 2012), 126.

6. Pace and Rikard, *Staging Sex*, 1.

7. Pace and Rikard, *Staging Sex*, 12.

8. Holly L. Derr, "The Art and Craft of Intimacy Direction," HowlRound, January 30, 2020, https://howlround.com/art-and-craft-intimacy-direction.

9. Carey Purcell, "Intimate Exchanges," *American Theatre Magazine*, November 2018.

10. Hadley Kamminga-Peck, "Make It Less Weird: Theatrical Intimacy Education and How a Fence Can Lead to Intimacy," *Theatre Topics* 30, no. 3 (November 2002).

11. Kamminga-Peck, "Make It Less Weird."

12. Maureen Dowd, "Ewan McGregor: Dahling, He's Halsted," *New York Times*, May 7, 2021.

13. Casey Mink, "Sex on Camera," *Backstage*, December 27, 2018.

14. Pace and Rikard, *Staging Sex*, 40.

11. EXTERIOR FITTINGS AND FINAL TOUCHES

1. William Shakespeare, *Hamlet*, Act 5, scene 2

2. Sanford Meisner and Dennis Longwell, *Sanford Meisner on Acting* (New York: Vintage, 1987), 11.

12. WHEN THERE'S NO BLUEPRINT

1. Joseph Chaikin, *The Presence of the Actor* (New York: Theatre Communications Group, 1992), 67.

2. "Stefan Brun, "Creating Authentic Stories through Collaboration: On Devised Theater in the U.S.," HowlRound, July 23, 2020, https://howlround.com/creating-authentic-stories-through-collaboration.

3. Alison Oddey, *Devising Theatre: A Practical and Theoretical Handbook* (London: Routledge,1994), 1.

4. Deirdre Heddon and Jane Milling, *Devising Performance: A Critical History* (New York: Palgrave Macmillan, 2006), 3.

5. Davis Robinson, *A Practical Guide to Ensemble Devising* (New York: Palgrave, 2015), 1.

6. Michael Rohd, *Theatre for Community, Conflict and Dialogue: The Hope Is Vital Training Manual* (Portsmouth, NH: Heinemann Drama, 1998), 2.

7. Stephan Wangh, *An Acrobat of the Heart* (New York: Vintage, 2000), xxxvii–xxviii.

13. NEW CONSTRUCTION

1. Joan Harrington, ed., *Playwrights Teach Playwriting* (New York: Smith and Kraus, 2006), 117.
2. Heather Helinsky, "Rules of Engagement for New Play Development," HowlRound, January 22, 2017, https://howlround.com/rules-engagement-new-play-development.
3. Edward Cohen, *Working on a New Play: A Play Development Handbook for Actors, Directors, Designers and Playwrights* (New York: Prentice Hall Press, 1988), 70.
4. David Kahn and Donna Breed, *Scriptwork: A Director's Approach to New Play Development* (Carbondale: Southern Illinois Press, 1995), 134.
5. Based on an informal online survey by the author, completed anonymously by seventeen directors, fifteen playwrights, and four dramaturgs, 2015.
6. Susan Letzer Cole, *Playwrights in Rehearsal* (New York: Routledge, 2001), xv.

14. THE FAST BUILD

1. Jenna Fischer, *The Actor's Life: A Survival Guide* (Dallas, TX: BenBella, 2017), 151.
2. Michael Caine, *Acting in Film* (New York: Applause, 2000).

15. MOVING IN

1. Gray, Frances. *Noel Coward*. New York: Macmillan International Higher Education, 1987. p. 94.
2. Plaque at the Globe Theater, London.
3. Lauren Gunderson, Twitter, May 6, 2019, 3:04 p.m., https://twitter.com/LalaTellsAStory/status/1125476499715268608.

CONCLUSION

1. Crosby, Harry. *Transit of Venus: Poems*. Foreword by T. S. Eliot. Paris: Black Sun Press, 1931.

Appendix A

Recommended Play Reading List

As we refer quite often to these plays, we recommend that you read them as we work through examples and exercises. The following four plays are referred to quite often. The subsequent list of plays are also mentioned and are well worth reading or having on your bookshelf.

PRIMARY PLAYS

Gogol, Nikolai. *The Government Inspector.* 1836.
Ibsen, Henrik. *Hedda Gabler.* 1891.
Lonergan, Kenneth. *Lobby Hero.* 2001.
Nottage, Lynn. *Intimate Apparel.* 2003.

SECONDARY PLAYS

Butterworth, Jez. *Jerusalem.* 2009.
Chekhov, Anton. *Uncle Vanya.* 1898.
Cruz, Nilo. *Anna in the Tropics.* 2002.
Elice, Rick. *Peter and the Starcatcher.* 2009.
Hudes, Quiara Alegría. *Elliot, A Soldier's Fugue.* 2006.
Jospeh, Rajiv. *Gruesome Playground Injuries.* 2009.
Letts, Tracy. *August: Osage County.* 2007.
Nottage, Lynn. *Sweat.* 2015.
Rebeck, Theresa. *What We're Up Against.* 2017.
Ruhl, Sarah. *Eurydice.* 2003.
Schebetta, Dennis. *The Albatross.* 2008.
Wilde, Oscar. *An Ideal Husband.* 1895.
Wilson, August. *Fences.* 1985.
———. *Ma Rainey's Black Bottom.* 1982.

Appendix B

Recommended Reading & Resources

GENERAL ACTING

Caine, Michael. *Acting in Film*. New York: Applause, 2000.

Caldarone, Marina, and Maggie Lloyd-Williams. *Actions: The Actor's Thesaurus*. London: Nick Hern Books.

Cranston, Bryan. *A Life in Parts*. New York: Scribner, 2017.

Esper, William, and Damon Dimarco. *The Actor's Art and Craft*. New York: Anchor Books, 2008.

———. *The Actor's Guide to Creating a Character*. New York: Anchor Books, 2014.

Fischer, Jenna. *The Actor's Life: A Survival Guide*. Dallas, TX: BenBella, 2017.

Hagen, Uta. *A Challenge for the Actor*. New York: Scribner, 1991.

Johnstone, Keith. *Impro: Improvisation and the Theatre*. New York: Theatre Arts Books, 1981.

Meisner, Sanford, and Dennis Longwell. *Sanford Meisner on Acting*. New York: Random House, 1987.

Merlin, Joanna. *Auditioning: An Actor-Friendly Guide*. New York: Vintage Books, 2001.

Odom, Leslie, Jr. *Failing Up: How to Take Risks, Aim Higher, and Never Stop Learning*. New York: Fiewel & Friends, 2018.

O'Gorman, Hugh. *Acting Actions: A Primer for Actors*. Lanham, MD: Rowman & Littlefield, 2021.

Otos, Kevin, and Kim Shively. *Applied Meisner for the 21st-Century Actor*. New York: Routledge, 2021.

Persley, Nicole Hedges, and Monica White Ndounou. *Breaking It Down: Audition Techniques for the Global Majority*. Lanham, MD: Rowman & Littlefield, 2021.

Rosenfeld, Carol. *Acting and Living in Discovery*. Newburyport, MA: Focus, 2014.

Roznowski, Rob. *Roadblocks in Acting*. London: Palgrave, 2017.

Silverberg, Larry. *The Sanford Meisner Approach: Workbook Two: Emotional Freedom*. Hanover, NH: Smith & Kraus, 1997.

Sloan, Gary. *In Rehearsal*. New York: Routledge, 2012.

Stanislavsky, Konstantin. *An Actor's Work*. Translated by Jean Benedetti. New York: Routledge, 2008.

———. *An Actor's Work on a Role*. Translated by Jean Benedetti. New York: Routledge, 2010.

Tucker, Patrick. *Secrets of Screen Acting*. New York: Routledge, 2015.

TEXT AND LANGUAGE

Ball, David. *Backwards and Forwards: A Technical Manual for Reading Plays.* Carbondale: Southern Illinois University Press, 1983.

Basil, John, with Stephanie Gunning. *Will Power: How to Act Shakespeare in 21 Days* (New York: Applause Books, 2006.

Carey, David, and Rebecca Clark Carey. *The Verbal Arts Workbook.* London: Methuen Drama, 2010.

Kaplan, Steve. *The Hidden Tools of Comedy: The Serious Business of Being Funny.* Studio City, CA: Michael Wiese Productions, 2013.

Kiely, Damon. *How to Read a Play: Script Analysis for Directors.* New York: Routledge, 2016.

Rodenburg, Patsy. *The Actor Speaks: Voice and the Performer.* London: Methuen, 2019.

STAGE COMBAT

Najarian, Robert. *The Art of Unarmed Stage Combat.* New York: Focal Press, 2016.

Lane, Richard. *Swashbuckling: A Step-by-Step Guide to the Art of Stage Combat and Theatrical Swordplay.* New York: Limelight Editions, 2003.

Society of American Fight Directors (SAFD). 2014. https://www.safd.org.

INTIMACY

Intimacy Directors and Coordinators (IDC). Accessed September 12, 2021. www.idc professionals.com.

Intimacy Directors of Color. 2020. https://intimacydirectorsofcolor.com.

Pace, Chelsea, with Laura Rikard. *Staging Sex: Best Practices, Tools and Techniques for Theatrical Intimacy.* New York: Routledge, 2020.

Theatrical Intimacy Education (TIE). 2020. www.theatricalintimacyed.com.

DEVISING, ENSEMBLE-BASED DEVELOPMENT, AND SITE SPECIFIC

Boal, Augusto. *Theatre of the Oppressed.* New York: Theatre Communications Group, 1993.

Graham, Scott. *The Frantic Assembly Book of Devising Theatre.* 2nd ed. New York: Routledge, 2014.

Johnston, Chloe, and Coya Paz Brownrigg. *Ensemble-Made Chicago: A Guide to Devised Theater.* Chicago: Northwestern University Press, 2019.

Kaufman, Moises. *Moment Work: Tectonic Theater Project's Process of Devising Theatre.* New York: Vintage, 2018.

Oddey, Alison. *Devising Theatre: A Practical and Theoretical Handbook.* London: Routledge, 1994.

Robinson, Davis. *A Practical Guide to Ensemble Devising.* New York: Palgrave, 2015.

Rohd, Michael. *Theatre for Community, Conflict and Dialogue: The Hope Is Vital Training Manual.* Portsmouth, NH: Heinemann Drama, 1998.

NEW PLAY DEVELOPMENT

Cohen, Edward M. *Working on a New Play: A Play Development Handbook for Actors, Directors, Designers and Playwrights.* New York: Prentice Hall Press, 1988.

Kahn, David, and Donna Breed. *Scriptwork: A Director's Approach to New Play Development.* Carbondale: Southern Illinois Press, 1995.

Bibliography

Ball, David. *Backwards and Forwards: A Technical Manual for Reading Plays.* Carbondale: Southern Illinois University Press, 1983.

Basil, John, with Stephanie Gunning. *Will Power: How to Act Shakespeare in 21 Days.* New York: Applause Books, 2006.

Berne, Eric. *Games People Play: The Basic Handbook of Transactional Analysis.* New York: Ballantine, 1964.

Brun, Stefan. "Creating Authentic Stories through Collaboration: On Devised Theater in the U.S." HowlRound. July 23, 2020. https://howlround.com/creating-authentic-stories-through-collaboration.

Butterworth, Jez. *Jerusalem.* London: Nick Hern Books, 2009.

Caine, Michael. *Acting in Film.* New York: Applause, 2000.

Caldarone, Marina, and Maggie Lloyd-Williams. *Actions: The Actor's Thesaurus.* London: Nick Hern Books, 2004.

Chaikin, Joseph. *The Presence of the Actor.* New York: Theatre Communications Group, 1992.

Chekhov, Anton. *Uncle Vanya.* 1898. https://www.gutenberg.org/files/1756/1756-h/1756-h.htm.

Cohen, Edward M. *Working on a New Play: A Play Development Handbook for Actors, Directors, Designers and Playwrights.* New York: Prentice Hall Press, 1988.

Cole, Susan Letzer. *Playwrights in Rehearsal.* New York: Routledge, 2001.

Derr, Holly L. "The Art and Craft of Intimacy Direction." HowlRound. January 30, 2020. https://howlround.com/art-and-craft-intimacy-direction.

Dowd, Maureen. "Ewan McGregor: Dahling, He's Halsted." *New York Times*, May 7, 2021.

Elice, Rick. *Peter and the Starcatcher.* New York: Disney Editions, 2014.

Esper, William, and Damon Dimarco. *The Actor's Art and Craft.* New York: Anchor Books, 2008.

Fischer, Jenna. *The Actor's Life: A Survival Guide.* Dallas, TX: BenBella, 2017.

Flores, Miguel, R. Christopher Maxwell, John Meredith, Alexander Murphy, Quinn O'Connor, Phyllis Smith, and Chris Waters. "Hold Please: Addressing Urgency and Other White Supremacist Standards in Stage Management." HowlRound. October 15, 2020. https://howlround.com/hold-please.

Furness, Hannah. "It Has Become Fashionable for Actors Not to Learn Their Lines, Bill Nighy Complains." *Telegraph*, October 5, 2017. http://www.telegraph.co.uk/news/2017/10/15/has-become-fashionable-actors-not-learn-lines-bill-nighy-complains/.

Gogol, Nicolai. *The Government Inspector.* Adapted by Jeffrey Hatcher. New York: Dramatists Play Service, 2009.

Gunderson, Lauren. "The big note, as you might have picked up, is pace. Pacing is structural not aesthetic. If the rest of the scene clips along, the break of that pace will tell . . ." Twitter, May 6, 2019, 3:04 p.m. https://twitter.com/LalaTellsAStory/status/1125476499715268608.

Hagen, Uta. *A Challenge for the Actor.* New York: Scribner, 1991.

Hall, Peter. *Exposed by the Mask.* New York, Theatre Communications Group, 2000. p. 100.

Harrington, Joan, ed. *Playwrights Teach Playwriting.* New York: Smith & Kraus, 2006.

Heddon, Deirdre, and Jane Milling. *Devising Performance: A Critical History.* New York: Palgrave Macmillan, 2006.

Helinsky, Heather. "Rules of Engagement for New Play Development." HowlRound. January 22, 2017. https://howlround.com/rules-engagement-new-play-development.

Hudes, Quiara Alegría. *Elliot, A Soldier's Fugue.* New York: TCG, 2012.

Ibsen, Henrik. *Hedda Gabler.* Translated by Edmund Gosse and William Archer. 1906. https://www.gutenberg.org/files/4093/4093-h/4093-h.htm.

Johnstone, Keith. *Impro: Improvisation and the Theatre.* New York: Theatre Arts Books, 1981.

Kahn, David, and Donna Breed. *Scriptwork: A Director's Approach to New Play Development.* Carbondale: Southern Illinois Press, 1995.

Kamminga-Peck, Hadley. "Make It Less Weird: Theatrical Intimacy Education and How a Fence Can Lead to Intimacy." *Theatre Topics* 30, no. 3 (November 2020).

Kelly, Anita E. "Lying Less Linked to Better Health, New Research Finds." American Psychological Association. August 2012. https://www.apa.org/news/press/releases/2012/08/lying-less.aspx.

LeTraunik, Brian. *A History of Contemporary Stage Combat.* New York: Routledge, 2020.

Meisner, Sanford, and Dennis Longwell. *Sanford Meisner on Acting.* New York: Random House, 1987.

Mink, Casey. "Sex on Camera." *Backstage*, December 27, 2018.

Oddey, Alison. *Devising Theatre: A Practical and Theoretical Handbook.* London: Routledge, 1994.

Odom, Leslie, Jr. *Failing Up: How to Take Risks, Aim Higher, and Never Stop Learning.* New York: Fiewel & Friends, 2018.

Pace, Chelsea, with Laura Rikard. *Staging Sex: Best Practices, Tools and Techniques for Theatrical Intimacy.* New York: Routledge, 2020.

Purcell, Carey. "Intimate Exchanges." *American Theatre Magazine*, November 2018.

Robb, Alison E. "Exploring Psychological Wellbeing in a Sample of Australian Actors." *Australian Psychologist* 53, no. 1 (2018). https://doi.org/10/1111/ap.12221.

Robinson, Davis. *A Practical Guide to Ensemble Devising.* New York: Palgrave, 2015.

Rodenburg, Patsy. *The Actor Speaks: Voice and the Performer.* New York: Methuen, 1997.

Rohd, Michael. *Theatre for Community, Conflict and Dialogue: The Hope Is Vital Training Manual,* Portsmouth, NH: Heinemann Drama, 1998.

Roznowski, Rob. *Roadblocks in Acting.* London: Palgrave, 2017.

Silverberg, Larry. *The Sanford Meisner Approach: Workbook Two: Emotional Freedom.* Hanover, NH: Smith & Kraus, 1997.

Slepian, Michael. "Why the Secrets You Keep Are Hurting You." *Scientific American*, February 5, 2019. https://www.scientificamerican.com/article/why-the-secrets-you-keep-are-hurting-you/.

Sloan, Gary. *In Rehearsal.* New York: Routledge, 2012.

Stanislavski, Konstantin. *An Actor's Work.* Translated by Jean Benedetti. New York: Routledge, 2008.

Tran, Diep. "10 Out of 12: How the Other Half Techs." *American Theater*, June 2015.

Villada, Diego. Interview with the author, May 20, 2021.

Wangh, Stephan. *An Acrobat of the Heart.* New York: Vintage, 2000.

Wilde, Oscar. *The Ideal Husband.* London: Methuen, 1893. https://www.gutenberg.org/files/885/885-h/885-h.htm.

Wilson, August. *Fences.* New York: Penguin, 1986.

Zinoman, Jason. "Lynn Nottage Enters Her Flippant Period." *New York Times*, June 13, 2004.

Index

actions, 13, 32, 43, 66–67, 98, 103, 176; beats, 32, 171; character, 29, 31, 44, 66; eight major categories, 67–70; physical, 72; reviewing, 137; rhetoric, 108; status, 79; verb, 33
Actions: The Action Thesaurus , 33, 34
acting, definition, 32
Actors Equity Association (AEA), xvi, 119
affective memory, 105
agreements and disagreements, 91–92
The Albatross, 48, 96–97, 99
Albee, Edward, 28
alcohol: *See* physical modifications
Aristotle, 18
audience, 11, 23, 23–24, 25, 41, 46, 60, 61, 73, 85, 90, 94, 101, 103, 137, 147, 148, 178, 181; audience-actor relationship, 149; listen, 73; reading as audience, 3–5; readings, formal, 155; readings, staged, 157; watch, 73; watch and listen, 74
auditions, 54, 121; backers, 155; devised plays, 144; preparing, 7; sides, 3, 168
audition disclosure form, 121
August: Osage County, xiii, 8, 22, 28, 30, 35, 60, 61, 104, 116

backstage, 134, 136
beats, 32–33, 75, 107, 109
Beckett, Samuel, 18, 39, 41 Berne, Eric, Dr., 81

bits. *See* beats
The Big Lebowski (film), 116
Ball, David, 18
Black acting methods, 148
Blanchett, Cate, 115
blocking, 43, 59, 71, 81, 113, 129, 133, 135, 156, 157, 160; film, 168–169
boundaries, xv, 120–121, 123, 128, 129, 154
Boseman, Chadwick, 112
Breaking Bad, 28, 31, 46, 83, 85
breath, 94, 99, 101, 126, 177
Bridges, Jeff, 116
Brook, Peter, 141
British Academy of Stage and Screen Combat, 122
Butterworth, Jez, 24
button, self-care cue, 129

camera, 60, 129, 149, 165–166, 169, 171, 172
Caine, Michael, 171
Caldarone, Marina, 33, 34
Cat on a Hot Tin Roof, 28, 42, 115
Chaiken, Joseph, 141
character, ix, xii, 6, 77, 81, 92, 134; actions, 32, 66–67; costumes, 135; descriptions, 4; development, 23, 24, 41; devising, 145, 146; disclosure, discovery, decision, 95; emotional dynamics, 103; endowment, 60; etude

exercise, 37; given circumstances,
13; language, physical, 42; language,
verbal, 41–42; lies, lying, 83–84,
86; names, 28; need, 30, 30–31, 66;
new plays, 151, 153, 154, 156, 157,
158; obstacle, 71; other character
interactions, 57; other character
says, 8; physical activities, 112;
physical modifications. *See* physical
modifications; physical language, 44;
props, 45, 61, 62; psychological roles,
82; relationships, 61; repetitive words,
7, 9; secret, 84; stage combat, 124;
status, 77, 80, 81; story, 21–22
Chekhov, Anton, 39, 69; *Uncle Vanya*, 10;
Three Sisters, 69
Chekhov, Michael, 125
choreographer, 121; fight, 122, 124, 125;
intimacy, 126, 127, 128, 129
Churchill, Caryl, 12, 41, 142, 160; *A
Number*, 12
circumstances. *See* given circumstances
communication, intimacy, 127, 128
collaboration, 53, 56, 132, 142, 154
comedy, 28, 94, 98, 181
comparisons and contrasts, 92–93
conciliation project, xiii
conflict, xvi, 9, 20, 31, 35, 66, 70, 90, 91
consent, xv, 120–121
consent-based practices, xiv, xv, 120–121,
128
costume, 37, 59, 132, 135, 156
Coward, Noel, 41, 175
Cranston, Bryan, 85
Cruz, Nilo, xiii, 39; *Anna in the Tropics*,
47, 63, 69, 91
cue, line or word, 100, 177

Davis, Viola, 104, 172, 173
designer: collaborating with, 53,
58–60; costume, 135; lighting, 180;
presentations, 58; technical rehearsal,
132
designer run, 131
design team, 132
devising, 141; companies, 141; definition,
142; rehearsal process, 142–144;
rehearsal room, 147; site-specific, 148;
text, 5; writing, 145

dialects, 6, 7, 101, 102
directors, 32, 45, 73; auditions, 3; actions,
32; bad, 56; boundaries, 121; devising,
142, 147; fight. *See* fight director; film,
129, 166, 168, 170; improvisation, 160;
intimacy. *See* intimacy director; line
readings, 180; new play, 153, 155, 156,
158, 159; notes, 47, 136, 151, 160,
170, 175; power dynamics, xv, 120;
rehearsal, 54, 126, 132
Diresta, John Michael, 178
downward inflection, 101–102, 179
dramaturg, 144, 147, 152, 155, 158, 159,
160, 162
dress rehearsal, 74, 133, 135, 175, 178, 181
DuVernay, Ava, 166

Embler, Scott, 161
emotional preparation, 104, 105–106, 173
endowment, 58, 60–61, 167
end stops, 98; *See also* punctuation
Eno, Will, 41
equity, xiii, xiv, 120, 127
Esper, William, 35, 36, 65, 114
Eustis, Oscar, 159
exposition, 23, 25, 95

fear, xv, 54, 85, 126, 152, 161, 175
fight director, 119, 122, 124, 125
film & TV, 165; blocking, 168; emotional
scene, crying, 172–173; emotional
preparation, 173; location shooting,
172; table read, 167–168; rehearsal, on
set, 168; script, 166
Fischer, Jenna, 168
focus, 4, 45, 55, 110, 178, 179; camera,
169, 170; stealing, 179; taking, 179
Fornes, Maria Irene, 18, 39
fourth-wall, 40, 148

Gilligan, Vince, 28
Gogol, Nicolai, xiii; *See also* Jeffrey
Hatcher
given circumstances, 11, 34, 41, 43;
definition (*see also* Stanislavski), 11;
exercise, 13; first rehearsal, 55; five
"W"s, 12; script analysis sheet, 13;
two kinds, 35; *See also* six steps; Uta
Hagen

Gunderson, Lauren, 178
Gurira, Dania, 68
Gyllenhal, Maggie, 128

habits, 53, 65, 71, 137, 183
Hagen, Uta, 39, 105; endowment, 60; six
    steps, 13; stage descriptions, 43
Hedda Gabler, xiii, 31, 37, 68, 70, 91–92
Halston, 128
Hamilton (play), 163
The Hangover (film), 114 Hanks, Tom,
    104, 184
Hatcher, Jeffrey: *The Government
    Inspector*, xiii, 19, 29, 31, 44, 68, 73,
    79; *See also* Gogol, Nicolai
Hedwig and the Angry Inch , 158
Helinsky, Heather, 152
Holsinger, Holly, 141
Howe, Tina, 151
Hudes, Quiara Alegria, 40; Elliot, *A
    Soldier's Fugue*, 40

Ibsen, Henrik, xiii, 9
improvisation, 142, 145, 146, 148, 160
intellect, 32, 43, 57
instinct, 32, 34, 57, 162
intimacy, xv, 119, 121, 126–130; love, 30
intimacy coordinator. *See* intimacy
    director
intimacy director, 119, 126
intimacy coordinators & directors (IDC),
    119; five pillars, 127

Jerusalem, 24, 28, 30, 40–41
Johnstone, Keith, 78
Joint Stock Theater, 142, 160
justification of lines, 44, 170

Kingsley, Ben, 15, 169

Leong, David, 125, 127
Letts, Tracy, xiii, 117
Lewis, Robert, 89
Lloyd-Williams, Maggie, 33
Lonergan, Kenneth: *Lobby Hero*, xiii, 16,
    20, 31, 34, 41, 43, 66, 69, 80, 84, 90,
    132, 134
*Love's Labor's Won or Benvolio is Alive
    and Well in the Bahamas*, 161

Lucas, George, 28
Luckett, Sharell, xiii

Ma Rainey's Black Bottom (play), 112
major dramatic question, 18, 19, 21
Marlin-Jones, Davey, 19, 177
Marsalis, Branford, 112
McKellen, Ian, 107
Meisner, Sanford, ix, 71; definition of
    acting, 32; emotional preparation, 104–
    105, 173; Meisner-based classes, 4, 36,
    114; Meisner technique, 35; reality of
    doing, 32; text, 138
memorizing lines, 75, 100, 168; *See also*
    Nighy, Bill; *See also* off-book
Mitchell, John Cameron, 158
music, 11, 16, 37, 40, 89, 157, 159, 162,
    176
My Date with Adam (film), 98

names, meaning, 27–28
Ndounou, Monica, xiii
needs, 30, 56, 90, 115, 128; five basic
    needs, 30–32, 66; psychological, 72
new play, 151; development,
    153; production, 158; reading,
    developmental, 158; reading, informal,
    154–155; reading, formal, 155–157;
    reading, staged; rewrites, 161–163;
    workshops and labs, 153
Nighy, Bill, 75
notes, 55, 125, 153; common notes, 175–
    181; director notes, 66, 136, 160; line,
    74, 133; receiving, 133, 136, 175,
    181
Nottage, Lynn, 9, 18, 29, 31; *Intimate
    Apparel*, xiii, 29, 31, 42, 63, 82, 83;
    Sweat , 9, 10, 46
nudity, 121, 126, 129; *See also* intimacy

objective, 19, 33, 176, 178
obstacle, 70–71
Oddey, Alison, 142
Odom, Jr., Leslie, 3
off-book, 74; *See also* Nighy, Bill; *See
    also* memorization
open theater, 141
operative word, 93–94, 101, 180
O'Neill, Eugene, 12, 43

The O'Neill Center, 153
Ostrenko, Sergio, 35

pace, 177, 178
Pace, Chelsea, xv, 119, 126
pacing, 176
Parks, Suzan-Lori, 18, 39
parenthesis. *See* punctuation
pauses, 98, 99, 177–178
Pettiford-Wates, Tawyna, xiii; *See also* conciliation project
Pace, Chelsea, xv, 126, 127
paraphrasing, 111, 161
Parks, Suzan-Lori, 162
Persley, Nicole, xiii
Peter and the Starcatcher (play), 25, 45–46, 59, 62, 73, 74
physical modifications: alcohol, drunk, 114, 115; drugs (marijuana, cocaine), 115; hangover, 114; headache, 113–114; temperature, 116–117
Pinter, Harold, 39, 177
placeholder, 121, 129
playwrights, 11, 16, 28, 40, 42, 46, 151, 152, 156, 158, 159
postdramatic syndrome, xv
producer, 121, 129, 155, 167
props, 45, 61–63; endowment, 61
Punch Drunk Theater, 148
punctuation, 97–100; colon, 99; comma, 99; dash, 100; ellipsis, 99; end-stops, 98; exclamation marks, 46; parenthesis, 99; semi-colon, 99

questions & answers, 90–91

raising the stakes, 47, 178
reading: reading the text, 3–13; *See* new plays
realism, 148
Rebeck, Teresa, xiii, 39; *What We're up Against*, 24
rehearsal: 10 out of 12, xiv; cue-to-cue, 135; dress, 135; first dress, 136; first rehearsal, 53–57; on-set rehearsal (film/TV), 121, 165, 167–170, 172; previews, 137; read-through, 54–55; technical run-throughs, 135, 180
Reeves, Keanu, 8

relationships, 35, 58, 80, 86, 105; character, 22, 34, 35–37; playwright, 153; props, 45, 62; spatial, 13, 17, 61, 136, 149, 172; status, 81
repetition, 11, 42, 53, 89
rhetoric, 39, 42, 110, 160, 162
rhetorical devices, 89–93
rhythm, 39, 40–41, 89, 98, 102, 132, 145, 157, 159, 162, 178
Rikard, Laura, 119, 126, 127
Rodenburg, Patsy, 101
Rodis, Alicia, 127, 129
Rohd, Michael, 146
Romeo & Juliet, 30, 161
Rosenfield, Carol, 13
Rostova, Mira, 30
Royal Shakespeare Theater, 107
Roznowski, Rob, 106
Ruhl, Sarah, xiii, 12, 39; *Eurydice*, 12
run-through: crew run, 131; designer run, 131; film/TV, 168; technical run, 135
Rylance, Mark, 24

Safety, xiv, 119, 120, 121, 122, 124, 128, 129, 135, 175
schedule, 58, 76, 129; film & television, 22, 167, 173; technical rehearsal, 133, 134
screenplay, 167; *See also* script, film & TV
script: analysis, 3–13, 16; devising, 143; film & TV, 166, 168; new, 154–158; notating in, 110, 169; reading, first, 3–5; rehearsal reading, 54; research, 16; stage directions, 42–43; structure, aristotelian, 17, 18–19, 143; structure, film, 21; structure, PASTO, 19–21; titling scenes, 22–23
Screen Actors Guild (SAG), xvi, 119
self-care, xiv–xv, xvi, 134, 148, 178
Seton, Mark, xv
sexual content. *See* intimacy
Shakespeare, 9, 18, 27, 31, 39, 40, 77, 90, 94, 107, 161
sides. *See* auditions
Silverberg, Larry, 104
Sina, Tonia, 127
site-specific, 143, 148–149
SITI Company, 141

Smith, Will, 104
Society of American Fight Directors
 (SAFD), 119, 122
Spolin, Viola, 141
spontaneity, 5, 71, 74–75, 165, 166
stage crew, xiv, 4, 59, 131, 132, 136
stage managers, 6, 43, 59, 74, 125, 128,
 132, 134, 136, 155, 160, 175
Stanislavski, Constantin, xvii, 6, 11–12,
 65; affective memory, 105; *See* beats
 (bits); *See* given circumstances;
 psychological needs, 72; subconscious, 57
Star Wars, 28, 110
status, 77–81, 84
Stoppard, Tom, 39
Stewart, Patrick, 107, 111
substitution, 35, 105, 109, 111
subtext, 34, 70, 72, 79, 80, 101
Sudeikis, Jason, 47
Synetic Theater, 144

table-read, 23, 54
Ted Lasso, 23, 42, 47
Theatrical Intimacy Education (TIE), 127,
 130
transactional analysis, 81
Twelfth Night, 28

upstaging, 179

viewpoints, ix, 120, 145
Villada, Diego, 122
verb, playable, 33, 34, 66, 79; *See also*
 action
volume, 48, 93, 98, 176

Wagner, Arthur, 81
Walken, Chrisopher, 165
Wangh, Stephen, 147
Warden, Claire, 127
warm-ups, xvi, 146, 148, 177, 179
Washburn, Anne, xiv
Wellman, Mac, 19
We See You White American Theater, xiii
West Wing, 23
*Will Power, How to Act Shakespeare in 12
 Days*, 17, 30, 77, 81, 107
Wilde, Oscar, 41, 77; *An Ideal Husband*,
 91, 94, 108–109
Williams, Tennessee, 28, 39
Wilson, August, xiii, 16; *Fences*, 24,
 30, 42, 104, 172; *Ma Rainey's Black
 Bottom*, 112; *Seven Guitars*, 39
Wright, Edgar, 166

Zhao, Chloe, 166

About the Authors

John Basil is associate professor at Marymount Manhattan College. He has directed twenty-seven of the thirty-seven Shakespeare plays, many of them as a founding member and producing artistic director of American Globe Theater. John also directed on the NBC soap opera *Another World* and seven seasons at Sarasota Opera, helped launch the Sedona Shakespeare Festival, and worked regionally as a director. He trained with Stella Adler, Uta Hagen, and Mira Rostova, as well as with John Barton at the Royal Shakespeare Theater. He is the author of the book *Will Power: How to Act Shakespeare in 21 Days* (2006).

Photo by Basil Rodericks

Dennis Schebetta is an actor, writer, and director for film and theater. He is assistant professor at Skidmore College, where he teaches acting and directing. He has worked off-Broadway and regionally in works ranging from Shakespeare to devising to new play development at such organizations as Ensemble Studio Theater, 13th Street Rep, Vital Theater, Pittsburgh Playhouse, Saratoga Shakespeare, and the NY Fringe. A graduate of the William Esper Studio, where he studied with William Esper, he also holds an MFA from Virginia Commonwealth University.

Photo by Dan Doyle